ONE ELECTORATE UNDER GOD?

THE PEW FORUM DIALOGUES
ON RELIGION AND PUBLIC LIFE

E.J. Dionne Jr., Jean Bethke Elshtain, Kayla M. Drogosz

Series Editors

THE PEW FORUM ON RELIGION & PUBLIC LIFE

This book series is a joint project of the Pew Forum on Religion and Public Life and the Brookings Institution.

The Pew Forum (www.pewforum.org) seeks to promote a deeper understanding of how religion shapes the ideas and institutions of American society. At a time of heightened interest in religion's public role and responsibilities, the Forum bridges the worlds of scholarship, public policy, and journalism by creating a platform for research and discussion of issues at the intersection of religion and public affairs. The Forum explores how religious institutions and individuals contribute to civic life while honoring America's traditions of religious liberty and pluralism.

Based in Washington, D.C., the Forum is co-chaired by E. J. Dionne Jr., senior fellow at the Brookings Institution, and Jean Bethke Elshtain, Laura Spelman Rockefeller Professor of Social and Political Ethics at the University of Chicago. The Forum is supported by the Pew Charitable Trusts through a grant to Georgetown University. Luis Lugo, the director of the Trusts' religion program, serves as the Forum's executive director.

The Pew Forum Dialogues on Religion and Public Life are short volumes that bring together the voices of scholars, journalists, and policy leaders engaged simultaneously in the religious and policy realms. The core idea behind the dialogues is a simple one: There are many authentically expert voices addressing important public questions who speak not only from their knowledge of the policy issues at stake, but also from a set of moral concerns, often shaped by their religious commitments. Our goal is to find these voices and invite them to join in dialogue.

OTHER TITLES IN THIS SERIES

Is the Market Moral? A Dialogue on Religion, Economics, and Justice
Rebecca M. Blank and William McGurn

Lifting Up the Poor: A Dialogue on Religion, Poverty, and Welfare Reform
Mary Jo Bane and Lawrence M. Mead

Liberty and Power: A Dialogue on Religion and U.S. Foreign Policy in an Unjust World (forthcoming)
J. Bryan Hehir, Michael Walzer, Louise Richardson, Shibley Telhami, Charles Krauthammer, and James Lindsay

ONE ELECTORATE UNDER GOD?

A DIALOGUE ON RELIGION AND AMERICAN POLITICS

E.J. DIONNE JR.

JEAN BETHKE ELSHTAIN

KAYLA M. DROGOSZ

EDITORS

BROOKINGS INSTITUTION PRESS
Washington, D.C.

Copyright © 2004
THE BROOKINGS INSTITUTION
GEORGETOWN UNIVERSITY

Library of Congress Cataloging-in-Publication data
One electorate under God? : a dialogue on religion and American politics /
E. J. Dionne Jr., Jean Bethke Elshtain, and Kayla M. Drogosz, editors.
p.   cm.   —(The Pew Forum dialogues on religion and public life)
Includes bibliographical references and index.
ISBN 0-8157-1643-5 (pbk. : alk. paper)
1. Religion and politics—United States. I. Dionne, E. J.
II. Elshtain, Jean Bethke, 1941– III. Drogosz, Kayla Meltzer. IV. Title. V. Series.
BL2525.O53 2004
322'.1'0973—dc22   2004011096

4 6 8 9 7 5 3

The paper used in this publication meets minimum requirements of the American National Standard for Information Sciences—Permanence of Paper for Printed Library Materials: ANSI Z39.48-1992.

Typeset in Adobe Caslon

Composition by R. Lynn Rivenbark
Macon, Georgia

Printed by Victor Graphics
Baltimore, Maryland

CONTENTS

PART II
EXPANDING THE DIALOGUE

Contents

FOREWORD

LIKE BILL CLINTON and Jimmy Carter before him, George W. Bush has included in his speeches references to his religious beliefs. During a presidential debate in 2000 he identified Jesus as the greatest influence on his political philosophy. "When you accept Christ as savior," he said, "it changes your heart—it changes your life."

Declarations of faith by our presidents have engendered little controversy, nor should they. What has prompted debate is the question of how religious convictions and sensibilities should relate to the obligations of public office in a political system that insists on the separation of church and state.

This book is intended as a contribution to that debate. Two of the series editors, my colleague E.J. Dionne Jr. and Jean Bethke Elshtain of the University of Chicago, have been accomplished scholars of religion and politics for several years and together helped found and cochair the Pew Forum on Religion and Public Life. The third editor, Kayla M. Drogosz, has had a serious commitment to understanding the civic purposes of religion and helped develop this series from the beginning. She is the senior research analyst in governance studies at Brookings and a visiting faculty member with the Center for Democracy and the Third Sector at Georgetown University.

As E.J. and Kayla write in the introduction, "With the growing popularity of 'God bless you, and God bless America' as a standard close for political speeches, it seems that an increasing number of candidates are devoutly wishing for Divine endorsement and assistance. . . . But the fact that God's political intentions are not easily discerned does not stop mere mortals from speaking with great certainty about the meaning of religion in politics—and holding a great many prejudices on the subject."

It is also evident to E.J. and Kayla that policy and public office in the United States are inevitably shaped by the moral and religious commitments of its citizens and its elected officials. They believe it is important to be explicit about faith so that public deliberation can be more honest, more searching—and more democratic.

This is the core proposition behind this book, the third volume in the Pew Forum Dialogues on Religion and Public Life. The series is based on the premise that religious communities have a great deal to contribute to debates about politics and policy.

At the center of the discussion captured in this volume is the exchange between Mario Cuomo, the former governor of New York and a liberal Catholic, and Mark Souder, a Republican member of the House of Representatives and a conservative Evangelical—two experienced politicians with strongly held religious beliefs. Cuomo writes of the universal principles he draws from the Jewish tradition, which he claims are "shared by most if not all of our nation's religions, whether they include God or not." Cuomo also describes how political questions and real policy choices always involve moral judgement.

Souder does not disagree. "To ask me to check my Christian beliefs at the public door," he writes in this book, "is to ask me to expel the Holy Spirit from my life when I serve as a congressman, and that I will not do. Either I am a Christian or I am not." In a way, each politician thinks it is not possible to check his beliefs at the door and each believes that, to quote Souder, "the challenge is to find ways to continue to allow personal religious freedom in America, as guaranteed by our Constitution, while working through the differences."

The conversation between Cuomo and Souder raises many questions that E.J. and Kayla have encouraged others to address. They have invited contributions from across the political—and religious—spectrum, including journalists, practitioners, policymakers, elected officials, social scientists, and religious leaders.

The purpose of the Pew Forum dialogues is not to impress a particular viewpoint on readers, and it certainly is not to suggest that there is only one answer to any of the questions posed. These dialogues are intended to open the debate.

We are deeply grateful for the support of the Pew Charitable Trusts and the Pew Forum on Religion and Public Life, which are committed to an expanded effort to bring policy experts and civic leaders together to discuss the relationship between faith, politics, and public office.

It is customary to close with a disclaimer: the opinions expressed in this volume are those of the authors alone and do not necessarily reflect the views of the Pew Forum, the Pew Charitable Trusts, or the trustees, officers, or staff of the Brookings Institution. That said, this volume fits perfectly with the Brookings tradition of nonpartisan public policy research on important national and international topics. In exploring the complexities of faith and public office, it combines serious scholarship with the insights of policy practitioners. As the contributors show, the public obligations of faith are an essential and enduring part of the American experiment. Our hope in publishing this book is that the essays will spark a renewed national discussion on a topic that will be relevant for a long time to come.

STROBE TALBOTT
President, Brookings Institution

May 2004
Washington, D.C.

ACKNOWLEDGMENTS

Most of the time, we hope that we won't have to choose between our religious convictions and our public obligations. But sometimes politicians and citizens are required to make tough choices and to explain why they've done so. Democratic politics is about principle and compromise, standing up for strongly held beliefs and making the deals that make a free government run. Former Governor Mario Cuomo and Congressman Mark Souder are fine examples of politicians who understand the obligations and paradoxes of public service and who respond with clarity and candor in these pages about these difficult questions.

We applaud their courage, patience, and perseverance in being so firmly committed to their faith and their responsibilities as public officials. We are also grateful to have such a diverse and extraordinary group between these covers. Elected officials, community leaders, some of our most distinguished scholars, advocates, and others across religious communities and the political spectrum join together in this volume.

This is the third volume in a series designed to encourage public discussion about matters that lie at the intersection of religion and public life. Our authors have been clear and honest about what they believe and why they believe it. In the first volume, *Lifting Up the Poor: A Dialogue on Religion, Poverty, and Welfare,* authors Mary Jo Bane and Larry Mead use their exceptional experience to debate their contrasting perspectives on faith and policy in discussing the challenges facing the most burdened among us. In the second volume, *Is the Market Moral? A Dialogue on Religion, Economics, and Justice,* Becky Blank and Bill McGurn lend their expertise in economics in considering the morality of the market.

In this book, Congressman Souder and former Governor Cuomo help us understand the role played by their faiths in their decisionmaking as elected officials. The dialogue series is based on the idea that we can learn from others who have strong religious convictions, whether or not we share their faith, and that, to paraphrase the political philosopher Glenn Tinder, each of us can give and receive help on the road to truth. All gathered within these pages advance that cause.

We are deeply grateful to Rebecca Rimel, the president of the Pew Charitable Trusts, and Luis Lugo, the director of its religion program and the executive director of the Pew Forum on Religion and Public Life. Lugo has generously supported our projects for several years, not just in material terms but with excellent advice and a passion for the issues that are at the heart of the Pew Forum and its dialogue series.

For permission to reprint, expand on, or revise pieces that were published previously, we thank the following organizations and individuals: David Brooks for granting permission to draw from two articles previously published in the March 2003 and September 2002 issues of the *Atlantic Monthly.* Portions of Martha Minow's essay grew from her article "On Being a Religious Professional: The Religious Turn in Professional Ethics," 150 *University of Pennsylvania Law Review* 661 (2001).

The editors also are extremely grateful to Strobe Talbott, president of the Brookings Institution, for his deep and energetic commitment to this project; to Carol Graham for her leadership as director of the Brookings Governance Studies program; to Tom Mann, Paul Light, and Pietro Nivola for their friendship and for doing so much to make our projects possible; to Katherine Moore for being a wonderful colleague and for helping in countless way to bring this series to life; to Sierra Ferguson for her background research; to Robert Wooley and Bethany Hase for administrative assistance; to Staci S. Waldvogel, whose gifts we've been blessed with since the Pew Forum was created; to Bob Faherty, the director of the Brookings Institution Press, who never, ever fails us, embracing our projects with deep intelligence and exceptional understanding; to John Sherer and Nicole Pagano for making sure that this publication saw the light of day and made it into the right hands; to Janet Walker and Diane Hammond for being gifted, patient, and careful editors; to Carlotta Ribar for proofreading; and to

Susan Woollen and Sese Paul Design for creating just the right cover for each volume in the dialogue series.

We are also grateful to Melissa Rogers, who served as the Pew Forum's first executive director and whose leadership has helped to shape the Forum since the beginning. Her generosity, professionalism, and deep commitment to these issues continue to inspire us to live up to the Forum's mission. This project would not have been possible without Sandy Stencel. As the Forum's associate director, Sandy works with warmth and understanding to ensure all the pieces of our project come together at just the right time. We are truly blessed to have her and all our other exceptional colleagues at the Pew Forum.

Above all, we thank our authors. Arguments about the proper role of religion in the public square are in newspapers and on television and radio every day, but these debates are sometimes harsh and unforgiving. In wrestling with each other's positions and commitments, the authors here allow all who enter into their conversation the chance to sort out for themselves why they believe what they believe about the public purposes of religion. And because of their willingness to grapple with some of the toughest questions and their courage in being so open about their assumptions, all of our authors have, we think, raised the moral seriousness of our nation's debate on this essential subject.

HOW WOULD GOD VOTE?
AN INTRODUCTION

E.J. DIONNE JR. AND KAYLA M. DROGOSZ

OF COURSE NO ONE knows whom God would vote for, though most religious people do think—or at least hope—that the Almighty would come down on the side of their party, their cause, their candidates. With the growing popularity of "God bless you, and God bless America" as the standard close for political speeches, it seems that an increasing number of candidates are devoutly wishing for divine endorsement and assistance.

But the fact that God's political intentions are not easily discerned does not stop mere mortals from speaking with great certainty about the meaning of religion in politics—and holding a great many prejudices on the subject. Consider claims that are made all the time: Religious people are conservative. Liberals are hostile to religion. President Bush talks about religion far more than other politicians. Democrats just do not know how to talk about God or invoke the scriptures. Whenever religious people get involved in politics, all they care about are abortion, homosexuality and "family values."

Then consider the following, from a president who found Saint Paul's letter to the Ephesians an excellent guide to public policy. "Ephesians says we should speak the truth with our neighbors for we are members one of another," the president said. "I believe that. I think that is the single most important political insight, or social insight, in the Bible. And I think it is what should drive us as we behave together." Then he got to the compassionate God talk. "Is my destiny caught up in yours?" he asked. "Are we part of the same family of God? It is not enough to say we are all equal in the

1

eyes of God. We are all also connected in the eyes of God." And the crowd applauded.

Does it bother you that our president talks that way? If it does, consider this: The speech quoted here was not given by President George W. Bush. It was given at Washington's Metropolitan Baptist Church in December 1997 by a president named William Jefferson Clinton. Bush is not the first president to invoke God and the scriptures, nor will he be the last.

There are many reasons to cheer the dialogue that Mario Cuomo and Mark Souder kick off in this book—and to thank the many distinguished thinkers who have generously added their voices here. The most important may be the contribution they collectively make to exploding prejudices about religion's role in politics. Religious voices are not confined to the Right—or to the Left or the Center. Worries about improper entanglements between religion and government are not confined to liberals. Moral passion rooted in faith is not limited to the ranks of religious conservatives. Religious politicians and intellectuals are perfectly capable of "doing" and living with nuance. They also understand contradiction, paradox, and irony. Indeed, it can be argued that religious faith, properly understood—yes, that is a dangerous phrase—is usually a sign of contradiction, an invitation to paradox, a reminder of the ironies of the human condition.

Richard Fox captures this sense of irony when he notes in these pages that the twentieth century's great American theologian Reinhold Niebuhr knew that "politics needed religion to keep itself pointed toward justice, but he also knew that the struggle for justice was threatened by the power of religion." Niebuhr, Fox continues, insists that "a consciousness of one's own inveterate sinfulness is a basic component of a religious person's public responsibility." And Fox argues that "awareness of sin—of their often hidden desire for fame, power, privilege, and other kinds of self-aggrandizement—can counteract religious people's temptation to see themselves as chosen instruments for divinely sponsored action." One can only wish that this were consistently true.

This volume is part of the Pew Forum Dialogues on Religion and Public Life. The series is based on a simple proposition, one that its editors see as obvious but that others might see as controversial: Religious voices and insights rooted in faith have a great deal to contribute to our public deliberations about politics and public policy. As our coeditor Jean Bethke Elshtain puts it in her essay here, "American politics is indecipherable if it is severed from the interplay and panoply of America's religions."

The series is also rooted in the idea that religious people—including people who share the same faith and live the same religious tradition—can disagree fundamentally on political questions not only because they see the facts differently but also because they read and experience their traditions differently. The series emphatically rejects the idea that faith commitments render the messy facts about politics and policy irrelevant. On the contrary, we have sought out people of faith who respect the facts and have genuine knowledge about the issues about which they speak.

The first volume of the series, *Lifting up the Poor: A Dialogue on Religion, Poverty, and Welfare Reform*, brings together in dialogue Mary Jo Bane and Larry Mead, two of the nation's premier experts on poverty and welfare policy. Both care profoundly about the facts—and their faith. In *Is the Market Moral? A Dialogue on Religion, Economics, and Justice*, Rebecca Blank and William McGurn show how their reflections on economics, rooted in years of engagement with the subject, interact with their moral commitments rooted in faith. Bane and Mead, Blank and McGurn all perform a service in demonstrating that faith speaks to questions that are not easily pigeon-holed as "religious issues." And they provide a model in demonstrating the obligations of the person of faith in the public realm: They make arguments accessible and engaging to those who may not share their particular brands of faith, their specific approaches to theology.

The inspiration behind the series is reflected well by Martha Minow, a professor at Harvard Law School who notes in these pages that "religiously inflected arguments and perspectives bring critical and prophetic insight and energy to politics and public affairs." Minow writes, "There is something woefully lacking in any view that excludes religion entirely from the public sphere." One can believe this, she notes, and still accept that "difficulties arise if government actions cross over from reflecting religious sources of vision and energy to preferring one kind of religion over others." Figuring out how a polity can be open to religious insights without succumbing to the temptation to impose specific religious beliefs through the state might be said to describe the fundamental challenge of religious freedom.

As Representative David Price, a North Carolina Democrat, writes here: "There are compelling reasons, rooted in the theology of divine transcendence, human freedom and responsibility, and the pervasiveness of sin and pride, for refusing to identify any particular ideology or political agenda with the will of God and for rebuking those who presume to do so." This also means that it is far better that those who bring their religious beliefs to the public square be explicit about what they are doing and not be intimidated into muting or hiding their religious commitments. As Jeffrey Stout, a professor of religion at Princeton University, argues in these pages: "If . . . a large segment of the citizenry is in fact relying on religious premises when making political decisions, it behooves all of us to know what those premises are. Premises left unexpressed are often premises left unchallenged."

This volume differs from the earlier ones in form because it differs in content. Where the earlier volumes discuss specific issues, this one deals with the broader question of what faith has to say about politics. In tribute to the broad range of religious voices that jostle with and inspire each other in the United States, it includes many contributors, representing a wide range of traditions, political points of view, and experiences. In these pages are practicing politicians and theologians, preachers, pollsters, and intellectuals. There are voices from the trade union movement, the law, history, sociology, journalism, and the clergy. The essays go back and forth from Left to Center to Right, from Catholic and Jew to Protestant and Muslim.

We do not pretend that this collection in any way exhausts the possibilities for this discussion, but we do believe that this unusually diverse and thoughtful group of writers has much to contribute to the public discussion of religion and public life. In their diversity, they challenge the stereotypes that insist that when religion enters the public square civility inevitably gives way, tolerance disappears, and rational argument becomes impossible. On the contrary, these writers can only strengthen the hope that when religion's relationship to politics is discussed openly, civility, tolerance, and rationality are advanced.

The anchor of this collection is a dialogue between Mario Cuomo, a Democrat who served three terms as governor of New York, and Mark Souder, an experienced Republican member of the House of Representatives from Indiana. Cuomo and Souder first came together at an event sponsored by the Pew Forum on Religion and Public Life in Washington on October 2, 2002. Cuomo, a Catholic and a liberal, and Souder, an Evangelical Protestant and a conservative, were asked to offer their reflections on faith and politics.

The result, at least we think, was dazzling because two men from profoundly different political and religious traditions were able to illuminate such a large portion of our nation's cultural and moral landscape. (Cuomo also showed how very particular the relationship between religion and politics can be. He told the story of Fishhooks McCarthy from Albany, N.Y., a city that was long the home of a legendary political machine. Fishhooks, Cuomo reported, "would start every day of his political life the same way, in Saint Mary's Church . . . on his knees, uttering the same prayer: 'Oh, Lord, give me health and strength; I'll steal the rest.'")

Readers themselves will enter into the dialogue between Cuomo and Souder—and think through the ways in which these two men, who have profound differences, may also share significant areas of common ground. But it is worth offering here a taste of what is to come.

At the heart of Cuomo's view—it can be fairly described as a liberal religious view—is an emphasis on what our traditions have in common. Cuomo speaks of two principles "shared by most if not all of our nation's religions, whether they include God or not."

"Look at the earliest monotheistic religion, Judaism," Cuomo writes. "Two of Judaism's basic principles, as I understand it, are *tzedakkah* and *tikkun olam*. *Tzedakkah* is the obligation of righteousness and common sense that binds all human beings to treat one another charitably and with respect and dignity."

"The second principle, *tikkun olam*, says that, having accepted the notion that we should treat one another with respect and dignity, we come together as human beings in comity and cooperation to repair and improve the world around us. *Tikkun olam*."

"Well," Cuomo continues, "that is also the essence of Christianity, founded by a Jew and built on precisely that principle. Jesus' words, approximately, were, Love one another as you love yourself, for the love of me. And I am Truth. And the truth is, God made the world but did not complete it, and you are to be collaborators in creation."

"Would it not be nice," Cuomo asks, "to find a way simply to announce at once to the whole world that before we argue about the things that we differ on we concentrate on the two things we believe in? We are supposed to love one another, and we are supposed to work together to clean up this mess we are in, because that is the mission that was left to us. I cannot think of any better guidance."

Souder by no means disagrees with all of this. But his emphasis is different. "Conservative faiths, even sects within these faiths, differ on how involved the City of God should be with the City of Man," he says. "But this much is true: Conservative Christians as individuals do not separate their lives into a private sphere and a public sphere."

"To ask me to check my Christian beliefs at the public door," he goes on, "is to ask me to expel the Holy Spirit from my life when I serve as a congressman, and that I will not do. Either I am a Christian or I am not. Either I reflect His glory or I do not."

Souder says, and one doubts that Cuomo disagrees, that "most political issues are moral issues."

"When you serve in government, as I do, every day, every hour you make moral decisions—like making new laws to restrict cheaters like Enron executives. Why restrict cheating? Because it is a moral premise of society. When we deal with rape, with child support enforcement, with juveniles in trouble with the law, why do we not let both sides fight it out and let the strongest win? Because of certain moral premises that society shares."

"But I find that I am allowed to use these Christian values in speaking out for national parks and in speaking out against spouse abuse," Souder continues, "but not when I speak out against homosexual marriage, pornography, abortion, gambling, or evolution across species."

He continues: "Faith institutions are the key to developing a personal moral foundation. The government may foster these institutions, encourage them, nurture them; or it may discriminate against them, harass them, undermine them. But it is not the job of government to replace these institutions as the primary moral agents of society. The Founding Fathers clearly wanted no part of an official sectarian religion." On that last point, all might agree.

Souder's conclusion is that it is "unfair" to ask believers to "check those beliefs at the public door. It is not going to happen. The challenge is to find ways to continue to allow personal religious freedom in America, as guaranteed by our Constitution, while working through the differences."

To build on the Cuomo-Souder dialogue, we invited others to join in, and it was exciting to discover how many thoughtful people were eager to share in this discussion. It would be foolhardy to try to summarize so many thoughtful essays here, but it is worth pointing to the essential themes that will inevitably inform any discussion of religion and politics.

One theme that emerges repeatedly is how complicated it is in a free and pluralist society to find the right balance between the two halves of the First Amendment to our Constitution. How should we as a people properly interpret the amendment's guarantees of the free expression of religion *and* its prohibitions on the establishment through government of any particular religion? In our time, this debate is often expressed in less constitutional terms. How much should religion enter our public debate? How can we guarantee the rights of religious people in the public sphere without threatening the rights of those who are not religious? More simply, how much in any given political argument or campaign do we want to hear about the religious commitments and beliefs of political candidates? As M. A. Muqtedar Khan argues in these pages: "Today, as all religions experience revivals, we must find ways to guarantee religious freedom without proscribing the scope of religion." And, yes, that is not easy.

Robert Bellah, one of our country's premier interpreters of religious and ethical questions, is acutely aware of the difficulties. It is, he writes, "perfectly appropriate to base one's political stand on the particular faith tradition to which one is committed and to explain that tradition in arguing one's case." But he continues: "The only caveat is that one's argument must appeal to general moral principles in persuading others. One does not have the right to demand that others accept the tenets of one's own faith in making a political decision."

And Bellah knows perfectly well that matters get more complicated still. "But if public action is legitimately, and perhaps inevitably, based in significant part on the religious beliefs of public persons, as both Cuomo and Souder seem to agree," he writes, "then the nature of those religious beliefs is also legitimately part of the public discussion." In other words, the public square cannot be bathed in any particular religion, and it cannot avoid religion.

The many conservative voices gathered in this volume help explode stereotypes on this question, specifically the idea that religious conservatives simply want to impose their beliefs on the willing and unwilling alike. It is striking how many of our conservative contributors emphasize the importance of respecting our country's religious diversity. Many of the voices gathered here suggest that it is possible to share the hope of one of our contributors, Republican Representative Amory Houghton of New York, that our destiny is a to be a special nation that "could draw strength from its religious pluralism."

Michael Cromartie of the Ethics and Public Policy Center, for example, argues forcefully that conservative Christians "would be more effective if they developed a public language, a public philosophy, and a public posture that communicates a concern for the common good of all and not just of fellow believers."

Terry Eastland, the publisher of the *Weekly Standard*, is just as clear. "Were I an officeholder or candidate for office," he writes, ". . . I would be willing to state what my faith is, though I would not want to use my faith as an instrument of politics, something to hold up before certain audiences to gain their support. . . . I would want to be persuasive, and on most issues arguments from explicit doctrine . . . are not likely to persuade majorities drawn from a religiously pluralist society."

And Stephen Monsma, a professor of political science at Pepperdine University, also insists that "there are . . . proper and improper uses of religion in the public realm."

"One way that religion is sometimes improperly used in the public realm is as a symbol to garner votes," he writes. "Another improper use of religion is to seek a preeminent place for one's own religion in the public policy realm . . . an improper goal in a religiously pluralist society."

Liberals in these pages also operate against stereotype. Michael Kazin, a professor at Georgetown University who is working on a biography of William Jennings Bryan, uses Bryan's example to show how important religious commitment is—and has been—to social progress. "Bryan transformed his party from a bulwark of conservatism—the defender of states' rights and laissez-faire economics—into a bastion of anticorporate Progressivism that favored federal intervention to help workers and small businesses," Kazin writes. "Undergirding [his] stand was a simple, pragmatic gospel: Only mobilized citizens, imbued with Christian morality, could save the nation from 'predatory' interests and the individuals who did their bidding."

"The Left," Kazin declares in an insightful sentence that will provoke much debate, "has never advanced without a moral awakening entangled with notions about what the Lord would have us do."

And Paul Begala, an architect of Bill Clinton's victories in the 1990s and the staunch liberal of *Crossfire* fame, is uneasy with how progressives treat religion—and how everyone treats those who are religious and liberal. "My friends in what the media calls the religious Right sure know how to fight," Begala writes. "But too many religious progressives do not. And what is worse, the very phrase *religious progressive* is seen as an oxymoron, like jumbo shrimp or compassionate conservative, because much of the Left is far too secular, even antireligious."

We offer here just a modest hint of what is to come. In his powerful 1973 book *The Seduction of the Spirit*, Harvey Cox, one of our contributors, speaks of the importance of respecting the religious beliefs of individuals and communities in their specificity.[1] There is no such thing as generic religion, which is why conflicts between those who hold deeply conflicting views are inevitable in a democracy and why religion's engagement with politics will always be vexing. Cox also discusses how religion can be used and misused. Religion can certainly be both used and misused in politics. But secular political ideologies are also subject to use and misuse. If those of strong views, whether secular or religious, are ruled out of the public discussion, then democracy will only be impoverished.

Jeffrey Stout poses an excellent question in his recent book *Democracy and Tradition*: "Is religion a conversation stopper?" At the risk of reducing Stout's elegant argument to a single word, it seems fair to conclude that he believes the answer is no. Stout insists that "it is possible to build democratic coalitions including people who differ religiously and to explore those differences deeply and respectfully without losing one's integrity as a critical intellect."[2]

This book is offered in the hope and belief that it is possible for religious people to join our democratic conversation and to explore each other's views deeply, respectfully, and constructively. If they cannot, our democracy is in very deep trouble. If they can, our democratic conversation will be decidedly enriched.

Notes

1. Harvey Cox, *The Seduction of the Spirit* (Simon and Schuster, 1973).
2. Jeffrey Stout, *Democracy and Tradition* (Princeton University Press, 2004), p. 91.

PART I

FAITH AND POLITICS
IN PUBLIC OFFICE

IN THE AMERICAN CATHOLIC
TRADITION OF REALISM

MARIO CUOMO

I HAVE BEEN ASKED to share with you my reflections upon the experience of elected officials who try to reconcile personal religious conviction with a pluralist constituency.

In discussing the matter, I do not pretend to be a theologian or a philosopher. I speak only as a former elected official and as a Roman Catholic baptized and raised in the pre-Vatican II Catholic Church. I am attached to the church both by birth and by decision.

In the interest of space constraints, I will try to keep my reflections plain.

Catholicism is a religion of the head as well as of the heart. To be a Catholic is to commit to certain dogmas. It also means a commitment to practice the faith day to day. The practice can be difficult. Today's America, as we all know, is a consumer-driven society, filled with distractions and temptations for people struggling to live by spiritual impulses as well as material ones. Catholics who also hold political office have an additional responsibility. They have to try to create conditions under which all citizens are reasonably free to act according to their own religious beliefs, even when those acts conflict with Roman Catholic dogma regarding divorce, birth control, abortion, stem cell research, and even the existence of God.

Catholic public officials, like all public officials, take an oath to preserve the United States Constitution, which guarantees this freedom. And they do so gladly, not because they love what others do with their freedom but because they realize that, in guaranteeing freedom for others, they guarantee their own right to live their personal lives as Catholics, with the right to reject birth control, to reject abortions, and to refuse to participate in or contribute to removing stem cells from embryos.

This freedom is perhaps the greatest strength of America's uniquely successful experiment in government, and so it must be a dominant concern of every public official. There are other general legal principles that affect the official's decisions operating at the same time. The First Amendment, of course, which forbids the official preference of one religion over others, also affirms one's right to argue that his or her religious belief would serve well as an article of universal public morality, that this belief is not narrowly sectarian but fulfills a universal human desire for order or peace or justice or kindness or love or all of those things—values most of us agree are desirable, even apart from their specific religious priority.

So I can, if I choose, argue—even as a public official—that the state should not fund the use of contraceptive devices, not because the pope or my bishop demands it but because I think that for the good of the whole community we should not sever sex from an openness to the creation of life. And surely I, as a public official, can, if I am so inclined, demand a law to prevent abortions or stem cell retrieval from embryos, not just because my bishop says it is wrong but also because I think that the whole community, regardless of its religious beliefs, should agree on the importance of protecting life, including life in the womb, which is, at the very least, potentially human and should not be extinguished casually. I, even as a public official, have the right to do all of that.

The Constitution, which guarantees your right not to have to practice my religion, guarantees my right to try to convince you to adopt my religion's tenet as public law whenever that opportunity is presented. And it is presented often.

The question for the religious public official, then, is not, Do I have the *right* to try to make public law match my religious belief? but, *Should* I try? Would the effort produce harmony and understanding? Or might it instead be divisive, weakening our ability to function as a pluralist community? For me, as a Catholic official, the question created by my oath of office, by the Constitution, and by personal inclination was, When should I argue to make my religious value your morality, my rule of conduct your limitation? As I understood my own religion, it required me to accept the restraints it imposed in my own life, but it did not require that I seek to impose all of them on all New Yorkers. For example, although the pope, while I was in office, renewed the Roman Catholic Church's ban on birth control devices,

I was not therefore required to veto the funding of contraceptive programs in my state if I did not believe that to be in the interest of the whole community I was sworn to serve. My church understands that. My church understands that our public morality depends on a consensus view of right and wrong. Religious values will not be accepted as part of the public morality unless they are shared by the community at large. The plausibility of achieving that consensus is a relevant consideration in deciding whether or not to make the effort to impose those values officially.

Catholics have lived with these truths of our democratic society fairly comfortably over the years. There is an American Catholic tradition of political realism, which has always made prudent, practical judgments with respect to its attempts to inject Catholic principles into civil law. That was true of slavery in the late nineteenth century. It is true of contraceptives today. And it certainly appears to be true of stem cell retrieval. I have not heard any proposal from either the Roman Catholic Church or President Bush, who took such a hard stance on this subject, that there should be a law condemning stem cell retrieval as murder. As I understood the president's position, we cannot take stem cells from embryos because the embryo is human life; this is the Catholic position as well.

Religion's place in our government is dependent on legal precedents and social attitudes, which are complex, shifting, and sometimes contradictory. Even trying to define the basic words can be an adventure. Most non-lawyers, maybe even most lawyers, would assume that religion necessarily implies belief in a god, perhaps even implies monotheism. Not so. The word *religion* has been defined by the Supreme Court to include belief systems like secular humanism, Buddhism, ethical culture—belief systems that by and large reject the notion of God. The term *God* is even more difficult. *Black's Law Dictionary* does not even attempt a definition.

And some authorities say that the concept of God is too big to be literally embodied. The word *God* implies an infinite power, infinitely effectual. The human race is only a couple of hundred thousand years old, just learning to reflect, struggling to understand large concepts with tiny intellects. It is therefore no surprise that the word *God* appears nowhere in the Constitution. Even in the Declaration of Independence, which is not a law and therefore not subject to legal interpretation and enforcement, the word appears only in reference to the laws of nature and nature's God.

As I understand it, natural law is law derived from human nature and human reason without the benefit of revelation or a willing suspension of disbelief. It is the law, as I perceive it, that would occur to us if we were only 500,000 people on an island without books, without education, without rabbis or priests or history, and we had to figure out who and what we were. We can figure out two of the most basic principles of natural law just by looking around at our world. We see that although some creatures are similar to us, we seem to be different from all other creatures in our ability to communicate. That is the first principle. The second is that we should use our abilities to make the place as useful and as good as we can make it.

These two principles are shared by most if not all of our nation's religions, whether they include God or not. Look at the earliest monotheistic religion, Judaism. Two of Judaism's basic principles, as I understand it, are *tzedakkah* and *tikkun olam. Tzedakkah* is the obligation of righteousness and common sense that binds all human beings to treat one another charitably and with respect and dignity. Of course. What else would you conclude if you are on a desert island, and you saw other like kinds, and you knew you had to protect yourself against the beasts, and you knew that you had to raise children, and you knew you had to produce crops so you could eat? You would say that we should treat one another with respect. You would not need a whole lot of influence from on high or anywhere else to conclude that.

The second principle, *tikkun olam,* says that, having accepted the notion that we should treat one another with respect and dignity, we come together as human beings in comity and cooperation to repair and improve the world around us. *Tikkun olam.* Well, that is also the essence of Christianity, founded by a Jew and built on precisely that principle. Jesus' words, approximately, were, Love one another as you love yourself, for the love of me. And I am Truth. And the truth is, God made the world but did not complete it, and you are to be collaborators in creation. That is the message. Judaism describes it as the whole law, without need of ornamentation or elaboration. And on a desert island, it would work. Incidentally, it would work on this island, the globe, before we make it a desert.

All the religions that I am aware of share those two principles. The Koran, I am informed, honors them. It seems to me, as it did to Tocqueville and to many others, that these two principles are of great benefit to our nation and could be even more beneficial if encouraged. Would it not be nice to find a way simply to announce at once to the whole world that before we argue about the things that we differ on we concentrate on the two things we believe in? We are supposed to love one another, and we are

supposed to work together to clean up this mess we are in, because that is
the mission that was left to us. I cannot think of any better guidance. Nor
do I think it is difficult to apply these two grand, natural law, religious principles to day-to-day affairs, even in a world with the competing virtues of
individuality and community.

no mediating institutions

Abraham Lincoln provides the simplest and most useful instruction in
how to reconcile these two virtues. He said that people should collaborate
through government to do for one another collectively what they could not
do as well or at all individually. This instruction implies that there is a simple way to know whether the responsibility rests with the individual or with
the government. Do not ask me if I am a conservative, if I am a liberal. All
I have to do is apply this instruction to each set of facts as they occur—and
that is not hard. We may argue about it, we may differ about it, we might
even fight about it, but it is not intellectually complicated.

Education? You want to do it all privately? Terrific. We did that for a
long time. I do not think it works. I think we need to do it collectively,
because some people will not be able to pay, and we have to educate everybody. That is why we have free public schools.

Health care? It was not until 1965 that we had Medicare and Medicaid,
and so before that we had decided, according to Lincoln's prescription, that
we did not need collectivity here.

Unemployment insurance? Worker's compensation? When my mother
and father came to the United States from Italy and ran into the Depression there were none of these things. And so the decision we made for the
first hundred years or so was, We do not need any, we are fine. Not complicated. Maybe primitively stupid, but not complicated. And it is still not. To
answer the question of whether society or the government should be
involved in the reaping of stem cells, for example, all we have to do is apply
the simple test of the facts of a changing world as they confront us.

What our religious principles urge upon us comes down to this: We need
to love one another, to come together to create a good society, and to use
that mutuality discretely in order to gain the benefits of community without sacrificing individual freedom and responsibility. In these concededly
broad terms, that would be good government. This construction is also,
frankly, inviting to people who think of themselves, or want to think of
themselves, as religious, who want to believe in something bigger than they
are, which is the basis of all of this. I know I do; I know I do desperately

want to believe in something better than I am. If all there is is me in this society, then I have wasted an awful lot of time, because I am not worth it.

I conclude that religious convictions, at least mine, are not a serious impediment to efficient and proper service by a public official in today's America. In fact I am convinced that some of the fundamental propositions common to all religious convictions actually enrich, instead of inhibit, public service, and they make public service especially inviting to people who are trying to be religious.

A CONSERVATIVE CHRISTIAN'S VIEW
ON PUBLIC LIFE

MARK SOUDER

IT IS CLEAR that Mario Cuomo and I agree on one thing, and that is that most political issues are moral issues. If taxes are a moral issue, then we have a pretty wide berth to include just about any public issue.

We are to many degrees products of our background. I would like to lay out a little bit of the background that might shape a conservative Christian's view on how to approach public life. I begin with a quotation from John Adams: "Our Constitution was made for a moral and religious people; it is wholly inadequate to the government of any other."[1] That was once an uncontroversial statement. It is a little more controversial today.

Faith institutions are the key to developing a personal moral foundation. The government may foster these institutions, encourage them, nurture them; or it may discriminate against them, harass them, undermine them. But it is not the job of government to replace these institutions as the primary moral agents of society. The Founding Fathers clearly wanted no part of an official sectarian religion.

But a moment of silence in the classroom, the posting in the schoool-room of the Ten Commandments (as long as other expressions are also posted), and a Bible on a teacher's desk are not indications of state-sponsored religion. Quite frankly, extrapolations from these practices to accusations of a government-sponsored religion are downright ridiculous, particularly when these accusations are anchored in the so-called wall-of-separation argument. This argument stems from a court opinion about Evangelical revivalists who did not want to pay for Virginia's state church.

It is not an argument of the Founding Fathers, nor was the argument about religious views.

Conservative faiths, even sects within these faiths, differ on how involved the City of God should be with the City of Man. But this much is true: Conservative Christians as individuals do not separate their lives into a private sphere and a public sphere. Chuck Colson and Nancy Pearcey, in their important book *How Now Shall We Live*, clarify a key basis of the Christian worldview: "Creation, Fall, Redemption. There is no Salvation if there is no Fall. There is no Fall if there is no intelligent design. Those who believe in intelligent design and order, rather than some sort of random chaos and the survival of the fittest, have a fundamentally different view of the world."[2]

Let me give you another quotation: "Things have come to a pretty pass when religion is allowed to invade public life."[3] That is what Lord Melbourne said in response to the efforts of William Wilberforce and others to abolish the slave trade in America. Melbourne was interpreting the efforts of Wilberforce as religious and was arguing that religion should not be part of public discussion. However, devoutly religious individuals like Wilberforce have led almost every major social reform.

Here is what the famous Evangelist John Wesley wrote to William Wilberforce after Wilberforce's second or third defeat on the slavery argument:

> Unless God has raised you up for this very thing, you will be worn out by the opposition of men and devils. But if God be for you, who can be against you? Are all of them together stronger than God? Oh, be not weary of well doing. Go on in the name of God and in the power of His might, till even American slavery, the vilest that ever saw the sun, shall vanish away before it, that He has created you from your youth that you may continue strengthening in this and all things.[4]

If you believe you are specifically designed—if you believe in fact that you are not part of some random, inevitable progression of life—then you believe not only that you can change things, you believe also that you have an obligation to change things.

When you serve in government, as I do, every day, every hour you make moral decisions—like making new laws to restrict cheaters like Enron executives. Why restrict cheating? Because it is a moral premise of society.

When we deal with rape, with child support enforcement, with juveniles in trouble with the law, why do we not let both sides fight it out and let the strongest win? Because of certain moral premises that society shares.

I serve on the National Parks Committee. If I should be asked, Why preserve the national parks? Why do we want to preserve our heritage? I might answer, Because there is a logical order and a moral order to what we are preserving. But I find that I am allowed to use these Christian values in speaking out for national parks and in speaking out against spouse abuse but not when I speak out against homosexual marriage, pornography, abortion, gambling, or evolution across species. Then, it seems, I am supposed to check my religious beliefs at the public door. In other words, some moral views seem to be okay in the public arena but other moral views, no matter how deeply held, are not okay.

To again quote Colson and Pearcey, "Genuine Christianity is more than a relationship with Jesus, as expressed in personal piety, church attendance, Bible study, and works of charity. It is more than discipleship, more than believing in a system of doctrines about God. Genuine Christianity is a way of seeing and comprehending all reality. It is a worldview."[5]

To ask me to check my Christian beliefs at the public door is to ask me to expel the Holy Spirit from my life when I serve as a congressman, and that I will not do. Either I am a Christian or I am not. Either I reflect His glory or I do not.

Some time ago, a trendy Evangelical expression was WWJD—What would Jesus do? A better question, given that we are not God, would be: To the best of my limited capability to understand, what do I believe Jesus would have me, as a humble sinner, do? That is a legitimate question.

All this said, we might ask, How in a pluralist society do we implement our own deeply held beliefs? It is not easy. How should we, for instance, handle defeat in the public arena? How do we react to official decisions regarding abortion, for example. Do we resort to violence, or do we take up civil disobedience, or do we work to elect different decisionmakers? Do we respect those with whom we deeply disagree? Can there, for example, be a civil debate on abortion or not?

Few decisions were ever as hard for me as voting against three of the counts of impeachment of Bill Clinton. I was the only conservative in Congress to do so. I found Clinton's moral behavior abominable; I cannot tell you how disgusted I was at a personal level. But I also had sworn to uphold the Constitution. Based on how I interpreted the Constitution, having studied all the arguments looking for a way to vote yes, I concluded I could not do that on three of the counts. Chuck Colson did not agree with my position, but the night before I voted he advised me that if I did not vote my conscience, if I caved in to the political pressure from my base in my district, then I would be committing perjury, just like the allegation against Clinton. So I had a choice either to resign or to vote my conscience.

The only more difficult question than a constitutional one is a question about war. I come from an Anabaptist background, which espouses nonresistance. The Book of Romans, however, clearly states that although individual Christians have a responsibility for peace, it is the job of government to punish the evildoers. Opposition to war is the reason that many Anabaptists do not work in government. So, for me, a vote to support even a necessary and just war will never, ever, be easy because of my fundamental beliefs. I believe that such a vote should be exercised with grave caution.

Sometimes we who are members of a minority church behave as though being a minority is terrible, especially for children. The church in which I grew up did not believe in attending movies, for example. When the school I went to decided to take the students to see the movie *The Sound of Music*, I spent that time in a classroom all by myself. The ACLU did not come to defend me. On this and other issues the school did not try to accommodate my moral views.

Mind you, I was not persecuted, I was not intimidated. In fact, at the time, it did not even particularly bother me that I alone did not attend the movie. But what bothers me is that, in the public arena today, if I as a Christian am offended, I have to be the one to leave. If a liberal—or anyone of a different view from that of a conservative Christian—objects, then the conservative Christians are supposed to stop their objectionable action. Minority views are not given the same representation as majority views.

For example, a liberal may argue that debates about evolution are about science versus religion. But they are not about religion. They are about differing scientific viewpoints, anchored in differing views of how the world came to be. It is not a science versus religion debate, and it is unfair to describe it that way. It unfair to claim that other people's views are based on religion and therefore do not belong in the arena of public debate.

Thus I believe that society discriminates against the moral views of conservatives. In my case, such discrimination had a side benefit: It without a doubt built the character that enabled me to be able to dissent from the accepted view and to make my views heard. That is one of the benefits of learning to defend your belief.

America is clearly becoming more religiously diverse: More religions are represented and membership in these religions is growing. A significant percentage of this country is Evangelical, charismatic, fundamentalist, or conservative Catholic, or conservative Lutheran, or Orthodox Jewish, or fundamentalist Muslim, and these people hold passionate views, views that are essential to their very being. These believers will not—and it is unfair to ask them to—check those beliefs at the public door. It is not going to happen. The challenge is to find ways to continue to allow personal religious freedom in America, as guaranteed by our Constitution, while working through the differences.

In a republic, disagreements are decided in the public arena. At different times in American history, different moral views may prevail. Abortion may be legal in some periods and illegal in other periods. Will dissenters resort to violence or will they confine their protest to the ballot box? Sex with minors? The use of marijuana? Date rape? The spanking of children? The way we judge these depends on our moral view, on our worldview. The way society judges these depends on the worldview of legislators, of the president, and of the courts.

Notes

1. Charles Francis Adams, ed., *John Adams, The Works of John Adams, Second President of the United States*, vol. IX, October 11, 1798 (Boston: Little, Brown, 1854), p. 229.

2. Chuck W. Colson and Nancy Pearcey *How Now Shall We Live?* (Wheaton: Tyndale House Publishers, 1999).

3. Elizabeth Knowles, ed., *The Oxford Dictionary of Quotations*, 5th ed. (Oxford University Press, 1999), p. 504.

4. Charles Yrigoyen, Jr., *John Wesley: Holiness of Heart and Life* (Abingdon Press, 1999), p. 56.

5. Colson and Pearcey, pp. 14–15.

CONTINUING
THE CONVERSATION

JEAN BETHKE ELSHTAIN TO MARIO CUOMO   In the course of your presentation you note concerns about making an individual's religious faith the value of the wider community, and you also indicate that in attempting to do that, rather than creating or sustaining civic harmony, it might do quite the opposite. Do you believe there are times when a public official, who is also a deeply committed person of faith, should deepen divisions that may exist in the community for the sake of furthering values that may be religiously based? When is it your job to deepen that debate and to extend the debate in a direction that is consistent both with your religious values and with what you hope will be the values of the wider community at some point?

MARIO CUOMO RESPONDS   What you are asking for is examples—for me to tell you under what circumstances I would risk rejection for a greater good. That question should not be limited to religious issues. My position on the death penalty, for example, confuses a lot of people. In debating it against Ed Koch, which I did for years, he would say, "Mario is against the death penalty because he thinks it is a sin," which is a deprecating way to characterize my position. I have been against the death penalty all of my adult life. For most of my adult life the Catholic Church did not express an opinion against the death penalty. Notwithstanding, I wrote to the Vatican when I was governor and said, "Please, please, please, speak on this subject."

When I speak against the death penalty I never suggest that I consider it a moral issue. I seldom talk in terms of moral issues. I am against the death penalty because I think it is bad and unfair. It is debasing. It is degenerate. It kills innocent people. It eclipses other more significant issues that we should be addressing when we talk about murder and how to do away with it.

My position on the death penalty is based on reasons that are not religious nor it is based on questions of morality. My reasons are perfectly appropriate in this pluralist society. The question is, What is good for us, what is fair, what is reasonable? What works, what does not work? I have made a strong case for my position on the death penalty, but I got—pardon me—murdered at the polls, especially in 1994, when I lost 7.5 percent of the votes because of my position on the death penalty. And considering that I lost the election by only 2.5 or 3 points, that meant a lost election. But I believe it was better to make the point as insistently as I could than to walk away from it.

Why? Because it is an issue that goes way beyond executing somebody at Sing Sing. I pushed the issue because it goes far beyond the death penalty itself. It is a question of how one views human beings. It is a question of how one deals with anger. People favor the death penalty, to my understanding, because they are angry and because they want revenge. There is no other reason that I can find. And anger is corrosive. I think that the death penalty is bad and that it has to be objected to. And so I did.

So when do we take a potentially unpopular stand for a greater good? When we think we should. Should we take a stand against stem cell research? Should Catholics be arguing that there should be a law that declares that anybody who withdraws a stem cell from an embryo is a murderer? Should the government forbid it? Make the issue part of penal law? That seems to be the logic of those who object.

That is the logic of the argument against abortion. If we say that the fetus is a person, we should also say that there should be a law punishing abortion as murder. But, no—I do not think so. Why? I think such a law would be divisive. It would not work. People would not understand it, and we would not make our point.

I tried to make the point at Notre Dame in 1984 as a Catholic. I said, look, if we want to convince people that our position on abortion demonstrates a respect for life that would be good for all of us, let us start by example. At that time the statistics available to us showed that Catholics were having abortions to the same extent that everybody else was. How can we expect to convert this community to our point of view unless we lead the way by example and with love?

One of my disappointments with the Democratic Party is that, although it often talks in terms of morality on both Iraq and the tax cut, it has basically declined to take a stand on these issues. The tax cut was passed when we had the largest surplus in American history. The tax cut was passed with the rationale that we do not need the money. They gave us the money; we should give it back. And so most of it will go back to the rich people who gave us most of it.

Over the next few years, $500 billion will go to 1,120,000 taxpayers, more or less. The richest people in America will get $500 billion. This will happen in spite of the deficits that threaten states and local government, which means increases in real estate taxes and property taxes. These are regressive taxes, the taxes that hurt most of all working people and poor people.

Now, with all of that—with the lack of money for prescription drugs, with a war looming that they say will cost $200 billion, with Social Security money being used up in this process—should we go forward with a $500 billion distribution of money to people who are so rich they cannot reasonably be said to need it? When it would not even be invested in the economy? Are we going to switch our rationale now to say, Well, we had a great surplus then, we had a powerful economy then. Now we have a lousy economy. Now we want the tax cut because it will stimulate the economy.

But tax cuts for, say, my clients at Willkie, Farr, and Gallagher are not going to stimulate the economy. My clients are not going to buy automobiles with the money; they are going to invest it. Give the money to people who are going to spend it right away. Take half of the $500 billion and give it to state and local governments so as to avoid raising state and local taxes for poor people. Tell the rich people to wait four years. Tell me why that is not a totally moral position and fairer than our current position, which is, If it seems that we are raising taxes we will lose an election.

Now consider Iraq. Imagine Iraq without 9/11; just for a moment try to imagine there was, if only it could be so, no 9/11. And imagine that a year and a half or so into the presidency, without 9/11, the president announces that America is going to attack Iraq. What would have happened? Well, after the laughter stopped, people would have said to Bush, You have to be kidding. Make the case. You did not say this in the 2000 campaign. You have not said it for a year and a half. Why are you saying it now? What has happened? Did you learn something? Maybe you know something; maybe you found something; maybe the Israelis found something.

The Iraq issue was shoved into the draft of that great surging current of emotion created by 9/11. We did not even ask questions. But now we are coming to our senses, and we are asking questions. We say of Saddam Hussein, Look, he is a bad guy, he is Adolf Hitler. We want to get rid of him. We understand that. But is there a way to do it without sending 200,000 or 300,000 people to Iraq, some of whom will be killed, and without killing lots of innocent people? Is there another way to do it?

We are not making that argument because many politicians believe that people will not understand. They sanctify popularity. But is this not a good example of when to go forward? The issue does not have to be religious or moral. It could be something we believe in our hearts to be absolutely wrong. Why do we say nothing about them? Because we want to stick around, to stay in public service. We tell ourselves that in the long run we will do many good things that are heavier in weight than the good thing we might accomplish if we speak out. Or we say that we cannot accomplish anything good here anyway and so as a matter of prudence and pragmatism decide to sit back and not make waves.

Is it a sin to do nothing? Well, the God I trust in, I hope, is more supple than that. I am not sure it would be called a sin. But the question comes up all the time, and we have to decide it by our own lights.

E.J. DIONNE TO MARK SOUDER Non-Christian Americans look at Christianity in general as the majority faith, and they are therefore fearful of the injection of this majority faith into not so much the public square—there should be no argument about the right of people to bring religious arguments to the public square—but into public policy. Many times political arguments do break down along such lines, so that not only secularists but also members of minority communities worry about the injection of Christianity into public policy. On the other hand, your perspective is potentially helpful because you define a group of Christians—broadly speaking, Evangelical Christians—as yet another minority. Could you talk about whether this is an apt description of your view and about the fears of non-Christian religious minorities that their rights could be violated?

MARK SOUDER RESPONDS   That is a complex question, but it goes to the heart of one of the fundamental reasons that liberals and conservatives pass each other right by. It also highlights some differences inside what might be called *Christianity* or even *conservative Christianity*.

Let me first deal with the idea that some maintain that America was once considered a Christian nation. If you define America or another country as a Christian nation, you pretty well define the word out of existence, because the term *Christian* is so broad in interpretation and application that it does not really have meaning. Yet those who do not consider themselves Christian view the Christian movement as monolithic and, therefore, a danger.

I grew up in a fundamentalist church. Many people in my denomination felt that when John Kennedy got elected that there would be a direct phone line to the pope. They thought that the Catholic Church was monolithic and that every Catholic was alike. When I went to graduate school at Notre Dame, I found that no two Catholics agreed on anything. There were Sunday Catholics, daily mass Catholics, holiday Catholics, Catholics who believe in the Trinity, and those who do not. The idea that they were going to unite and crush us was absurd. It is also absurd to believe this about Christians.

Christians have in fact killed each other. I remember one time in Dan Coats's office, where I was a staffer, we were arguing about whether to fund drug-free school programs. A staffer who is Calvinist in background told me in jest that I advocated these programs because I was a dissenting, free-will Pelagian who believed that people could be changed. I argued that, in fact, people could be changed. He said, "And that is why my people killed your people 500 years ago." So the idea that Christians are going to unite on a church-state type of thing is just not even on our horizon.

MARGARET O'BRIEN STEINFELS   The Catholic Church has apparently never provided, as part of its insurance coverage for its employees or for people who get insurance from Catholic companies, contraceptive coverage. The New York legislature has voted to require all insurance companies in the state, including Catholic ones, to provide contraceptive coverage. One could make a case that violating the conscience of a religious institution by requiring it to do something that is against its strictures merits discussion and further thought.

MARIO CUOMO RESPONDS   The question is, How far should we go to accommodate religious liberty? There are Catholic hospitals that will not perform abortions, and we allow them the privilege of not providing abortion services, even as we give them a whole range of government services that we give to other hospitals. We do not insist that they surrender their reluctance to perform abortions.

Another question is, To what extent should we accommodate the Catholics' reluctance to cooperate materially in the distribution of contraceptives? I do not see that that would be terribly punishing to the rest of society to allow them that exemption—to allow them that conscience clause. What the courts would do with that is an entirely different matter. As you know, the law is far from clear on the question of giving people exemptions so they can practice their religion. The decision in *City of Boerne, Texas* v. *Flores* did not help. I am not sure there is a lot of logic at the Supreme Court level. Sometimes the Court has been more willing than at other times to decide in favor of religious groups.

MARK SOUDER RESPONDS   If the hospital were purely private, there would be little dispute. The problem comes with dependence on public money, when the question moves into the realm of public debate. I believe there should be a conscience clause. There are plenty of hospital options for people who choose abortion in big cities. But it is a much more difficult question if there is only one choice of a hospital or one choice of a health care plan and if government funds pay for a portion of those services.

JEAN BETHKE ELSHTAIN   Others would cast the question of Catholic hospitals being allowed the privilege of not performing abortions in a different political language and say they have a right, not simply a privilege, not to perform abortions. It is part of religious liberty, part of free exercise. That issue will be refracted in different ways, depending upon the rhetorical choices.

WILLIAM GALSTON   The greatest thinker in my tradition, Moses Maimonides, worked all of his life to reduce 613 commandments to 13 articles of faith. The governor of New York, without working too hard, has taken that 13 down to 2. With more work, we can probably take it down to a single, unitary article of faith.

The issue as I understand it is how to reconcile personal religious views with the practice of politics in a pluralist democracy. Mario Cuomo gives an interesting and clear response: The God who ought to enter the public realm of a pluralist constitutional democracy is nature's God, and the religious arguments that ought to enter the discourse of a pluralist constitutional democracy are the religious arguments that are the common property not only of all religions but also of all mankind. This is the classic natural law argument.

My question to Mark Souder is whether you agree with that formulation, and if you do not, what portion of faith that is not accessible to the common reason of mankind has a legitimate role in the public realm?

RON SIDER   I want to add to the natural law discussion. It would seem that simply taking the two principles (especially the second, working to repair and improve the common society) does not work because policymakers might have very different worldviews—views about the nature of persons and so on. Different and even contradictory public policies will flow from these different worldviews. Secular humanists and fundamentalist Christians, for example, have different worldviews and espouse different policies, though both will claim to be working to improve society.

So that general principle, it seems to me, is so general that it is virtually useless. We have to move to a more specific content, which is what Mark Souder does. But then the problem on the other side is that, yes, we have the right to bring our full-blown religious views into the public debate but then we have got to convince a broad range of people. And that need forces us to use common language, which pushes us back in the direction of Cuomo's position.

MARK SOUDER RESPONDS   The notion of a natural law common to all religions is in fact a worldview and a moral view that is different from a Christian worldview and moral view—and is unacceptable to me. So the question is, How do I reconcile that view with my Christian view in the public arena, since I believe that the Holy Trinity is nature's God, since I believe the Trinity is the God who created nature? I cannot relate to the idea of a generic, natural law God. My God is a particularly Christian God. If you ask, What is common to all religions? Well, what if child abuse is? What if date rape is? What if religions allow twelve-year-olds to have sex with adults? Does the law have to be common to all religions? Or just to major religions? And what if major religions disagree on the role of women? What is nature's God? I do not believe there is a common denominator that is workable in the American political system.

The question really comes down to, How do we respect one another? How do we resolve our differences? In other words, What is in the City of God realm and what is in the City of Man realm? But that is what we work through in the public arena.

MARIO CUOMO RESPONDS   If the natural law principle that says that we are all in this together is too general to be useful, well, that is of course true also of the American Constitution. Consider the Articles of Confederation—thirteen states decided they were interconnected and interdependent and ought to come together to *tikkun olam,* to repair the situation. They created a Constitution that has soaring general language about "for the common welfare," "to create a more perfect union." Talk about generalizations.

In the wake of 9/11, in dealing with hatred all over the planet, do we believe in a principle that says, Let us start with the proposition that we are interconnected and interdependent and that these others are part of our world? It is the first principle.

I was heartened to read President Bush's new strategy for defense. He says, "I acknowledge the importance of dealing with poverty in parts of the world where there is apparently hostility to us, and that until we help them to rid themselves of the problem of oppression and poverty, we will continue to have a problem." That is specifically a recognition of interdependent interconnectedness.

Those, of course, were Gorbachev's greatest words. They were Vaclav Havel's greatest words. They were their contribution—that we are all in this thing together. It is the difference between isolationism and getting involved.

I do not think such a principle is too general, any more than the Constitution is too general. The Constitution says, Get together for the sake of the whole place; and you states, give up some of your power, throw it into the pot so that we have a commonality here. America has worked it out for a couple of hundred years. The first hundred years did not have a whole lot of the commonality aspect; Americans were believers in rugged individualism. Thanks to the Depression we then moved into a new phase.

Too general? I do not think so. It is the heart of the matter. We are supposed to treat one another with dignity. That means that people in Africa who are dying from AIDS are just like people here who are dying from AIDS. We do not treat them that way, not nearly. We are not doing anything like what we would do for them if they were in our family. That is a violation of the principle I am enunciating. You have to apply it from moment to moment, as Mark Souder says. In the end it is always a matter of fashioning it to meet the practical situation. But too general? It is the whole game. It is the whole game. Unless the United States, particularly, understands that, we are finished.

We are talking about changing accounting irregularity to accounting regularity, through Sarbanes-Oxley, the Securities and Exchange Commission, and all sorts of specific rules. By 2005 the European Union will have 380 million people and its own set of accounting principles. Unless the United States also institutes new accounting regulations and an improved accounting system by 2005, the growing globalization in financing, which is important to both the European Union and the United States, will be slowed. That is a simple principle. Too general? No, of course not. We apply the principle to the situation. But in all cases, we work to cooperate.

If you take—I hate to say evolutionary—but if you take an evolutionary point of view, we are going from the slime to the sublime. We are going from a big bang to gas to liquid to fish to humans, who reflect, who get brighter and brighter, who become ever more civil. When we finally have perfect civility, then we are home. And the key to perfect civility is integration, not disintegration, not fragmentation. Maybe it is general, but it works very nicely for me.

ROBERT EDGAR   My question has to do with a concern that is growing in me as a former congressperson, as someone who has watched as capitalism has become, in a sense, a religion that has been lifted up high and honored, particularly by the conservative tradition.

I look at the fact that 80 percent of the world's population lives in substandard housing, that 70 percent of the world's population cannot read or write, and that 50 percent of the world's population will go to bed tonight hungry, and I see the rise in children being placed in factories, particularly offshore, to produce products that we profit from in our society, and I wonder, given both of your perspectives on your faith statements, how might our faith statements critique capitalism in a constructive way so that an economic system can be shaped for the future that is not based on having a percentage of our population poor? And as I understand it, all of our religious traditions fundamentally care about the least of these, our brothers and sisters.

Azizah Y. al-Hibri   I speak as a Muslim. I am aware in these comments of a very rudimentary knowledge of Islam and the Muslim community. I offer examples. In some cases, I think Islam could have been included in describing positive attitudes in this country, and it was not because we just do not know enough. And in other cases, assumptions were made about Muslims that are inaccurate. I will pick one of those simply to show that just as minorities fall into the trap of talking about Christians as one lump, the same is true of minorities—that we cannot talk about all of them as one lump, that there are differences among the various minorities. For example, in talking about bringing religion to the public square, it is often assumed that minorities do not like that, because they will be the losers. In fact, Representative Souder, I wrote an article in which I said that Muslims would rather live in a Christian state than a godless state. So that might come as a surprise to you, but it was after a lot of discussion with a lot of Muslims in my community.

These are good things to say about Muslims. My concern is that since we are very concerned about people bringing their faith to the public square, we have noticed that since 9/11 some of us have been left in the class alone. In fact, a lot has been said about Muslims that renders them powerless and voiceless. If religion is brought to the public square, is there a responsibility on the part of those we view as a majority to stand up, to make sure that certain minorities, even in the most difficult of times, are not rendered voiceless and are not being condemned in unfair ways?

J. Brent Walker   I am with the Baptist Joint Committee on Public Affairs; unlike our Anabaptist cousins, who are pacifists, we Baptists like to fight with one another all the time. I want to offer something that my Baptist sister, Barbara Jordan, once said when asked the same question about how she went about integrating her faith with her public service. "You would do well to pursue your cause with vigor while realizing that you are a servant of God, not a spokesperson for God, and realizing that God may well choose to bless an opposing point of view for reasons that have not yet been revealed to you." I think she spoke a lot of wisdom. And I would like the governor and the congressman to comment briefly on the role of humility as exemplified by Jesus and taught by Jesus in an otherwise ego-ridden arena of politics and public service.

JOANNA ADAMS   First, do our panelists sense a growing religiosity in the United States, or is the United States becoming increasingly secular in its values? And second, if the conclusion is that we are becoming increasingly religious, clearly we are becoming increasingly religiously diverse. Is this diversity a hair shirt, a problem that we must bear up under and figure out how to respond to, because it is a negative? Or is it in fact a blessing—I would use that word—a great opportunity for our democracy?

MARIO CUOMO RESPONDS   About the religiosity, this is a truly intriguing question and a very good one. What I have seen over my span is an increasing desire to be able to engage this world in spiritual terms, as distinguished from material terms. And I think, without making it too complicated, that is not always religion qua religion. It is a growing desire to find an explanation that goes beyond ourselves.

And this has always been true of humanity. We have always wanted to find an explanation that goes beyond our own me-ness and that is larger and more beautiful and will sustain us in all the confusion of this place, especially after things like 9/11, where the biggest question we are left with is not, Why did our religion fail, why did our intelligence fail? but Why did any good God allow this to happen? And that is the question asked of the Holocaust, and that is the question asked when a child dies in the crib without explanation, and that is the question that troubles religious people most. We read Rabbi Harold Kushner's book *When Bad Things Happen to Good People*, but it is never enough, no matter what we read.

Most people conclude at some point that the only thing they are sure of is the value of the next breath they draw, the value of their lives and of making more of their lives. And then they fall back to one of two possibilities: One, they see themselves as baskets of appetites and run around filling up their baskets as fast as they can because they know they are likely to be extinguished at any moment; that is what 9/11 reminds them of, and so they do sex or food or power, whatever it is.

But I think a larger number of people know that that is foolish, because they get older, and the basket falls apart, and they look for something really meaningful. And what is it? It is the people they love and the people who love them. It is their children, their home.

So the short answer: Spirituality, yes, a great desire for spirituality, but the sophistication—and I am using the term as a negative—that comes with a lot of education makes it a little bit harder for people to keep the religious tradition and to make a religious commitment, because more and more people think they are wise enough to challenge it: I cannot prove it, I do not understand it, and so I am going to reject it. And if you give them any provocation to give up on their so-called faith, they will lapse; they will say, Well, I am spiritual.

So if there are people who are trying more and more to be spiritual, more and more to find some truth, that is what the natural law is. It is a truth that appeals to reason, that does not have the benefit of bureaucracy and carefully etched, specific rules for specific situations, but that has the fundamental principles that make people believe in something bigger than themselves. And what is bigger than ourselves is the world we are part of and the contribution we can make to making it a little bit better.

Now, I am not smart enough to figure out Heaven and Hell and why any good God would burn us eternally for making us vulnerable and all of that (this is not me; I am talking about people who are spiritual but not religious). I detect—and that is a very good thing—people looking for something more to believe in. That is what religion is supposed to do for you.

Is it good? Bad? I think it is good because I think what we desperately need is some way to express a willingness to be a community, because we are going from the slime to sublime, and the only way you get there is through integration, and that means we have got to learn better than we know now how to come together. So I think it is good.

MARK SOUDER RESPONDS   I will give a couple fast answers to the questions, and then I want to zero in on the two related to the Muslims. I have some agreements and some disagreements about the religiosity question. I believe, in fact, we are losing a lot of the middle, that we are simultaneously moving to traditional faiths, which are growing, and also moving away from any organized religion at all in the sense of church attendance or a rule that mandates something other than a person's will.

I agree that 9/11, particularly, sparked people into looking for something bigger than themselves. But often, if there is not a standard that has a tradition, this search merely becomes looking for something that enables people to do what they want; or the method is really arbitrary, like finding guidance in a crystal or how the stars align. I believe the question, at least for Christianity, is, Do you accept Jesus Christ as your savior? Because without him, you will be lost in Hell forever. And then you honor and obey him. Other religious faiths have variations of that, but to me, that is what religion is, not what our personal desires are and the way we cope with them. It is how to honor the creator.

The poverty question is difficult. I am more of a neoconservative than a libertarian. However, all conservatives are really fusionists in the political arena, because that is how we get elected. I have more faith in the free market than many others might have, but I have always believed that corporations have a responsibility to be active in their communities. I am as angered by Enron as any liberal, because I believe the company is a shame to capitalism, hiding things off the books. I believe in openness and honesty. The Enron scandal shook confidence in the whole capitalist system, the system that I believe helps the poor the most.

That said, I believe that we will never eliminate the poor, because *poor* is a relative term. What we want to do is make sure that there is opportunity to rise and a decent standard of living for the poor. Eliminate not relative poverty but absolute poverty, as Nicholas Eberstadt of the American Enterprise Institute says, and with certain decent standards as a given. While I might have different solutions than Ron Sider would advocate, he has helped call attention to the fact that we in the Evangelical movement often get into thinking that our little fingernail is more important than anything else in the rest of the world. And we as Christians have obligations to the rest of the world.

I am an American. I am proud. I think this country is a beacon to the world. But I also think it is part of an international community. Christ talked more about the poor than he did about the rich, and I believe that we will be measured ultimately by how we help those who are hurting, not by how we help those who are powerful. In the public arena, however, that means we can differ over whether capital gains cuts will help the poor.

With regard to the question of diversity, which ties into the question about Muslims, I have a far more diverse base than establishment liberals or Democrats do. My campaign chairman is Armenian. I have a large Asian Indian community in my district, which actively supports me. I have never in any subpoll pulled less than 67 percent of any minority subgroup, including African American, Asian, and Hispanic, and it is partly because, by my nature, I am nondiscriminatory. I have strong views, and so I respect the strong views of others, and people sense that.

For instance, I am a very strong supporter of Israel. That, however, does not mean that I believe that Palestinians or Arabs or Muslims are subhuman, or that I am disrespectful of them, or that I do not want to try to work out the complexities, both international and domestic, with the Muslim faith. And it is not that I do not understand the diversity of the Muslim community in my district. There are 200 Iraqis in my district. About half of them came here before Saddam Hussein's reign in Iraq. About half of them are Shi'i from the southern part of Iraq, and the other half are Sunni. If Christians or others, particularly at this time, do not try to understand the complexities and the differences in the Muslim community, this is wrong.

The bad news for the Muslim community is that the potential war in Iraq and the terrorism question have exposed them to prejudice and discrimination in our society. The good news for the Muslim community is that others are trying to understand Islam and to learn how many Muslims are in America, in our communities. Americans are also learning that Muslims are not all one. Just as I said about the Catholic Church, it is clear that there is a wide diversity in the Muslim community. For instance, Iraqi Shi'i point out that Iranian Shi'i are not Arabs, although they are Muslims and a part of the Shi'i Muslim community. But still most Americans, including many in government, do not necessarily understand these distinctions.

Now, understanding the differences and the common traditions is going to be slow. But how we work through that is important. The ultimate question is, Do I think that the diversity will strengthen or weaken America? It depends on how we react. In fact, we have absorbed one wave after another of immigrants, and each wave of immigrants has felt some form of discrimination: the Asians did, the Irish did, the Germans did, the Mexicans do currently. The question is, How do we assimilate? And that goes in both directions: How much does American society expand to tolerate and understand the new people who have come in? And what things cannot be assimilated in the public arena? And how much do those who come accept the values of America in the public arena? So assimilation can take a while, but there still has to be an assimilation of certain values that people came to America for.

As we absorb people who practice Asian religions and Muslim religions in larger numbers than we have before, how in the public arena do we accommodate a legal system and an ethical system that is anchored in the Judeo-Christian tradition? How much are the people who are coming in going to assimilate into the Judeo-Christian tradition? How much do we have to change the framework? To answer these questions, we have to be far more understanding of the differences, and we have to work out how these differences and changes are going to work in the public arena.

PART II
EXPANDING THE DIALOGUE

WHAT IS A CHRISTIAN TO DO?

DOUG BANDOW

Not too many years ago religion seemed to have little to do with the national political debate, but few Americans likely remember that time. Consider the 2004 presidential campaign: George W. Bush was the most overtly observant Christian to hold the presidency in at least a quarter century. The Democratic primaries drew as candidates an Orthodox Jew and an ordained (Pentecostal) minister. Abortion passed the thirty-year mark as a divisive national issue, and gay marriage exploded as another bitter social controversy. Many Evangelicals looked at U.S. policy toward Israel, Iraq, the Palestinians, and Islamic terrorism through the prism of their faith.

In 2003 some religious conservatives cited God as the reason to jail gays across the nation and to raise taxes in Alabama. Liberal Christians used religious images and rhetoric to oppose the war in Iraq and tax cuts. Left-wing activists announced the formation of the Clergy Leadership Network to counter such conservative organizations as the Christian Coalition and the Family Research Council. So much for the naked public square, at least when it comes to political advocacy.

As America's political campaigns were heating up, with clergy and laymen in tow, sacred scriptures and ancient traditions were certain to suffer the indignity of being enlisted for ephemeral political causes. Many activists assumed that religious people—and particularly Christians, who nominally make up the vast majority of the American population—should think, act, and vote in a certain way because of their faith. But in what way? The proper role of government—the central concern of political theory—has long been a controversial issue within Christendom. Christians seem no closer to agreement today. The very pervasiveness and persistence of political disputes should be cause for humility. There is, it seems, no simple Christian view of the state. And for good reason: Holy scripture and church tradition provide guidelines and principles but no detailed blueprint for godly government. On most issues believers are left with the Apostle James's unsatisfying injunction to ask for wisdom, which God "gives generously to all without finding fault" (James 1:5). God provides Christians with principles to be applied with wisdom, rather than specific answers. Indeed, part of the Christian walk appears to be to work out our faith as we attempt to resolve problems in community with others.

Christians do have specific responsibilities toward government, such as prayer for public officials and obedience to the law. Yet those who take their religious faith seriously should have limited expectations for politics. Certainly Christians should not treat the state as either redemptive or eternal. Rather, it is the Lord who "will judge the world in righteousness and the peoples with equity" (Psalms 98:9). Beyond that, the Bible sets only general boundaries for political debate. For Christians the dominant message of the Gospel, as well as of the Hebrew writings, is our relationship to God and to our neighbors. Although many of the principles in this message have some application to politics, the Bible gives much more guidance on how we should treat people in everyday life than on when we should coerce them, especially through today's secular political order.

The state's fundamental role is to protect citizens from the sinful conduct of their neighbors. The Bible indicates that government is to help preserve order—people's ability to live "peaceful and quiet lives," in Paul's words, in a sinful world (1 Timothy 2:2). One goal of the state is just retribution. Deterrence, encouraging even evil people to respect others' rights, is another objective of government. Paul wrote that fear of punishment is one reason for compliance with the authorities (Romans 3:5). But even here, where government's role is clear, the exact means of achieving godly objectives is left to human discretion.

Another recurring theme is reflected in King David's observation: "The Lord is righteous, he loves justice" (Psalms 11:11). Civil rulers, like individuals, are to be just and righteous. However, corporate duty differs from personal responsibility. Individuals must respond generously to the needs and rights of their neighbors; government must regulate coercively yet fairly relations between both righteous and unrighteous people. In short, the contrast is personal virtue versus public impartiality. Thus government is to be a neutral arbiter and protector. Biblical justice protects all citizens in their enjoyment of God's blessings. It certainly is not to become a tool to rob and oppress, a constant risk in every political system, including American democracy. Protection of the needy is of special concern to God; they are, after all, the least able to look after their own interests, especially in the face of a government that is easily subverted to favor the powerful. However, extra sensitivity to the abuse of the poor does not warrant prejudice in their favor. God commanded: "Do not pervert justice; do not show partiality to the poor or favoritism to the great, but judge your neighbor fairly" (Leviticus 19:15).

In their focus on process, godly justice and righteousness are different from the modern notion of social justice, which demands equal economic and cultural outcomes. However appealing may be some proposals advanced under the rubric of social justice, they are not matters of biblical justice, which guarantees a fair civil government nested within a larger culture, in which the wealthy and powerful recognize their obligation to God to help those in need. Thus although seemingly problematic economic and social outcomes matter, they should be addressed directly, most obviously through charity, rather than by manipulating standards of justice.

In the Old Testament the government enforced many essentially "religious" rules, and some believers want those same rules to be enforced today since they are thought to be "God's law." For example, leftist Christians often point to ancient Israel's Jubilee laws, which limited property sales, to support income redistribution. Some conservatives look to Mosaic law for support for their social preferences. So-called reconstructionists have advocated the stoning of unruly children and similarly draconian punishments for other moral offenses. The Supreme Court decision voiding state sodomy laws caused even more mainstream religious conservatives—some associated with Concerned Women of America, for instance—to not only dispute the constitutional legitimacy of the Court's ruling but to also defend jailing homosexuals as a requirement of God's law. A number advocated similarly punishing adulterers and fornicators, which would put most of the teen and adult populations behind bars.

The willingness of fervent activists to pick and choose preferred provisions of Mosaic law to enforce is disturbing enough. But the enforcement of Old Testament law was tied to the nature of the political community in which it was applied and is not properly the province of civil government today. Most obviously, these strictures reflected the Israelites' status as the chosen people. That is, God established the law to mold the nation of Israel as part of his overall plan of salvation. Perhaps for this reason public enforcement of many Old Testament norms required the active intervention of God, something no secular state today is likely to rely upon. In fact, by the time Jesus began his ministry, the old Hebraic rules appear to have been largely abandoned, and the Jewish world at that time—under secular Roman leadership—looked much more like today's America than it did ancient Israel.

Indeed, the move from a geographically bounded Jewish state to a Jewish community under the rule of secular civil authorities, as well as the shift from the Old Covenant to the New Covenant, would appear to have changed the focus from national to individual responsibility and judgment. Obviously, even during Moses' time, Hebrews were liable for their own conduct, and even though today's Christian church has important corporate duties, the theological center of gravity has shifted. God warned the Israelites that compliance with his law would result in good harvests and national success; disobedience would bring disease, defeat, and dispersal (Leviticus 26:1–46; Deuteronomy 28:15–68). When Jesus ministered to an Israel ruled by the Roman Empire, he placed the burden of fulfilling the law on the people individually. Those who did not maintain the law would "be called the least in the kingdom of heaven" (Matthew 5:19).

Another reason to doubt that today's state is mandated to enforce moral and religious rules is that most of these rules ultimately deal with matters of the heart as much as conduct. Paul wrote, "A man is a Jew if he is one inwardly; and circumcision is circumcision of the heart, by the Spirit, not by the written code" (Romans 2:29). Meaningful enforcement of the moral law, then, requires God's direct intervention. However good the civil authorities may be at detecting and punishing, say, adultery, no official can judge lustful looks—or anger at one's brother, which Christ equated with murder.

Christians should be particularly hesitant to advance civil enforcement of essentially religious strictures because the church has taken over the theological role once reserved for the geographic nation of Israel. Although the objective of maintaining spiritual purity is the same, the institution (state or church) and the penalties (death or excommunication) are different. For instance, in his first letter to the Corinthian church Paul instructed believers to disassociate themselves from "anyone who calls himself a brother" but is immoral. He did not apply the same rule to nonbelievers, he explained, since "God will judge those outside" (1 Corinthians 5:9–13). And like it or not, Christians live in a society dominated by nonreligious neighbors. The very nature of the state, in contrast to the ancient Israelite monarchy, is to govern a disparate people of disparate beliefs. Today's state is designed to promote civil order and public good, not religious faith and individual salvation.

Just as scripture requires government to act in some circumstances—though not as often as many liberals and conservatives would like—it also restricts some government actions. The most important limitation flows from the first commandment given to Moses: "You shall have no other gods before me" (Exodus 20:3). Although the "other gods" were usually such supposed deities as Baal, some secular rulers, notably the later Roman emperors, also claimed to be divine. In at least two instances, Tyre's head and Israel's Herod, the Lord punished kings for making or tolerating such preposterous claims.

Most secular rulers are more discreet in their formal pretensions, but many nevertheless act as quasi-gods. From the pharaoh who held the Jews in captivity and ordered the murder of their newborn sons to the twentieth-century totalitarians with their personality cults, civil authorities often have usurped God's role. Even the modern welfare state has increasingly turned into what Herb Schlossberg calls "the idol state," using "the language of compassion because its intention is a messianic one."[1]

The Bible suggests that an expansive government is bad not only because it might demand to be treated like God but also because it will reflect the sinfulness of its participants and mistreat its citizens. The inescapable problem is that man is a fallen creature, often eager to do wrong. This sinful nature is exacerbated by the accumulation of power, which, warned Lord Acton, "tends to corrupt." Why else would God have instructed the Israelites that their king was neither to acquire too many horses and wives, gold and silver, nor to "consider himself to be better than his brothers"? (Deuteronomy 17:16–17, 20). In fact, when the Israelites requested that God give them a king, he cautioned, through the prophet Samuel, that such a ruler would oppress them and that they would receive no relief when they cried out. And history down through today certainly has shown that "power was on the side of their oppressors—and they have no comforter" (Ecclesiastes 4:1).

Although scripture is ultimately more concerned with spiritual freedom—particularly liberation from sin—than with political liberty, the latter remains an important theme for at least three reasons. First, the lives and dignity of human beings created in the image of God require respect by other people, including governors. In the end, the least important person for whom Christ died is of greater value than the grandest empire. Second, people must be free to respond to God's grace, to worship him, to integrate obedience to him into their daily lives, and even to sin. Indeed, the exercise of virtue is impossible without the freedom to sin. Finally, Christ's injunction that believers be salt and light requires them to have at least some autonomy from the state, whether totalitarian or the slightly less imperialistic welfare states that dominate the West.

To know what government must and must not do is critical, but it is only a start, since most issues fall in between. Some broad biblical principles may help resolve them. Consider poverty. God's concern for the poor, the vulnerable, and the weak is persistent, pervasive, and powerful. Little is clearer in scripture than the duty of believers to care for those in need, particularly the proverbial widows and orphans. Notably, however, the Bible does not vest this responsibility in the state. Although it does not proscribe a public role, it does imply that believers should fulfill their individual and corporate responsibilities before turning to government and that any state program should not violate biblical norms, such as family formation.

About many other current public controversies, like the Bush tax cuts, corporate accounting rules, and the Export-Import Bank, the Bible offers little specific guidance. Rather, these usually are more matters of prudence than principle and fall within the permissive area of government activity. That is, there is neither a mandate for nor a prohibition against the state, say, regulating who may trade which securities based on what disclosures. God has chosen to leave the issue up to us rather than to express his own preference.

Where God is silent, what role should we assign to the state? Although there is no formal Christian political philosophy, believers have good reason to be skeptical about the use of government to solve economic and social problems. The temptation to seize power in an attempt to do good is strong, the prospect of making people moral and righteous is alluring. But can there be greater hubris than the belief that one should forcibly remake individuals and transform entire societies—to save God the trouble of having to separate the wheat from the tare? Thousands of years of history suggest that such a project is fraught with peril and doomed to fail.

Moreover, believers must never forget that the basis of the state is coercion. The ultimate sanction behind every law and rule is prison and, should a citizen resist, death. In general, throwing someone in jail cannot be viewed as an act of love. Thus Christians should exhibit humility before resorting to force and then should do so only reluctantly. In some cases the only way to demonstrate love for one's neighbors is to punish miscreants, but we should be careful before turning disagreements, however serious, into crimes.

Finally, the lessons of practical experience are particularly powerful. Although private market outcomes are imperfect—the traditional justification for state action—that is not a sufficient basis for political intervention.

There also needs to be solid reason, rather than just wishful thinking, to believe that the government response will not be more imperfect. Given the problems inherent in the political process, the case for state action should be overriding necessity, not personal whim. In general, government should provide the legal scaffolding that allows people to collectively but voluntarily solve their problems. Only in extraordinary circumstances, where there is no other choice, should the state supplant private decisionmaking. Ultimately, a political system based on liberty will enhance man's ability to provide for his family and others in his community, exercise dominion in transforming God's creation, enjoy the many gifts of God, and seek to fulfill God's will.

Of course, freedom is not enough. As Pope John II explained, a market economy will work only "within a strong juridical framework which places [capitalism] at the service of human freedom in its totality and which sees it as a particular aspect of that freedom, the core of which is ethical and religious." Government can provide the juridical framework, but the church— the world body of Christian believers—must help provide the ethical and religious core. Without that core a free society will still be better than an unfree society, but it will be neither good nor godly. For Christians, politics is an important, but never the most important, calling.

Notes

1. Herb Schlossberg, *Idols for Destruction: Christian Faith and Its Confrontation with American Society* (Nashville, Tenn.: Thomas Nelson, 1983), p. 185.

RELIGION, POLITICS, AND THE AMERICAN EXPERIENCE

MICHAEL BARONE

Of course religion is part of American politics. Over the past two hundred-plus years, politics has split Americans more often along cultural than along economic lines. The efforts of New Deal historians to portray American political history as a battle between the rich and the rest bumps up against the fact that the rest have always far outnumbered the rich and fails to account for many of the most divisive political issues in American history—slavery, the Civil War, the treatment of sectarian schools, Prohibition, abortion, gun control, whether America should take military action in the Spanish American War, the Philippine insurrection, World War I, World War II, Vietnam, and the Middle East. Quite understandably Americans have brought to these issues the moral principles they have derived from their religious beliefs or lack thereof. And they have argued and contended for their positions with a fervor that very often reflects the fervor of their religion.

This is not new. "America is," Alexis de Tocqueville wrote in the 1830s, "still the place in the world where the Christian religion has most preserved genuine power over souls; and nothing shows better how useful and natural to man it is in our day, since the country in which it exercises the greatest empire is at the same time the most enlightened and the most free."[1] Tocqueville noted that priests—his word for clergymen, both Protestant and Catholic—carefully refrained from taking a direct part in politics. But priests and religion had a huge indirect effect on politics and government because they shaped the minds of individual voters, and religion had a firmer hold on people because it did not tie itself to the fortunes of transitory politicians.

Tocqueville came to America before Irish Catholic voters established a strong identification with the Democratic Party, and he tended to elide Catholicism and Protestantism. But for the next 130 years, Protestant-Catholic sectarian rivalry was often played out in politics. Just a few years after Tocqueville's time in America, the question of religious teaching in schools became a controversy, notably in New York; the result was that Archbishop John Hughes set up a system of Catholic schools because he felt the public schools promoted the Protestant religion. In the nineteenth century many Protestants believed that Catholics' loyalty to church superseded their loyal to country; work on the Washington Monument was postponed for decades because Protestants feared that a stone contributed by the pope contained some infernal device. Many Protestant churches strongly backed Prohibition; the Catholic Church and Catholic voters were strongly against. When federal aid to education was proposed in the 1940s, Catholics wanted parochial schools to be eligible; there was a fierce exchange of letters on this issue between a sulphurous Francis Cardinal Spellman and an emollient but unyielding Eleanor Roosevelt. Congress was unable to pass a federal aid to education bill from 1948 to 1965 because Catholic Democrats would not support it without aid to parochial schools, and Protestant (especially southern) Democrats would not support it with such a provision.

These sectarian differences were important in presidential elections as well. For years it was assumed that Americans would not elect a Catholic president (though there were many Catholic senators and congressmen and several Catholics on the Supreme Court, including one chief justice). Then in 1928 the Democrats nominated Governor Al Smith of New York, an Irish-German-Italian Catholic. Smith would probably have lost by a wide margin to Republican Herbert Hoover in any case, but his party could not help noticing that he lost eight ordinarily Democratic southern and border states; fewer noticed that he carried previously Republican Massachusetts and Rhode Island because of an outpouring of new Catholic voters. In 1960 the Democrats nominated another Catholic, John F. Kennedy. He won by an exceedingly narrow margin and ran behind congressional Democrats. The voting was heavily sectarian: According to Gallup, 78 percent of Catholics voted for Kennedy and 63 percent of white Protestants voted for Richard Nixon.

The 1960 election marked the last time that Catholic-Protestant sectarian differences played much of a role in American politics. Sectarian politics has deep roots in Anglo-American politics, going back to the religious struggles in Britain and the colonies in the sixteenth and seventeenth centuries. The fear that Catholics had an overriding loyalty to their church, which was after all a sovereign state, remained strong in the late nineteenth and early twentieth centuries, when the popes of the time remained hostile to electoral democracy and religious toleration. Kennedy's election and the contemporaneous reforms of Vatican II ended this fear forever.

In the years after 1960 religion seemed to be playing less of a role in American politics, and certainly sectarian differences were playing less of a role. But in fact religion was growing in importance. The civil rights movement, let us remember, was in very large part a religious movement; its greatest leader, Martin Luther King, and many other of its leaders were ministers, and the strategy of nonviolent protest was informed by deep religious beliefs. Blacks were then and are now more fervently religious than the average American, and it is impossible to imagine a purely secular civil rights movement making such a moral impress on the American mind. To a lesser extent, religious beliefs were a basis for the movement opposing the Vietnam War. Today we are inclined to see religiously based political action as an element of the political Right. But in the 1960s it was an important, even essential, component of political action on the political Left.

In the years since the 1960s the religious profile of America has changed. There has been a substantial increase in the number of Evangelical and Pentecostal Protestants, even as the mainline Protestant churches have lost thousands of members. The distinctiveness of American Catholics has become muted, and while Catholic numbers have increased (partly because of Latin American immigrants) the number of Catholics attending mass regularly has declined. There has also been an increase in the number of Americans who identify themselves as atheists, agnostics, or seculars—as members of no church.

At the same time, decisions by elites—courts and administrative agencies—have raised religiously charged issues. The *Roe v. Wade* decision in 1973 drew into active politics first many Catholics and then many Evangelical Protestants. Carter administration rulings on the tax deductibility of private schools drew the heated opposition of many Evangelicals and their entry into politics on the Republican side—a big change, since the born-again Jimmy Carter probably received the votes of most Evangelical Protestants in 1976. The role of the religious Right was noted by Ronald Reagan in a speech at the Republican National Convention in 1984. By the 1990s it was clear that religion was the demographic factor that most deeply divided Americans in partisan politics. Frequent church attenders in all denominations except black churches were more heavily Republican than infrequent attenders and nonattenders. Mormons and Evangelical Protestants were more Republican than mainline Protestants. Frequent-attender Catholics voted for George W. Bush and infrequent-attender Catholics voted for Al Gore. Jews and nonbelievers voted heavily for Gore. These patterns are apparent in election results since 2000 and in polls on the races of 2004.

Some commentators have decried the role of religion in politics and argue that Christian conservatives should not be using political means to achieve their goals. But on issues like abortion it was secularly inclined elites, operating through unelected officials, who were imposing their own moral principles on the larger society and trying to prevent the elected representatives of the people from deciding them. Handling such issues through electoral politics is arguably more likely to produce acceptable results than allowing elites to decide them insulated from popular response. Tocqueville did not take the view of today's secular elites. He saw religion as a factor restraining people from using politics and government to achieve all ends. "At the same time that the law permits the American people to do everything, religion prevents them from conceiving everything and forbids them to dare anything."[2] Religion prompts people to assert moral principles, as Martin Luther King did, but also to respect the rule of the majority, as King in counseling nonviolence did. Today's religious conservatives who try to prevail in the political arena observe similar limits more than today's seculars who seek victories from unelected judges and administrative agencies.

Notes

1. Alexis de Tocqueville, *Democracy in America*, translated by Harvey Mansfield and Delba Winthrop (University of Chicago Press, 2000), p. 278.
2. Ibid., p. 280.

THE CONSERVATORY OF VIRTUE

GARY L. BAUER

Call me an optimist, but I believe that 2004 can be a watershed year for the rediscovery of the vital, and positive, connection between religion and politics. After decades of retreat from a proper understanding of America's history as "a nation with the soul of a church," to use G. K. Chesterton's phrase, events abroad and at home have compelled us to take a second look at the origin of our deepest beliefs.[1]

This second look received its strongest impetus on September 11, 2001. The primordial evil of that single day drove us once more to our knees. Americans felt with a fresh immediacy how fragile we are in our daily pursuits. We saw again how, of all the thoughts and dispositions that rule human affairs, there are really but two polar ideas around which human action arranges itself and can be judged. At one pole is the idea that justice is a human construct with no universal meaning. At the other pole is the conviction that justice has a fixed star, that right and wrong are discernible, and that human beings are accountable to standards they cannot alter or ignore.

Throughout the American experience, from the Declaration of Independence forward, we have found those fixed meanings in enumerated rights that come to us not from the handbooks of government but from the hand of our Creator. Our greatest leaders have returned to this insight time and again, most especially when they sought to help the nation close the gap between its enshrined ideals and its actual practice. Moreover, they have done this, invariably, with the conviction of religion as an aid, not as a hindrance, particularly when the fate of the nation was at stake.

Lincoln affords the prime example. His understanding of the connection between religious conviction and just governance was profound and never merely rhetorical. He accused his critics of wishing to silence opponents of slavery at every turn. "We must not call it wrong in politics," he chided them as saying, "because that is bringing morality into politics, and we must not call it wrong in the pulpit because that is bringing politics into religion."[2] The truth about slavery, he knew, must be spoken in both settings.

This same heritage motivated Martin Luther King Jr. to actions and speeches that resonated deeply with the American character. In *The Culture of Disbelief: How American Law and Politics Trivialize Religious Devotion*, the

Yale law professor Stephen Carter cites King's example and points out how the civil rights movement showed "no reluctance to claim for their positions an 'exclusive alignment with the Almighty.'"[3] Carter goes on to criticize other specific applications of this principle to public policy issues, but the fact that such applications are made is in no way objectionable to him.

For religious conservatives like me, who hold with Lincoln and King on the issues of slavery and racial injustice and who apply similar concepts to such current issues as abortion and the definition of marriage, Carter's argument is essential. We see, and find it wholly in keeping with the best American tradition to see, a close nexus between religious ideas and our country's well-being. In addition, we do not welcome, but rather regret, the loss of a bipartisan determination to strengthen that nexus in public life.

In fact it can be said that the deepest divide between the liberal and conservative portions of the political spectrum today is precisely this idea of a vital role for religious and moral insight. Church attendance was the single most reliable predictor of voter preference in the 2000 presidential election. This is no accident. For the past four decades, middle America has seen its most cherished values scorned as mere religious impositions, as one by one—voluntary prayer, the sanctity of life, the control of pornography, parental rights, objections to sodomy—the legal protection of these values has been ruled out of bounds by a judicial elite.

The result is that religiously motivated or morally convicted Americans are today's "discrete and insular minority."[4] Their notion of community, of a good society, has been rendered socially suspect and constitutionally void. When candidate George H. W. Bush referred to Michael Dukakis in 1988 as a "card-carrying member of the ACLU," no further explanation to middle America was needed. The morally convicted American knew that with the ACLU ascendant they could not win, no matter how many legislators might be persuaded to their view of justice or the common good. By judicial fiat, the entire sphere of community and family values would be relegated to the status of mere religious dogma and annulled by an unelected few.

This trend continues unabated, to the point that even the ability of Americans to assemble and associate on the basis of their moral convictions is under severe challenge. In 2000 the U.S. Supreme Court came within a single vote of holding that the Boy Scouts of America could no longer base their membership and leadership rules on a conception of what constitutes acceptable character and behavior. Throughout the twentieth century the scouts were a model of the melding of civic activity with a nonsectarian but nonetheless traditional personal faith. This outlook is now endangered, and that fact has helped to shift the nation into a stark array of red and blue states.

The 2004 election may well see an intensification of these hues. It would be healthier for the nation if there were instead a recognition on all sides that our nation's religious heritage has been a source of its strength and goodness. For some that heritage means only the most radical separation of church and state. But for most Americans it means a far more complex idea: not only the freedom to choose among religions but also the necessity of forming communities of faith and virtue.

Law and public policy are appropriate expressions and conservators of that virtue. Indeed, all law is such an expression, whether it is a local ordinance against jaywalking (yielding common courtesy to others), a state law taxing tobacco (limiting the right to injure one's self and force others to pay for that injury), or the federal Medicare program (providing the elderly with medical care). A religiously and morally robust society can and will debate the moral precepts behind such laws and ponder whether one approach (for example, the privatization of Social Security) is superior to another currently in use. But it is an illusion to believe that all, or even many, of these laws can be understood and assessed purely in terms of secular values and duties. The moral sentiments of a people can and should properly influence them all.

As this is written, there are forces at work in the Democratic Party calling upon its leaders to reassess their understanding of the role of morality and religion in public affairs. The Democratic Leadership Council is expressing the wistful hope that the party's 2004 candidate will deal with "cultural issues, ranging from guns and abortion, to religion and the struggle of families to raise kids, to the responsibility of individuals and civil society, not just government."[5] These are precisely the topics that Robert Casey, the late governor of Pennsylvania, sought to address at the Democratic national conventions in 1992 and 1996. On both occasions he was barred from speaking to a national audience, leaving the party of the "little guy" without a single voice of passion for the unborn and other key family concerns.

Will that change in 2004? If the change is superficial, it will be worse than no change at all. Writing in the *Wall Street Journal* not long before the first 2004 presidential primaries, columnist Al Hunt ventured the hope that the party's contenders might do a better job of "connecting culturally" with Americans in those places "where a Democratic candidate has to do better than last time—Missouri, the Florida panhandle, West Virginia, Southern Ohio." These voters, says Hunt, "like to hear some God talk."[6] Unintentionally or not, Hunt's phrasing echoes the infamous language of a *Washington Post* reporter who wrote in the mid-1990s that conservative Christians are "uneducated" and "easily led."[7]

The last thing America wants or needs is more symbolic God talk to religious people as a pet constituency. Voters—Evangelicals, Jews, Catholics, mainline Protestants, and people of other faiths—are more sophisticated than that. Elements of the media and judicial elite have something odious in common if they believe that religious and moral conviction can be satisfied with nothing more than a little God talk, acceptable when it is trivial, dangerous when it is actually believed, and unconstitutional when it is expressed in public policy.

The truth is that most Americans care deeply—and have thought long and hard—about whether their country's actions domestically and overseas square with moral norms. As a religious nation, we strive, no doubt imperfectly, to root public policy in ideas that are more than mere social contracts. The God to whom our coinage, our national symbols and monuments, and our Pledge of Allegiance pay tribute is more than a ceremonial deity whose role in human affairs is negligible. For most of us, though we in our human weakness may see him "as through a glass darkly," the God named in our public testaments is not just a civil God but also the God of civility and even the God of civilization.

If the nature of our politics and the character of our nation honor that God, America will survive and prosper. If we think we can find the way forward without his favor, without the "protection of divine Providence" on which our Founders relied, we sail a sunless sea at midnight.

Notes

1. *The Collected Works of G. K. Chesterton*, vol. 21, *What I Saw in America* (San Francisco: Ignatius Press, 1990), pp. 41–45.

2. Speech at New Haven, Connecticut, March 6, 1860, text printed in the *New Haven Daily Palladium*, March 7, 1860, reprinted in Roy P. Basler, ed., *The Collected Works of Abraham Lincoln*, vol. 4 (Rutgers University Press, 1955), pp. 13–30.

3. Stephen L. Carter, *The Culture of Disbelief: How American Law and Politics Trivialize Religious Devotion* (Doubleday, 1993), p. 48.

4. This phrase owes its origin to the famed footnote 4 to *United States v. Carolene Products*, 304 US 144, 58 SCt 778, 82 L.Ed. 1234.

5. "The Right Way to Go South," Democratic Leadership Council, *New Dem Daily*, November 6, 2003 (www.ndol.org/ndol_ci.cfm?contentid=252174& kaid= 131&subid=192).

6. Al Hunt, "The Doctor Is in, but Can He Win?" People and Politics, *Wall Street Journal*, November 6, 2003 (//online.wsj.com/article/0,,sb10680842 4069239100-email,00.html).

7. Michael Weisskopf, "Energized by Pulpit or Passion, the Public Is Calling: 'Gospel Grapevine' Displays Strength in Controversy over Military Gay Ban," *Washington Post*, February 1, 1993, p. A1.

THE RELIGIOUS LEFT, TOO OFTEN LEFT OUT

PAUL E. BEGALA

An exchange student from New York goes to live with a family in Tokyo. While there, his Japanese family takes him to a sumo wrestling match. Sumo is an ancient sport, filled with ritual. After the contestants enter the ring, or *dohyo*, they stomp their feet. "Why do they do that?" asks the American boy. "To drive away demons," say his hosts. Then the fighters receive a ladle of water from another contestant. "That is power water. It symbolizes purity." Then the wrestlers throw handfuls of salt onto the *dohyo* and, squatting at the edge of the *dohyo*, facing each other, they clap their hands in unison. "This is to summon the gods." Finally, the wrestlers raise their hands and turn their palms upward. "That is to show the opponent they have no weapons."

The American boy loves the sumo match, so when a year later his Japanese family comes to visit him in New York, the boy's family takes its Japanese guests to a boxing match at Madison Square Garden. The boy explains the American rituals to his Japanese friends. "The referee wears a bow tie as a sign of civility," he says. "The fighters meet in the center of the ring and listen to the rules to show that this is a gentleman's contest, not a street fight," he continues. "Then the referee inspects their gloves to make sure there's no foreign object in them. Finally, the two fighters shake hands—a sign of mutual respect—and come out fighting."

After the handshake, one of the fighters makes the sign of the cross. "What does that mean?" ask the guests. "Not a damn thing if he doesn't know how to fight," says the boy.

My friends in what the media calls the religious Right sure know how to fight. But too many religious progressives do not. And what is worse, the very phrase *religious progressive* is seen as an oxymoron, like jumbo shrimp or compassionate conservative, because much of the Left is far too secular, even antireligious. For me, the low point in how the Left deals with religion came when a group of abortion rights protestors gathered outside the governor's mansion in Pennsylvania and chanted to the occupant, the heroic Bob Casey: "Casey, get your rosaries off my ovaries." There was precious little outcry over this religious bigotry. Imagine what people would say if right-wing protesters had mocked Joe Lieberman's Judaism.

In a speech he wrote but never lived to give, Franklin Roosevelt called upon "a strong and active faith." For much of our history such a faith was at the heart of liberalism. Not so long ago it was the Left that appealed to morality, spirituality, even God, as we sought public support for our political goals. After all, Martin Luther King Jr. led the Southern *Christian* Leadership Conference. To be sure, civil rights was an ecumenical movement and included Jews and Muslims and atheists, but it also explicitly used religion and morality as its touchstone. Read King's letter from the Birmingham jail and you will see a spiritual leader appealing to his brothers in faith. But by 1980 that was changing. Led by W. A. Criswell, Jerry Falwell, Pat Robertson, and Ronald Reagan, the Right moved religious conservatism into the public square. The Left answered the Right's fire and brimstone with derision and anger. I can understand that response, having tangled with Jerry Falwell myself. But it is far better for religious progressives to answer the Right's censoriousness with acceptance, its exclusion with inclusion, its hate with love.

I was raised in the Bible Belt and went to Vacation Bible School at the Church of Christ, even though I went to Sunday Mass at Holy Family Catholic Church. Although I was never tempted to leave my church for the Church of Christ, I developed a deep respect for Protestant Evangelicals (a respect most liberals lack) as well as a profound love of scripture (which some Catholics of a different generation lack). But while those Christian views led many of the people I grew up with to express their politics through conservatism, Christianity—especially Catholicism—drew me to liberalism.

Consider school prayer: I saw the only two Jewish kids in my school back in Sugar Land, Texas, get up and stand in the hall each morning as the principal read a fundamentalist Christian morning devotional. Funny, the devotional never quoted Matthew 6:5–6: "When you pray, you are not to be like the hypocrites; for they love to stand and pray in the synagogues and on the street corners so that they may be seen by men. Truly I say to you, they have their reward in full. But you, when you pray, go into your inner room, close your door and pray to your Father who is in secret, and your Father who sees what is done in secret will reward you." I decided to listen to the Gospel according to Saint Matthew rather than the Gospel according to our principal, Mr. Shaver.

I see the same tension in the way religious conservatives address the issues of today. When I read the painful story about Governor George Bush mocking Karla Fay Tucker's last desperate plea for life—a plea Pat Robertson and other Evangelicals took heed of—or watched Governor Bush smirk and giggle when asked about death penalty cases in which lawyers slept while their clients were condemned to die, I turned to John 8:4–5: "They said unto him, Master, this woman was taken in adultery, in the very act. Now Moses in the law commanded us, that such should be stoned: but what sayest thou?" Then the Jesus I worship stopped the lawful execution of a person guilty of a capital offense, saying, "He that is without sin among you, let him first cast a stone at her."

I see an evidently faithful Christian in the White House ask for regulations that would allow more arsenic in our drinking water, more mercury in our air, more logging in our national forests, more drilling in our national wilderness, more mining in our national parks. And I think of Revelation 7:3: "Hurt not the earth, neither the sea, nor the trees."

Is there a Christian position on taxes? Bob Riley, the conservative Republican governor of Alabama, seems to think so. He says he has studied the New Testament all his life and has come away with three things: First, love God with all your heart, mind, body and soul. Second, love your neighbor as yourself. And third, be good to the poor. Riley takes this to mean reduce the tax burden on poor Alabamians and increase it on wealthy corporations, a most decidedly liberal conclusion.

One of my favorite moments in the New Testament is when the Pharisees try to con Jesus into leading a tax revolt. Matthew 22:15–22 says:

> Then the Pharisees went and plotted how they might entangle him in his talk. And they sent to him their disciples with the Herodians, saying, "Teacher, we know that you are true, and teach the way of God in truth. . . . Tell us, therefore, what do you think? Is it lawful to pay taxes to Caesar, or not?" But Jesus perceived their wickedness and said, "Why do you test me, you hypocrites? Show me the tax money." So they brought him a denarius. And he said to them, "Whose image and inscription is this?" They said to him, "Caesar's." And he said to them, "Render therefore to Caesar the things that are Caesar's, and to God the things that are God's." When they had heard these words, they marveled, and left Him and went their way.

I read that as Jesus saying, Shut up and pay your taxes; worry about more important things. But Jesus did support progressive taxation—or at least I think he did. In Luke 12:48 he uttered a rule I was raised with: "For everyone to whom much is given, from him much will be required." Christ also understood the importance of budgets as moral documents, or so it seems to me. In Matthew 6:21 he says, "For where your treasure is, there your heart will be also."

We cannot look into George Bush's heart, but we can look at his budget, where he puts *our* treasure. As a liberal, as a Democrat—and also as a Catholic—I ask, Why not redirect a minuscule fraction of the Bush tax cut? Why not take the amount of money that is supposed to go to the wealthiest 1 percent and give it instead to the poorest 1 percent? The 2001 tax cut will give $85,000 a year to each of the 1.4 million Americans in the wealthiest 1 percent, a total of $121 billion. That is a lot of money, to be sure. But to people whose average income is already $1.5 million a year, an extra $85,000 will not be life altering. But for the poorest 1 percent, $85,000 is a king's ransom. It would literally change the life of the Vietnam veteran damaged by the demons of mental illness, the homeless family sleeping in their car, the man dying of tuberculosis, the woman dying of addiction, the baby dying of AIDS. Redirected to the bottom 1 percent, it could be the difference between life and death, between despair and hope, between dignity and squalor. Imagining such a world is an act of faith.

Still, I cannot criticize the speck in my conservative friends' eyes without acknowledging the plank in my own. Jefferson famously said he trembled for his country when he reflected that God is just. As someone who lives in a nice house, in a good neighborhood, and drives a nice car, I tremble when I read Acts 2:44–45: "And all that believed were together, and had all things common. And sold their possessions and goods, and parted them to all men, as every man had need." Or in the Gospel according to Luke, when John the Baptist commands: "He that hath two coats, let him impart to him that hath none; and he that hath meat, let him do likewise."

Building from the scripture, the teachings of the church speak powerfully to politics. *Faithful Citizenship* of the U.S. Conference of Catholic Bishops addresses the need for Catholics to respect the right to life: yes, of unborn children, but also of the needy, the elderly, the infirm, and even of the hated, the convicted murderer facing execution. I am moved when the Holy Father—one of the great men of modern history; a man I have been privileged to meet twice when I was a government official—writes in *Novo Millennio Ineunte:* "How can it be that even today there are still people dying of hunger? Condemned to illiteracy? Lacking the most basic medical care? Without a roof over their heads? . . . Christians must learn to make their act of faith in Christ by discerning his voice in the cry for help that rises from this world of poverty."

And I am disappointed when prominent Catholic politicians and bishops try to reduce the call to faithful citizenship to the issue of abortion alone. Abortion is an important issue but one in which the majority of Americans appear to be unpersuaded by the church's call to life. Sometimes I fear the call has been less clear, less courageous, less consistent on other life-and-death issues: the injustice of the death penalty, poverty, discrimination, lack of health care, housing, economic empowerment. When is the last time you read about a bishop chastising a Catholic politician for supporting the death penalty or a war that the church believes is unjust? When was the last time a Catholic politician was denied Holy Communion for failing to support a just wage or health care for working people? As a cradle Catholic I was blessed to be born into a community of believers stretching back to Saint Peter. I was nurtured by parents and godparents and priests who fed that faith through their examples and their lives and by the Catholic Youth Organization and Catholic retreats and so many other life-shaping experiences.

My wife of fourteen years came to the church just a year ago, in the depths of the worst church scandal in modern memory. The faith and the strength she has shown—the vision to look beyond the corruption and the cover-ups to see the true beauty of the true church—deeply impressed me. My wife saw a church that is open, inclusive, and committed, in President John Kennedy's words, to the notion that "here on earth, God's work must truly be our own." That mission—the Catholic social mission—is a big part of the church's appeal to converts like my wife. It is what Franklin Roosevelt called "a strong and active faith." That faith is still occasionally under fire. Governor Bush, a good man, disgraced himself when he appeared at an institution that teaches bigotry and bias. At Bob Jones University they expel you for dating someone of a different race; they call the pope an antichrist and the Catholic Church a cult. And George W. Bush—a good man to be sure—did nothing, said nothing, when he had a chance to confront those who hate my church. Not because he is a bigot; he is not. He did nothing because, I suspect, he wanted the votes of the anti-Catholic bigots.

In the aftermath of the Bob Jones controversy, Bush wrote Cardinal O'Connor, "I hope and intend that anyone closely examining my agenda will see reflections of a much greater tradition—a tradition of social justice defended and represented by the Catholic Church."[1] Bush wrote of his commitment to the Catholic tradition of social justice one day after presiding over the state-sanctioned killing of a sixty-two-year-old great-grandmother.

And so it goes: lip service instead of social service, salesmanship instead of leadership. We hear endless exhortations to "the armies of compassion" and faith-based organizations, as though people of faith were not already doing all they can. Ask Catholic Charities, ask Catholic Relief Services, ask the Campaign for Human Development, ask any parish priest or any nun, and they will tell you they are already up to their ears in alligators. The armies of compassion are indeed in full battle mode, and they are heroically fighting the good fight. But they need reinforcements. Most of all, they need leaders whose message is, We're all in this together; not, You're on your own.

My political impulse is communitarian, I suspect, because I was raised and I remain in a community of faith. I know the strength that comes from community and the isolation of excessive individualism. This is a difficult and dicey topic for me. I dare not judge anyone else's faith. My own sinfulness and selfishness makes that impossible. I worry when politicians tell me how pious and prayerful they are. And I worry when they tell me their faith does not inform their politics. Religion is deeply and intensely personal in a way politics is not. I am not entirely comfortable discussing my faith in public. It is easier for me to talk politics than religion. My politics are pretty important to me. Politics defines what I do and what I think. But my religion defines who I am and what I believe. That is why, while I make a living judging other people's political views, I do not ever want to be in a position of judging their religious views. Besides, I could not if I wanted to. As the man said, judging other people's religion is against my religion.

Note

1. Bush to O'Connor, February 25, 2000 (www.nytimes.com/library/politics/camp/022800wh-bush-text.html).

AMERICAN POLITICS AND THE DISSENTING PROTESTANT TRADITION

ROBERT BELLAH

Between them, Mario Cuomo and Mark Souder lay out the major dimensions of the role of faith in American political life. I find myself agreeing with both of them, even in the areas where they seem to differ most.

I believe, with Cuomo, that there is such a thing as natural law and that there is wide agreement on its basic tenets among people of various religions and people of no religion at all. Most of the time political debate in fact occurs within the context of this broad moral consensus. I am, however, sensitive to Souder's view that there is no such consensus and that there are beliefs of his that he does not share—and should not be required to share—with others. I would reconcile the apparently opposing positions by arguing that, although there is a broad consensus, there are varying understandings even of basic moral principles and great differences in how they should be applied to particular cases.

In practical terms, this means that it is perfectly appropriate to base one's political stand on the particular faith tradition to which one is committed and to explain that tradition in arguing one's case. The only caveat is that one's argument must appeal to general moral principles in persuading others. One does not have the right to demand that others accept the tenets of one's own faith in making a political decision.

An example may help clarify what might appear to be my contradictory stand. Mark Souder indicates that he is, under certain circumstances, willing to vote for what he believes to be a just war, even though, because of his fundamental beliefs coming from the Anabaptist tradition, he must exercise what he calls "grave caution" in doing so. It is my view that no Christian, and I include myself though I do not come from an Anabaptist tradition, can support any kind of war except in fear and trembling because of the clear teaching of Jesus in the New Testament.

Nor do I believe, as Souder seems to, that a Christian pacifist does not belong in government. It would, however, be the obligation of a Christian pacifist serving in Congress to make the argument as to why any particular war is a mistake in terms that those who are not pacifists could understand. One might say, "I am a Christian pacifist and so am opposed to all wars, but in the case of the invasion of Iraq I also oppose the war because it is fool-hardy and likely to result in more harm than good." This might be called a de facto just war argument. But if I simply abstain from voting on the issue of war and give no reason other than my own faith, then I would have to face the judgment of my constituency at the next election.

We need pacifists in office just as we need people on juries who do not believe in the death penalty. Arguments in particular cases must take account of the relevant facts. But if we are to exclude people from public responsibility because of their religious belief, then we are violating the free exercise clause. In short, the matters of conscience to which Souder alludes belong in the public sphere. And I agree with Cuomo as to the form that public debate should take.

But if public action is legitimately, and perhaps inevitably, based in significant part on the religious beliefs of public persons, as both Cuomo and Souder seem to agree, then the nature of those religious beliefs is also legitimately part of the public discussion. Some people may imagine that natural law is a kind of automatic machine that will always grind out the same answers to the same questions, but that is surely not the case. If a political argument is based even implicitly on natural law, then it is legitimate to raise questions about the particular way natural law is being used and to argue for an alternative understanding of natural law.

Similarly, if religious beliefs, even unconsciously, are influential in the general culture and in the political culture, then it is legitimate to criticize those religious beliefs. I am clearly treading on dangerous ground here—and could even be accused of violating religious freedom or the separation of church and state. One's religious views are, according to common American understanding, inviolably part of one's private self and cannot therefore be challenged, at least as long as they do not endanger others. But what if widely held implicit and explicit religious understandings have important public consequences, even to the extent of endangering society? Cannot they then be criticized?

I have taken this position publicly for a number of years. I argue that dissenting Protestantism, the majority religious tradition in America for more than two hundred years, has deeply influenced American culture, including all other religions on American soil. This influence has made America unique among the Atlantic nations, all the others of which have had traditions of an established church. This influence has been expressed in our predominant value of individualism, rooted in the dissenting Protestant view that the individual stands alone before God and that the church is a voluntary association formed by individual believers. Such an emphasis on individual conscience and individual responsibility has had positive consequences in American culture and character. But there has been a cost.

Those Christians who believe that the church is essential for salvation, that it is only as members of the Body of Christ that they will be saved, and that the church was here before they were born and will be here after they die and will last until the end of time—and that includes not only Catholics but also church Protestants (as opposed to dissenting Protestants)—have a much deeper understanding of and commitment to the common good as a moral standard. They do not see the common good, as dissenting Protestants do, as merely the sum of individual goods. A commitment to the common good implies an understanding of social solidarity not shared by many Americans. For those concerned for the common good, equality of opportunity is not enough; equality of outcome, at least at some level, is also essential.

That America accepts as natural a degree of income polarization and a poverty level that would be unacceptable in any other Atlantic society has, I am arguing, religious roots. We have recently learned that the percentage of Americans below the poverty level has risen in the past two years. But more striking to me than the rise is how poverty is defined: $18,100 annual income for a family of four. Where I live, in the San Francisco Bay area, $18,000 would not even pay the housing costs of a family of four. Even in areas where housing costs are lower, I cannot even imagine what life must be like for four people with such an income. Yet Americans, with our deep belief in individual responsibility, tend to view poverty as the fault of the poor, so the extraordinary poverty that exists in the richest country in the world rouses little moral outrage, and when there is such outrage it tends to come from Catholics and church Protestants, not from the majority dissenting tradition.

Unfortunately, the religiously based tradition of radical individualism that dominates American culture is expressed not only in our domestic life but also in our foreign policy. George W. Bush has publicly affirmed the right of the United States to act as it thinks right with or without the agreement of the international community. Many in the rest of the world who might have agreed to the removal of Saddam Hussein under United Nations auspices were appalled at America's unilateral resort to force, something that since World War II the international community has done its best to prevent. The American public, however—used to believing that the lone cowboy or detective committed to justice is often opposed by the townspeople or the police force—sided with Bush in his confrontation with the rest of the world. Only now, when things are not going so well, are doubts beginning to arise.

It is my belief that the majority dissenting Protestant tradition, for all that it has contributed to the development of democracy and capitalism in America, is not serving us well today either at home or abroad. We live in a society and a world in which no individual and no nation can make it all alone. We need one another as we have never done before. The web that connects all of us on the globe is growing tighter, and being excluded from it has consequences that are uniquely terrible. There are rich resources in the biblical tradition and in other religious traditions in America that could help to rectify our one-sidedness, to balance our individualism with a profound sense of solidarity. Since there is not and never has been a wall separating religion and politics in America, I believe religious criticism is an essential ingredient in serious thinking about our present political situation.

HOW NIEBUHR HELPS US KICK
THE SECULARIST HABIT:
A SIX-STEP PROGRAM

DAVID BROOKS

Like a lot of people these days, I am a recovering secularist. Until September 11, 2001, I accepted the notion that as the world becomes richer and better educated, it becomes less religious. Extrapolating from a tiny and unrepresentative sample of humanity (in Western Europe and parts of North America), this theory holds that as history moves forward, science displaces dogma and reason replaces unthinking obedience. A region that has not yet had a reformation and an enlightenment, such as the Arab world, sooner or later will.

It is now clear that the secularization theory is untrue. The human race does not necessarily get less religious as it grows richer and better educated. We are living through one of the great periods of scientific progress and creation of wealth. At the same time, we are in the midst of a religious boom. Moreover, it is the denominations that refuse to adapt to secularism that are growing the fastest: Islam, Orthodox Judaism, Pentecostal Christianity.

Secularism, then, is not the future; it is yesterday's incorrect vision of the future. It was, for example, challenged by the twentieth-century American thinker Reinhold Niebuhr. I am amazed in fact that Reinhold Niebuhr has not made a comeback since the events of September 11. After all, he was one of America's most profound writers on war and international conflict. At the start of World War II and then again at the dawn of the cold war, he wrote books that helped readers to connect their historical situations with broad truths about God and human nature. He became a spokesman for moral realism, arguing that reform had to be conducted by people who were acutely aware of the limits of human capabilities and the intractability of sin. Niebuhr's worldview was well suited to the era of total war: in 1939 he delivered a series of lectures in Edinburgh on his version of Christian realism; as he spoke, bombs from German aircraft could be heard falling around the city.[1]

The classic Niebuhr pose was to argue the middle against both ends—to argue for reform but against the pride of idealists, who hope to achieve too much, and against the cowardice of standpatters, who are afraid to get their hands dirty. Niebuhr could be bloody-minded in his realism: every action causes some collateral damage, he acknowledged, but people must act nonetheless, begging forgiveness for the evils they commit in the service of good.

Niebuhr's great foe was idealism. American idealism, he believed, comes in two forms: the idealism of noninterventionists, who are embarrassed by power, and the idealism of imperialists, who disguise power as virtue. The noninterventionists, he argued, seek to preserve the purity of their souls either by denouncing military actions or by demanding that every action taken be unequivocally virtuous. They exaggerate the sins committed by their own country, excuse the malevolence of its enemies, and, as later polemicists have put it, blame America first. This is all just a pious way of refusing to face real problems, according to Niebuhr. Though his subject was the isolationist response to Nazi Germany, he might as well have been referring to some of the left-wing reactions to today's war on terror.

Niebuhr conceded that the United States was founded on utopian hopes, on the dream of transforming a new land into a second Eden, where the oppression and misery of the Old World would be supplanted by happiness, prosperity, virtue, and freedom. But Americans, Niebuhr believed, fail to appreciate the limitations of what can be achieved. They think the United States has a mission to spread democracy around the world, but nations in the grip of this sort of hubris, according to Niebuhr, seek "greater power than is given to mortals." They become inflamed by hatred for their foes and corrupted by that hatred—even if their foes deserve to be hated. And these nations become enraged when they discover barriers to the realization of their ideals.

But perhaps Niebuhr's insights were constrained by the times he was living in. Because communism and fascism were fomented by zealous idealists, he came to suspect all displays of passion, all righteous indignation. Idealism in defense of democracy, however, is no vice, at least not on balance. Our problem today is not, as Niebuhr might have predicted, excessive zealotry. Our problem is that most people are disengaged from great public matters. Consumed by private pleasures, they almost never invest their passions in dreams of a better world. We could use a little more idealistic zeal, a little more hope and confidence.

And Niebuhr was wrong to try to disabuse Americans of a sense of democratic mission, which he treated as a self-flattering appendage to the American character. In fact this sense of mission is the essence of the American character. Our Founders pledged their sacred honor because they thought they were leading a democratic revolution for all mankind. After all, the highest points of American history—the abolition of slavery, the Marshall Plan, the civil rights movement—were driven by the idea of mission.

This other side of the coin of idealism—and the realization that it thrives in today's religious revival—drives old secularists like me into recovery. I suspect I am not the only one who since September 11 has found himself reading a paperback edition of the Koran (bought a few years ago in a fit of high-mindedness). I am probably not the only one boning up on the teachings of Ahmad ibn Taymiyya, Sayyid Qutb, and Muhammad ibn Abd al-Wahhab.

We recovering secularists are also driven to a six-step recovery program. The first step is to accept the fact that we are not the norm. Western foundations and universities send out squads of researchers to study and explain religious movements. But religious groups should be sending out squads of researchers to study and explain those who do not feel the constant presence of God in their lives, who do not fill their days with rituals and prayers and garments that bring them into contact with the divine, and who do not believe that God's will should shape their public lives. Once we secularists accept this—which is like understanding that the earth revolves around the sun, not vice versa—we can begin to see things in a new way.

The second step toward recovery involves confronting fear. For a few years it seemed that the world was heading toward a benign end of history, one in which our biggest worry would be boredom. Liberal democracy had won the day. Yes, we had to contend with globalization and inequality, but these were material and measurable concepts. Now we are looking at fundamental clashes of belief and a truly scary situation—at least in the Southern Hemisphere—that brings to mind the Middle Ages, with weak governments, missionary armies, and rampant religious conflict.

The third step is getting angry. I now get extremely annoyed by the secular fundamentalists who are content to remain smugly ignorant of enormous shifts occurring all around them. A great Niagara of religious fervor is cascading down around them while they stand obtuse and dry in the little cave of their own parochialism—and many of them are journalists and policy analysts who are paid to keep up with these things.

The fourth step toward recovery is to resist the impulse to find a materialistic explanation for everything. When secularism seemed the wave of the future, Western intellectuals developed social science models of extraordinary persuasiveness. Marx explained history through class struggle; other economists explained it through profit maximization. Professors of international affairs used conflict-of-interest doctrines and game theory to predict the dynamics between nation states. All these models are seductive and all are partly true. This country has powerful institutions, such as the State Department and the Central Intelligence Agency, that use models like these to try to develop sound policies. But none of the models can adequately account for religious ideas, impulses, and actions, because religious fervor cannot be quantified and standardized.

Fifth, recovering secularists must acknowledge that we have been too easy on religion. Because we assumed that religion was playing a diminishing role in public affairs, we patronized it. We condescendingly decided not to judge other creeds. These are all valid ways of approaching God, we told ourselves, and ultimately they fuse into one. After all, why stir up trouble by judging another's beliefs? It is not polite. The better option, when confronted by some nasty practice performed in the name of religion, is simply to avert one's eyes. But in a world in which religion plays an ever larger role, this approach is no longer acceptable. One has to try to separate right from wrong. The problem is that, once we start doing that, it is hard to say where we will end up.

The sixth and final step for recovering secularists is to understand that America was never secular anyway. Americans long for righteous rule as fervently as anybody else. They are inculcated with the notion that, in Abraham Lincoln's words, they represent the "last, best hope of earth." Many Americans have always sensed that the country has a transcendent mission, if not a theological one. They instinctively feel, in ways that people from other places do not, that history is unfulfilled as long as there are nations in which people are not free. It is this instinctive belief that led George W. Bush to respond so ambitiously to the events of September 11 and that has led most Americans to support him.

If he were alive today Niebuhr would no doubt have qualms about the good-versus-evil rhetoric that President Bush uses to mobilize public opinion in the war on terror. He would be alarmed by American unilateralism: He believed it was necessary for America to work with European nations in order to check its hubris. No doubt Niebuhr overlearned the lessons of his age. No doubt these lessons are not ideally suited to this moment in history.

Still, America could use a Reinhold Niebuhr today, to police its excesses—to make the country aware of its prejudices, both religious and secular, and the way these prejudices prevent a fine-tuned understanding of this new world.

Note

1. The lectures were eventually collected in two volumes titled *The Nature and Destiny of Man* (1941, 1943).

ONCE MORE, THE CROSS
AND THE FLAG

HARVEY COX

Has the time come to look seriously for a better way to organize the world community than into a hundred plus competing and sovereign national states? Could this be the main theological problem confronting us in the twenty-first century? Can we even conceive of what a formidable undertaking this might be? Has anyone noticed how many national flags incorporate a cross, sometimes two or more crosses?

A very early Christian thinker once wrote that Christians have no homeland to which they owe supreme loyalty. But that insight got lost somewhere between Constantine and Charlemagne. The former made the cross, formerly a symbol of disgrace to the Romans and of defiant hope against imperial tyranny to the Christians, into his escutcheon: *In hoc signo vinces!* The latter, in cooperation with the pope, refounded a "Christian empire." Later, when the nation-states began to emerge, the melding—both symbolically and actually—of Christian with national symbolism became established practice. By World War I British soldiers under the crosses of Saint George and Saint Andrew slew and were slain by Germans with the slogan *Gott Mitt Uns* on their belt buckles.

Still, the Christian sanctifying of nationalism did not proceed without opposition. During the nineteenth century the popes opposed, often vociferously, the emerging unified national states. Pope Pius IX, now often viewed as a hopeless reactionary, was very nervous about these new centers of power. Those who supported him were dismissed as ultramontanists. But maybe the pope and his supporters were only being prescient. Did they foresee how much blood and gore was to flow in the interest of nationalism in the twentieth century? Still—and despite the blood that had just flowed at the Marne and Chateau-Thierry and the blood that was about to flow on the Normandy beach and later in the frozen forests of Belgium during the Battle of the Bulge—I was dutifully taught in high school that Garibaldi and Bismarck were to be viewed as heroes since they had effected the "unification" of Italy and Germany.

In the introduction to his thoughtful book, *Theopolitical Imagination,* William T. Cavanaugh asks the following question: "How does a provincial farm boy become persuaded that he must travel as a soldier to another part of the world and kill people he knows nothing about? He must be convinced of the reality of borders and imagine himself deeply, mystically, united to a wider national community that stops abruptly at those borders."[1] The answer is, he does so because he has been swept up in what has been called an imagined community. Indeed most of our thinking about politics today, both domestic and international, takes these so-called communities for granted, simply and uncritically.

Consciousnes still lags behind reality. (Was it Yogi Berra who first said that?) The brute fact is that national states, though they retain a certain hold on our imaginations and our loyalties, are losing their place of preeminence today. Pollution and plagues do not respect national borders. Neither do terrorists nor multinational corporations. Will the time come when our young people will no longer be willing to die for Bolivia or Nigeria (or America) but will put themselves in harm's way for al Qaeda or Microsoft? If nation-states are doomed to fade—and this is the big, big question— what will take their place? Will it be the United Nations or a successor international organization? If so, an international organization of what? Of a congeries of national states? Or of something else?

At its core Christianity is about the appearance in the world of a radically new kind of community. Jesus called it the reign of God. It was to be one in which Greeks and barbarians, Jews and Gentiles were to be included around a single table. Christians have not always remembered this founding impulse. But recently Christian leaders and organizations have begun (again) to question the validity of nation-states or at least their claim to our highest loyalty. Some years ago the Roman Catholic bishops of the southwestern American states issued a pastoral letter declaring that a hungry person in Mexico had an undeniable right to cross the border into the United States in search of employment or of food for the family. More recently, the National Council of Churches, the World Council of Churches, the U.S. Catholic bishops, and the pope all opposed the American invasion of Iraq. There are other examples. Christians, it seems, are at times willing to question the validity of the sovereignty of national states.

One problem, and not a minor one, is that Christianity is itself divided. And the world religions are divided from each other. But there are signs of hope. Despite communal massacres, Hindus and Christians and Muslims are in touch with each other in ways they rarely have been in previous history. John Paul II received some nasty criticism from conservative elements

in his own church (even from those who consider themselves staunch supporters) when he invited religious leaders from several faith traditions to
meet with him at Assisi some years ago to pray. We need more such prayer
meetings. And we need some hard thinking about how those of us who
believe we live in a universe we did not create ourselves, and on a planet we
were meant to share with each other, can transcend our divisions, celebrate
our diversity, and prepare for the inevitable arrival of a postnational state
world.

Note

1. William T. Cavanaugh, *Theopolitical Imagination* (New York: T. and T. Clark,
2002), p. 1.

COMMON GRACE, NATURAL LAW, AND THE PUBLIC ARENA

MICHAEL CROMARTIE

The presentations by Mario Cuomo and Mark Souder highlight the different ways that the Catholic tradition and the Evangelical Protestant tradition approach responsibilities of the public arena. "My church," Cuomo argues, "understands that our public morality depends on a consensus view of right and wrong. Religious values will not be accepted as part of the public morality unless they are shared by the community at large. The plausibility of achieving that consensus is a relevant consideration in deciding whether or not to make the effort to impose those values officially."

And how should such efforts be made? According to Cuomo, the Catholic tradition has long had respect for political realism, a realism that has necessitated making "prudent, practical judgments with respect to its attempts to inject Catholic principles into civil law." Making such judgments requires having a public theology that seeks to find common ground and consensus in a pluralist society. It means finding a public grammar that speaks across traditions and worldviews to find points of agreement. Cuomo suggests that such a vocabulary can be made by appeals to the natural law tradition, a tradition he reminds us receives far too little attention today. He says that "natural law is law derived from human nature and human reason without the benefit of revelation or a willing suspension of disbelief. It is the law, as I perceive it, that would occur to us if we were only 500,000 people on an island without books, without education, without rabbis or priests or history, and we had to figure out who and what we were." Similar to the argument C. S. Lewis makes in his classic *The Abolition of Man*, Cuomo asserts that natural law principles are "shared by most if not all of our nation's religions, whether they include God or not."[1]

In the discussion that follows Cuomo's and Souder's presentations, William Galston agrees with Cuomo by saying that religion that "ought to enter the public realm" is that portion of religion accessible to the natural reason of mankind. He wonders if Souder agrees with that formulation. Mark Souder's response is that of a prominent wing of his Evangelical heritage: "The notion of a natural law common to all religions is in fact a worldview and a moral view that is different from a Christian worldview and moral view—and is unacceptable to me. . . . I cannot relate to the idea of a generic, natural law God. My God is a particularly Christian God."

Unfortunately, this perspective is shortsighted. The particularly Christian God that Souder refers to is a God who also reveals himself, among other ways, in nature. Prominent Protestant thinkers as diverse as John Calvin, Emil Brunner, and C. S. Lewis hold that the natural law tradition is the more distinctively Christian view in that this law is written on the hearts of all men and women, believer and unbeliever alike. When the Protestant Reformers assert that nature teaches or that nature dictates they are arguing that this is what God teaches. The Reformers believed that people of all races, cultures, and religions have access to a universal law through their natural reason and that this law could be grasped without the aid of divine or special revelation. The Reformation scholar John T. McNeill argues that "there is no discontinuity between the teaching of the Reformers and that of their predecessors with respect to natural law . . . not one of the leaders of the Reformation assails the principle. Instead . . . they all on occasion express a quite ungrudging respect for the natural law implanted in the human heart and seek to inculcate this attitude in their readers."[2]

Moreover, they argue that many issues in political life pertain to the created and fallen order—not the redemptive order of salvation. The civil order, specifically the state, is an institution of God's common grace. In the words of the theologian John Murray: "Civil government as such is not a redemptive ordinance. But it provides, and is intended to provide, that outward peace and order within which the ordinances of redemption may work . . . the tranquility and order established and preserved by the ordinances of government are benefits enjoyed by all. This blessing arising from divine institution we must regard therefore as a common blessing and therefore as of the institution of common grace."[3] The fruits of common grace include the ability to perform what has been called civic righteousness, whereby religious believers and nonbelievers alike are used, by the power of the state, to promote justice and restrain evil.

As Mark Souder knows, when moral concerns are debated in the public arena the debate is often hampered by lack of a moral vocabulary acceptable to both religious and secular interlocutors. A proper appropriation of the natural law tradition can provide a public grammar for making appeals in the public arena to people who hold diverse philosophical worldviews and presuppositions. These theological points are important for conservative

Christians to ponder as they continue to influence contemporary policy disputes. Too often, when issues of great import are at stake, they use polemical language that projects an us-versus-them approach to politics.

Conservative Christians would be more successful if they recovered a proper understanding of common grace and natural law, thus forming allies of those whom they otherwise would disagree with on matters of religious truth. They would be more effective if they developed a public language, a public philosophy, and a public posture that communicates a concern for the common good of all and not just of fellow believers. Living in the intersection between the City of God and the City of Man, conservative Christians would do well to develop what the sociologist John Murray Cuddihy calls an esthetic for the interim, which encourages patience and "puts a ban on all ostentation and triumphalism for the time being."[4]

Working for social and political change often requires the patience of Job. Or as Max Weber observed, politics is "a strong and slow boring of hard boards." It frequently requires prudent and principled compromise while building coalitions with people who are often unlikely allies. It is the marketplace of the common, everyday person and not the courtroom of rarefied saints. And many have learned, and will continue to learn, through the hard knocks of battles fought, victories won, and disappointments beyond measure that politics is, because of the effects of the fall, "the method of finding proximate solutions to insoluble problems."[5] It is important for all of us to remember this, whatever our religious or political persuasion.

Notes

1. C. S. Lewis, *The Abolition of Man* (New York: Macmillan, 1947).

2. John T. McNeill, "Natural Law in the Teaching of the Reformers," *Journal of Religion* 26 (1946): 168.

3. John Murray, "Common Grace," in *Collected Writings of John Murray*, vol. 2 (Edinburgh: Banner of Truth, 1978), p. 112.

4. John Murray Cuddihy, *No Offense: Civil Religion and Protestant Taste* (New York: Seabury Press, 1978), p. 201.

5. Reinhold Niebuhr, *The Children of Light and the Children of Darkness* (Charles Scribner's Sons, 1944), p. 118.

FAITHFUL CONSENSUS

JOHN J. DiIULIO JR.

The twentieth century's premier Western intellectual defender of plural-ism, the late Oxford don Sir Isaiah Berlin, once quipped that there is no reason for supposing that the truth, once it is discovered, will necessarily prove interesting. The truth about so-called faith-based initiatives is not very interesting and would, in fact, be a dreadful bore were it not for the fact that orthodox sectarians, orthodox secularists, and their respective allies in the media and other places continue to distort, deride, or simply ignore it.

Let us begin with the historical truth, namely, that for all the secular sound and sectarian fury about religion's role in the public square, for all the ink spilled and voices raised, there is broad bipartisan consensus, buoyed by mass public approval and backed by federal laws and court decisions, favor-ing public-private, religious-secular partnerships that serve people in need.

On May 24, 1999, Democratic presidential candidate Al Gore, speaking at a Salvation Army drug treatment center in Atlanta, declared that our "severest challenges are not just material, but spiritual." Noting that "free-dom of religion need not mean freedom from religion," he praised faith-based groups that "nationwide have shown a muscular commitment to fac-ing down poverty, drug addiction, domestic violence, and homelessness." When these community-serving groups "have worked out a partnership with government," he said, "they have woven a resilient web of life support under the most helpless among us."[1]

Two months later, on July 22, Republican presidential candidate George W. Bush echoed Gore. Surrounded by inner-city clergy in Indi-anapolis, Bush said that "economic growth is not the solution to every problem" and promised that, if elected, his administration would "look first to faith-based organizations, charities, and community groups that have shown their ability to save and change lives." Noting that it "is not enough to call for volunteerism," he stressed that the nation's "armies of compas-sion" are "outnumbered and outflanked and outgunned" and needed "more support, public and private." "Government," he concluded, "cannot be replaced by charities, but it can welcome them as partners, not resent them as rivals."[2]

On December 17, 2001, Democratic Senator Hillary Rodham Clinton spoke at New York City's Abyssinian Baptist Church. "The Founders," she began, "had faith in reason" and "faith in God, from whom the ability to reason is a great gift." Clinton warned that when "government goes too far, and seeks to go beyond separation to outright hostility toward religion, you can end up with something like the Soviet Union." "Government," she concluded, "works in partnership with religious institutions . . . to promote public purposes—feeding the hungry, sheltering the homeless. Faith inspires those good works, to be sure. But tax dollars are properly used to channel the energies of the faithful in a direction that helps our society as a whole."[3]

Five years earlier, in 1996, President Bill Clinton had signed into law a bill espoused by Republican Senator John Ashcroft. It was the first and farthest-reaching of several so-called charitable choice laws that President Clinton signed. It debuted as a provision (section 104) of the Personal Responsibility and Work Opportunity Reconciliation Act of 1996, better known as the federal welfare reform law. Charitable choice was intended to ensure that religious nonprofit groups, large or small, national or local, could form public-private partnerships to deliver social services, participate in the government grant-making process, administer federal and federal-state social programs, and receive public funds on the same basis as other nonprofit organizations. The laws applied to tens of billions of grant-making dollars flowing through dozens of social programs across several federal cabinet departments and agencies.

Charitable choice fell squarely within constitutional boundaries. As Philip Hamburger documents in *The Separation of Church and State*, most Americans, like most jurists, have "no more wanted" strict separation than they have "wanted an establishment" of religion. Union and separation "are overgeneralizations, between which lies much middle ground."[4] Charitable choice finds that middle ground by embodying five interlocking, constitutionally correct, public administration principles:

—Sacred places, civic purposes: Diverse partnerships between government and religious institutions are entirely permissible provided that faith-based organizations use public funds only to fulfill social service goals or other civic or secular purposes as directed by law and relevant administrative rules. As the 1996 charitable choice law states, public funding is not to be used for or diverted to such religious activities as worship services, sectarian instruction, or proselytizing.

—Full citizenship for the faithful: The leaders, employees, and volunteers of faith-based programs are eligible to compete for public funds with which to administer public programs and supply social services, and they may do so on the same basis as other citizens and will be neither excluded nor included because they are religious, too religious, or of the wrong religion. They are subject to the same accountability standards and administrative protocols as others who seek or receive public support as leaders, employees, or volunteers working with or through nonprofit organizations.

—Respect for clients without regard to religion: Like other nonprofit organizations, religious organizations that choose to compete to administer federal social programs must operate under existing civil rights laws (including titles 6 and 7 of the 1964 Civil Rights Act) and program-specific administrative rules, regulations, and performance standards. In administering programs supported in whole or in part by public funds, religious organizations may not discriminate against an individual on the basis of religion, a religious belief, or refusal to participate in a religious practice. If a person objects to the religious character of a program, the government must guarantee that a secular alternative is available.

—Respect for staff without regard to religion: The vast majority of faith-based social service delivery programs are small, community based, and volunteer driven. They have few if any paid employees, and most of their volunteers are coreligionists. But in cases in which an individual (coreligionist or not) wishes to do paid work in a social service delivery program administered by a faith-based organization that receives public funds dedicated to staffing, the organization may take religion into account in making hiring, retention, and promotion decisions—but only to the extent provided under the so-called ministerial exemption afforded under civil rights and other laws.

—Respect for religious partners: Subject to the first four principles, faith-based organizations that receive public funds to administer social services (either independently or through interfaith, ecumenical, or religious-secular partnerships) retain control over the definition, development, practice, and expression of their religious beliefs. No government may require a religious provider to remove religious art, icons, scripture, or other symbols in order to compete for and receive public funds, to administer programs funded with public funds, or to be certified as being in compliance with relevant public laws and administrative rules, regulations, and performance standards.

During the 2000 presidential campaign, both Al Gore and George Bush called for implementing existing charitable choice laws and expanding charitable choice to a few other domestic and social policy domains. On January 29, 2001, the morning of the first day of the Bush administration's first full week in power, President Bush announced that he was nominating the former Indianapolis mayor Stephen Goldsmith to become chairman of the Corporation for National Service and appointing me to serve as the first director of a new White House office empowered by executive orders to coordinate his administration's "faith-based and community initiatives" and to conduct and complete within 180 days a charitable choice–focused grant-making "performance audit" across five cabinet departments (Health and Human Services, Housing and Urban Development, Education, Labor, and Justice).

The *New York Times* termed "the encouragement and government financing of faith-based programs . . . a signature campaign issue for Mr. Bush": "Mr. Bush and his aides are trying to blunt the impression that what the president is doing amounts to an evangelical endeavor. . . . Indeed, the president's goal is to find new ways for the federal government to encourage private charities—including but not limited to religious groups—to provide more social services. . . . A more thorough integration of faith-based and other not-for-profit groups into federally financed social services is a cornerstone of compassionate conservatism."[5]

The week after the announcement I met with more than a dozen Senate Democrats, and all agreed both that the Clinton-era charitable choice laws needed to be studied and implemented more fully and that a new bipartisan charitable choice bill would be desirable. Instead, House Republican staff preemptively drafted and released a remarkably (and needlessly) contentious "faith bill," H.R. 7, the Community Solutions Act.

The Wheaton College political scientist Amy Black chronicles the bill's rise and demise.[6] From the morning after the president's January 29, 2001, announcement on, those whom Black terms "religious purists," joined by conservative leaders intent on rolling back social welfare spending, demanded that the president and the Congress go beyond charitable choice. These critics, including several who had once publicly cheered charitable choice, now dismissed Ashcroft's bipartisan legislative achievement as weak tea brewed to suit the tastes of antireligious liberal Democrats. They variously insisted that the bill permit religious organizations to proselytize with public funds, to enjoy virtually unfettered rights to discriminate against publicly funded employees on the basis of religion, and to defund social programs administered through direct grant making, while authorizing the universal use of vouchers and other indirect disbursement arrangements. They thereby brought on legislative and media battles that drove even "religious pragmatists" and faith-friendly centrist Democrats into opposing the president's plans.

On July 19, 2001, the bill passed the House on a party-line vote (all Republicans plus fifteen Democrats voting in favor). Two weeks later, on July 26, 2001, Democratic Senator Joseph Lieberman and Republican Senator Rick Santorum met in the Oval Office with President Bush and me. The senators agreed, as the president phrased it, to "get things back on track" by considering the results of the administration's performance audit, redoubling efforts to implement existing charitable choice laws, and drafting a new bipartisan "faith bill" that would track closely with the 1996 charitable choice law.

On August 16, 2001, the White House released a report summarizing the preliminary results of its five-agency study. Titled "Unlevel Playing Field," the report documents a number of critical facts about how federal social programs really work.

The report observes that most national antipoverty and social programs are administered via state and local governments, for-profit firms, and nonprofit organizations. Within this government-by-proxy system, a small group of large national nonprofit organizations, both secular and religious, have for decades received the lion's share of public funding without, however, ever undergoing any meaningful performance audits or independent evaluations. In marked contrast, small community-based nonprofit organizations—especially urban churches, synagogues, mosques, and independent local faith-based organizations—received little or no public funding even though they supplied many major social services to low-income populations. For reasons ranging from outright antireligious discrimination to innocent bureaucratic inflexibility to sheer lack of information, charitable choice laws—and concomitant government performance and results regulations—have not yet been widely or effectively implemented.

As the report also notes, national studies have consistently suggested that, even when they operate, as the vast majority do, without receiving one penny of public funds, most urban community-serving ministries cost-effectively supply social services without proselytizing. Their primary beneficiaries, as the research shows, tend to be neighborhood children and families who are not themselves members of the congregation that serves them. Indeed, few African American, Latino, and other grass-roots urban religious groups make entering their buildings, receiving their services, or participating in their programs contingent upon present or future expression of particular religious beliefs.

But despite this well-documented "social services, not worship services" reality—despite a dozen-plus major social science studies highlighting how literally thousands of community-serving religious nonprofit groups across urban America have sponsored programs to mentor at-risk youth or help recently released prisoners get a fresh start—there continues to be a perverse government-grassroots funding gap. For example, in 2001 the Justice Department awarded a mere 0.3 percent of its discretionary funds to faith-based organizations (that is, $1.9 million of $626.7 million). Likewise, in cities from coast to coast many local religious charities have run exemplary after-school education and literacy programs, but in 2000 faith-based organizations received less than 2 percent of Education Department discretionary grants across eleven grant-making programs (about 25 of 1,091 grants).

As numerous national opinion surveys suggest, most Americans of virtually every socioeconomic status, demographic description, region, and religion strongly support public-private partnerships involving faith-based organizations, provided that these partnerships do not violate clear-cut constitutional restrictions on using public funds to proselytize, offer sectarian instruction, or subsidize worship services. Gore, the two Clintons, Ashcroft, Lieberman, and Santorum, among other leaders, reflect that balanced popular consensus. But through the first few months of 2001 and again during his May 20, 2001, commencement address at Notre Dame University, nobody articulated it better or with greater heart than President Bush. For Bush charitable choice is anchored by at least two broadly bipartisan points of public philosophy.

First, protecting civic pluralism: As the president has often repeated, both in public and in private, "faith initiatives" can arise from "Methodists, Muslims, Mormons, *and* good people of no faith at all." As he stated the point in one of the two executive orders he signed on January 29, 2001, the "delivery of social services must be results oriented and value the bedrock principles of pluralism, nondiscrimination, evenhandedness, and neutrality." As he stated in remarks made before signing the order: "We will not fund the religious activities of any group, but when people of faith provide social services, we will not discriminate against them." And as he stated during a public tour of a local community-serving ministry on the day after the announcement: "Government, of course, cannot fund, and will not fund, religious activities."

Second, going beyond volunteerism: As the president suggested in his aforementioned July 22, 1999, speech and throughout his campaign as a "compassionate conservative," it is "not enough to call for volunteerism," it is wrong to ask community groups "to make bricks without straw," and it is wrong to deny that many public programs, such as "Medicaid for low-income children," deserve to be expanded. As he repeated on February 28, 2001, during his first address before the U.S. Congress, government "cannot be replaced by charities or volunteers."

I believed in 2001, and I believe now, that the president genuinely wants to make "faith initiatives" and "compassionate conservatism" a living public policy reality that demonstrably benefits millions among America's "least of these." I believed then, and I believe now, that he sees charitable choice laws as part of his special "charge to keep" and essential to fulfilling his overarching "no child left behind" pledge. For that reason, it remains my hope that the president, whether reelected or not, can and will yet act to revive this public-spirited consensus, these faith-friendly laws, for the millions and millions of needy and neglected Americans who would benefit from their effective implementation and timely expansion.

The Pepperdine University political scientist Stephen V. Monsma reports that about half of all faith-based welfare-to-work providers receive some public support.[7] About three-quarters of these providers (whether or not they receive public funds) do not hire only coreligionists. Indeed, among the majority of faith-based welfare-to-work providers that are "faith segmented" (those that keep expressly religious elements separate from their service delivery), only 2.8 percent hire only coreligionists. None, including the "faith integrated" (those that integrate expressly religious elements into the services they supply), reports that partnering with government has made them "less efficient" or has reduced their volunteer manpower. Only 8 percent responded that partnering with government caused them to "cut down" on their religious emphases and practices. Finally, more than 90 percent want to expand their services "greatly" or "somewhat," and about 60 percent want to apply for public support.

Monsma notes that faith-based programs' "staff and clients" are mostly African Americans and that, barring further policy, administrative, and technical assistance efforts "to emphasize faith-based programs," most of these programs will continue to be ignored or disfavored. The White House and its faith centers, working in tandem with the CNCS, could ensure that these programs receive due consideration and support. This might happen most effectively if the White House's faith-based and community initiatives effort were anchored in those communities. Jim Towey, my successor in the White House office, has held information-sharing and technical assistance–oriented "town meetings" in cities all around America. Why not consider setting a goal—say tripling public assistance for qualified urban faith-based social service delivery organizations over the next five years—and reorganizing the office and its operations at the grass roots accordingly? Why not bring the public "generals" closer to where urban civil society's "armies of compassion" really are?

In conjunction, the president, if reelected, might consider appointing a national commission, cochaired by Senators Lieberman and Santorum and assisted by Stephen Goldsmith, to do far more systematically and thoroughly what "Unlevel Playing Field" did on the fly (short staffed and, given when the cabinet "centers" actually got up and running, in much less than 180 days), namely, study how federal social programs really work and how the government-by-proxy system might be reformed so as to translate social policy rhetoric and public laws into more cost-effective and socially beneficial administrative action. It could well be that integrating faith-based programs more fully into the system would have many salutary civic effects. But even with all the supporting evidence, that remains an assumption to be tested, not a dogma to be defended.

Of course, there is a chance that President Bush will not be reelected in 2004 and that the White House's "faith initiatives" effort and its associated centers will go the way of the Gore "reinventing government" effort and its national performance review units. In that case, George Bush could make the faith initiatives program his signature postpresidency issue, much like the government reform effort in the 1940s directed by Herbert Hoover. Government reform was a theme of Bush's 2000 presidential campaign, and while holding office he has been responsible for the largest reorganization of the federal government—through the Department of Homeland Security—since the end of World War II. Leading an overarching government reform effort, focused in part on the proper place of public-private partnerships involving religious organizations, would be a natural course for him.

Another path to reviving consensus on this issue would be for President Bush to pick a single faith-based program that epitomizes his vision for faith initiatives and to work to publicize and expand it so that, at last, no child is left behind. One obvious choice is the Philadelphia program Amachi, a public-private, religious-secular program for mentoring the children of prisoners. Bush has twice visited Philadelphia to celebrate this program, which is administered mainly by Big Brothers and Big Sisters of America in partnership with networks of community-serving churches. (*Amachi* is a West African word that means, "Who knows what God has brought us through this child.") The president, by significantly expanding federal support for programs that mentor prisoners' children (by every measure the most severely at-risk population in the nation), could claim this as among his most important social policy accomplishments. While there are as yet no experimental research or impact evaluation studies, the development of the Amachi program and its potential for improving the life prospects of children with a parent behind bars has been documented.[8]

In his 2001 inaugural address President Bush lamented the "proliferation of prisons" and subsequently spoke about "young, innocent kids" with "moms or dads in jail," including "decent dads who made a mistake but want to help their children grow up right and live better." "These children deserve a fair start," he said, "somebody to love them" and help their families. Win or lose reelection, President Bush is a good bet to revive the faithful consensus that calls us all to be charitable toward these fellow citizens while giving religious leaders and volunteers who wish to serve them and others in need a real charitable choice.

Notes

1. Vice President Al Gore, remarks on the role of faith-based organizations, May 24, 1999 (www.algore2000.com/speeches/speeches_faith_ 052499.html).

2. George W. Bush, "The Duty of Hope," July 22, 1999 (www. georgebush.com/speeches/72299_duty_of_hope.htm).

3. Hillary Rodham Clinton, remarks at the Abyssinian Baptist Church, New York, December 17, 2001, p. 17.

4. Philip Hamburger, *The Separation of Church and State* (Harvard University Press, 2002), pp. 486–87.

5. Frank Bruni and Laurie Goodstein, "New Bush Office Seeks Closer Ties to Church Groups," *New York Times,* January 29, 2001, p. A1.

6. Amy Black, *Of Little Faith* (Georgetown University Press, forthcoming).

7. Stephen V. Monsma, with Carolyn Mounts, "Working Faith: How Religious Organizations Provide Welfare-to-Work Services," Center for Research on Religion and Urban Civil Society, University of Pennsylvania, 2000.

8. Linda Jucovy, "Amichio: Mentoring Children of Prisoners in Philadelphia," Public/Private Ventures, Philadelphia, 2003.

RENDERING TO CAESAR AND TO GOD

TERRY EASTLAND

The question at hand is how faith informs one's understanding of policy and public office. In their dialogue, neither Mario Cuomo nor Mark Souder answers this question from the standpoint of some generic faith. Each speaks from his own faith. I propose to answer the question as if I were holding or running for office—and from the perspective of my own faith.

I am a Christian, a Protestant, and a Presbyterian, specifically a member of Fourth Presbyterian Church of Bethesda, Maryland, an EPC (Evangelical Presbyterian Church) congregation. My church is squarely in the Reformed tradition. It holds to the scripture as the inspired Word of God and has a high regard for the distinctive contributions to the church made by Luther and especially Calvin but also many others who preceded them.

In thinking about religion and politics, I start where you might expect someone in the Reformed tradition to begin—with scripture. My text is actually three texts, since they all tell the same story. The three are found in Matthew, Mark, and Luke, and the story is the one in which Jesus makes his famous statement about tribute money.

Jesus is in the last week of his earthly life. He has made the triumphal entry into Jerusalem and soon will be arrested and crucified. His growing following is a matter of deep concern to the religious and political leaders among the Jews, the Pharisees and the Herodians. They are eager to "lay hands on him," writes Luke, but because they fear how the people might respond, they instead watch him—and decide to lay a trap. They send his way "spies," who pretend to be honest, in order to "catch him in something," he says, so that they might "deliver him to the power and the authority of the governor"—one Pontius Pilate.

The spies ask Jesus a religion-and-politics question: "Teacher, we know you are a man of integrity and that you teach the way of God in accordance with the truth. You are not swayed by men, because you pay no attention to who they are. Tell us then, what do you think? Is it lawful to pay taxes to Caesar, or not?" Knowing what his inquisitors are really up to, Jesus charges them with hypocrisy and demands, "Show me the coin used for paying the tax." In Mark's account, Jesus also says, "and let me look at it." His inquisitors then bring him a denarius, and he asks them, "Whose image and inscription is this?" They answer, "Caesar's." To which Jesus speaks words for the ages: "Render unto Caesar the things that are Caesar's and to God the things that are God's."

You will notice that Jesus does not answer the question yes or no. He refuses to be caught in the trap. If he says no, the Herodians, Jewish rulers allied with the Roman regime, will accuse him of treason. If he says yes, the Pharisees, zealous for the Jewish religion, will accuse him of compromising with a pagan regime and indeed also with a pagan religion, since the inscription on the denarius shown to Jesus is very likely "Tiberius Caesar, son of the deified Augustus, and Augustus."

In his reply Jesus draws a distinction between Caesar—that is to say, civil government—and God. This is not a distinction you find in the Old Testament, where state and church, so to speak, are united, Israel being a theocracy. With the advent of Jesus, however, and the coming of the Kingdom of God, the Old Covenant is superseded by the new. Among the many things that means, of importance here is that the limitation of the Old Covenant to one nation is no more. The people of God are now from everywhere. There is no nation to which God is uniquely committed. No longer is it God's plan to have a state enforce the true religion.

Still, the New Testament does have something to say about civil government in the new age that dawns with the advent of Jesus. Simply stated, civil government is an institution ordained by God for ruling and maintaining order (see Romans 13). It is (just as ministers and parents are) a means of common grace; that is, it exists for the benefit of all humanity so that things might be a bit or maybe even a whole lot better than they otherwise would be. Generally speaking, a Christian must not ignore but must acknowledge the civil authority and render unto it what it is owed.

What it plainly is not owed, of course, is all that is owed God. And what is owed God? The answer, drawn from the scriptures and the great creeds and confessions of the church, is certainly this: our worship and ultimate obedience. If government forbids what God requires or requires what God forbids, a Christian is compelled not to submit and may find it necessary to engage in some form of civil disobedience. And what is owed government? The Bible says that laws are to be obeyed and taxes paid, the importance of taxes being that they underwrite the work of this institution of common grace: defending borders, administering justice, building roads, and so on.

Notably, a Christian is not relieved of the duty to render unto Caesar if Caesar believes not in God but in some other god (or none at all). Civil government is still ordained, regardless of whether those who execute a particular government believe in the God who has done the ordaining. Jesus would pay taxes to Caesar notwithstanding the presence of Caesar's blasphemous religion on the very coin used to pay those taxes. Jesus would do that even though "all authority on heaven and earth had been given" to him. God is sovereign over all. He uses the nations as he will to achieve his ends. As the scripture says, the nations rise and fall in his hands.

William S. Barker of Westminster Theological Seminary further illumines Jesus's statement about the tribute money.[1] He persuasively argues that implicit in the statement are the two great commandments, the first being to love God and the second being to love your neighbor as yourself. The first concerns an individual and God; the second, an individual in community. Barker correctly writes that civil government may not reach into the first area and compel people to do, or not to do, their duty to God. They must be free to do whatever they do in this area of eternal importance. But they also must love their neighbor, and in doing that they are engaged in the area where God has ordained civil government to function—the area Barker calls human relations.

Conscientious Christians thus cannot avoid thinking about the policies and performance of government. They will take an interest in politics and elections. And the second great commandment provides the starting point for their political thinking and involvement. It may be stated in the question, What is best for my neighbor? Importantly, the neighbor in scripture is not an abstraction but particular men and women (think of the man in the road whom the Good Samaritan helped out). Indeed, the second great commandment teaches concern for people as individuals, each of whom is created in the image of God.

The Christian life is, of course, not a solitary one. The New Testament assumes that every Christian will be part of a local church, worshipping with other believers and sharing in witness and ministry—rendering unto God the things that are God's. Although not every member of a church may be a Christian—only God knows what is in the heart—all genuine Christians are members of the church universal, what Paul called the body of Christ. The church clearly is one of those "things of God," and so a Christian will guard against state involvements that might corrupt it. Thus does the Westminster Confession state, "Civil magistrates may not assume to themselves the administration of the Word and sacraments; or the power of the keys of the kingdom of heaven."

The church, the body of believers, has an eternal destiny. But a Christian, duly mindful of the second great commandment, cannot let the world go to hell in the proverbial handbasket. By God's grace, the life of a community can improve. So too can the life of a nation. But Christianity also teaches realism about this world. It is passing away. It will not last. And Christians are not to put their ultimate hope in it—or in any human endeavor. "Keep yourselves from idols," says the First Epistle of John. Including, it should go without saying, the idol of nationalism.

My own faith, then, provides ground for accepting religious pluralism—for living in a country whose citizens can be of any faith or none at all. Indeed, I would argue that Jesus' statement about the tribute money points to a politics of religious liberty and thus to a religiously pluralist nation of the sort we have. To be sure, Jesus did not declare a right to believe whatever you want. He used the language of duty ("render unto"). Yet there must be freedom to carry out the duty to worship the one true God. So there must be a right of conscience that government may not violate—notwithstanding that many people may abysmally fail in rendering to God what is owed God. Again, it is not the job of the civil authority to enforce the true religion.

Strikingly, the historic Virginia Declaration of Rights speaks of the "duty which we owe to our Creator" as it declares religious liberty for all. The U.S. Constitution also assumes that there is such a right. The First Amendment was added in case there was any doubt. And religious pluralism has been the inevitable result: America has become a nation with a wide diversity of groups enjoying equal liberty to believe as they do. The church historian Martin Marty reports that America is now home to more than two hundred thousand denominations and that some twelve hundred religious groups are alphabetized in standard encyclopedias of American religion.[2] Protestants and Catholics still dominate the American religious scene, but the other main world religions also have a presence in the United States. So do many alternatives to these traditional religions.

Were I an officeholder or candidate for office, how would I conduct myself? For starters, I would be willing to state what my faith is, though I would not want to use my faith as an instrument of politics, something to hold up before certain audiences to gain their support. That, it strikes me, would come close to rendering to Caesar the things that are God's.

As for political argumentation, I would not rule out making a theological point when relevant; consider the debate over whether the invasion of

Iraq was a "just war." But I doubt that my arguments would often draw upon the particulars of Christian faith. I would want to be persuasive, and on most issues arguments from explicit doctrine (mine or anyone else's) are not likely to persuade majorities drawn from a religiously pluralist society. However, because I believe that there is such a thing as moral law that God has engraved on every human conscience, I would seek to make arguments that might resonate with the inner convictions of most Americans.

In addition, my politics would assume the need to join forces with people of faiths other than mine or no faith at all in working toward common moral goals. Nothing in my faith counsels otherwise, and indeed the injunction to love thy neighbor compels one to act, I think, with whatever allies can be found. Of course, it is hard to see how politics in a religiously pluralist democracy could otherwise be practiced. The other option, which I do not think is theologically correct, for it fails to love thy neighbor, is separation, as in the case of the historic Anabaptists, who chose to remain separate from society in order to stand as a witness to it.

On a specific issue much in the news recently, I would not feel compelled by my faith to suggest ways that government might formally "acknowledge" God. Here I refer to the case of the chief justice of the Alabama Supreme Court, Roy Moore, who installed a two-and-half-ton Ten Commandments monument in the rotunda of the Alabama judicial building. A federal lawsuit was filed, Moore lost, he was ordered to remove the monument—and he refused. Others carried out the order, and a state judicial ethics panel removed Moore from office for defying the order. Moore said the issue in his case was whether the people of Alabama may acknowledge God. Citing the preamble to the Alabama Constitution, which indicates the state's ongoing reliance on God, Moore saw that he was acting under its authority. Putting to the side the legal issues in the case, Moore also presented himself as compelled by his Christian faith—Moore is a Southern Baptist—to take the action he did. In that, I think, he was mistaken: It is hardly one of the essentials of the Christian faith that the people of a state acknowledge God by having a Ten Commandments monument placed in the judicial office building. The government of Alabama is no less an institution ordained by God for having had the monument removed. And throughout the dispute, the obligation of the citizen to obey the laws of Alabama remained the same.

On a general matter, I would be open to applications of the principle that where government assistance is being provided to a broad class of beneficiaries, defined without reference to religion and including both public and private institutions, entities that are religious should not be denied such assistance if they otherwise are eligible for it. That is, religious entities should be treated equally. Now, I would not support that principle because I wanted government assistance for something involving my faith. In fact if I were pastor of a church I would probably not seek a government grant, since I would worry about potential government influence (making sure that I was rendering rightly). But the principle seems correct for the religiously plural-ist nation we have, one in which plenty of religious groups are engaged in charitable undertakings. Of course, whether a particular application of the principle works will turn on the results that government is seeking. Those are not going to be theological in character, nor should they be.

On one other general matter: Precisely because of our religious pluralism I would be concerned about the operation of valid law upon particular reli-gious groups. I would want to see whether the burden upon conduct moti-vated by faith might be so great as to suggest the need for exemption from a law. The question of burden is complicated, as litigation in this area shows. Yet there are cases in which an exemption might be warranted.

There is a last point: I hope that, as a politician, I would keep politics in perspective, bearing in mind where ultimate authority, and the Christian's abiding hope, truly lies.

Notes

1. William S. Barker, "Theonomy, Pluralism, and the Bible," in William S. Barker and W. Robert Godfrey, eds., *Theonomy: A Reformed Critique* (Grand Rapids, Mich.: Academie Books, 1990), p. 237.

2. Martin Marty, quoted in Daniel G. Reid and others, eds., *Dictionary of Chris-tianity in America* (Downers Grove, Ill.: InterVarsity Press, 1990), p. 912.

GOD TALK AND
THE CITIZEN-BELIEVER

JEAN BETHKE ELSHTAIN

God talk, at least as much as rights talk, is the way America speaks. American politics is indecipherable if it is severed from the interplay and panoply of America's religions. American democracy from its inception was premised on a complex intermingling of religious and political imperatives. The majority of Americans were religious seekers and believers who saw in communal liberty the freedom to be religious rather than freedom from religion.

That is the easy part. More difficult is sorting out a question that has become exigent in civic life, namely, How should those with religious convictions speak when they go public? Does the believer enter the civic arena using a full-blown faith-based and confessional vocabulary? Or should the believer be compelled to translate every religiously derived conviction into some ostensibly neutral vocabulary of civic discussion? Those who answer yes to the last question—that believers are obliged to neutralize their speech for the purposes of civic life—insist that, if they are not obliged to do this, the faithful enjoy an unfair advantage over nonbelievers because their religious claims enjoy some sort of epistemological privilege: They lie beyond challenge.

Is this plausible? The record of American history and current politics suggests that this is not a credible worry. Indeed, what is striking is just how much division and contention there is within the universe of religious believers on just what is required politically, given their faith convictions. Religious believers have never spoken with a single voice or used the same vocabulary. For example, does Christianity require taking a stand against slavery and Jim Crow? In joining the ranks of abolitionism and antisegregation, thousands of Americans answered this question with an enthusiastic yes. At the same time, however, other Christians, especially those in the antebellum South, pointed to scriptural passages that justified certain sorts of ordering of relationships and that could be used (or twisted, some would say) to underwrite race-based inferior or second-class status. (Certain passages from the Old Testament were often drawn upon for this purpose.)

Over time, one interpretation—that Christianity and slavery are not compatible—won the day. This example—and one could point to many others—indicates that religious conviction invites civic contestation rather than a uniform religious perspective or set of religious demands in, or on, civic life. It does seem to me appropriate—and it is prudent politics besides—for religious believers to try to state their concerns in a vocabulary that reaches out to the widest possible audience of Americans, whether they share one's faith or not. That is how social change is effected, after all. What is called for is contextual engagement: The citizen-believer evaluates a political issue depending upon the nature of the issues involved and the spheres of human social existence affected by a proposed policy. Are there issues of common good here? Does the issue touch at the heart of the Christian commitment to the dignity of the human person? (I assume that faithful Jews, Muslims, and others will have their own version of such questions.) There are times when a particular issue—like cloning, or euthanasia, or for that matter abortion—calls for a more robust display of faith-based concerns than some other issue—like a balanced budget.

There is no easy tick list to guide citizens, whether religious believers or not, to engage issues in the public square. Those who claim that believers enjoy an unfair advantage because they can make absolute claims based on unargued premises are quite simply wrong. It is not merely that believers contend with one another within the parameters of their beliefs but that believers often contend with secularists who are also adamant about their beliefs. One way or the other, all citizens operate from relatively stable reference points concerning public life and the goods it sustains and promotes. No one should be ruled out of the conversation a priori, whether on the grounds of being too religious, too irreligious, or some other. Only those whose preachments are steeped in hate and violence should find their speech limited. But that is another conversation.

THE POLITICS OF RELIGION
IN A SINFUL WORLD

RICHARD WIGHTMAN FOX

Both Mario Cuomo and Mark Souder want to bring Christianity—the religion of Christ's love—into politics. Religion is not private, according to them, not a set of convictions to be left at the archway as you stride into the public sphere. The so-called wall of separation between church and state refers only to official preference for one religion over another. Christian politicians should proudly bring their beliefs to bear on their political activities. As Christians, Cuomo and Souder see politics as an opportunity to respond lovingly to the pervasiveness of sin.

By *sin* they do not just mean the evils out in the world that a politician may wish to attack or reform. Sin, for Cuomo and Souder, resides in the human person. They announce that they are sinners themselves. Cuomo concludes by saying that he "desperately" wants to believe in a force "better" than himself. If he has fought all his political battles for nothing greater than himself, he explains, then he has "wasted an awful lot of time, because I am not worth it." Souder, meanwhile, identifies himself as "a humble sinner" who finds the popular phrase, What would Jesus do? presumptuous. How could a sinner like him dare aspire to doing what God would do? The question he prefers is, What do I believe Jesus would have me . . . do? Discipleship is not "the imitation of Christ," as Thomas à Kempis famously put it, but obedience to the stirrings of Christ's spirit in your heart.

It might seem oddly quaint in this day and age for politicians to speak of sin as a deep-seated unworthiness rather than a discrete immoral act of the sort we have come to expect from athletes, actors, revivalists, and priests, as well as politicians. But as Reinhold Niebuhr, the great twentieth-century American theologian and political journalist, argued—from his classic *Moral Man and Immoral Society* (1932) to *The Irony of American History* (1952)—a consciousness of one's own inveterate sinfulness is a basic component of the religious person's public responsibility. Seeing themselves as sinners, and also as creatures made in the image of God, enables believers to struggle for justice in the world without ever identifying their position with God's standpoint. Knowing themselves as sinners allows them to withstand the temptation to turn their cause into a righteous mission on God's behalf. Awareness of sin—of their often hidden desire for fame, power, privilege, and other kinds of self-aggrandizement—can counteract religious people's temptation to see themselves as chosen instruments for divinely sponsored action.

In the 1930s Niebuhr saw religiously derived fanaticism blossoming on the Left and on the Right. He knew politics needed religion to keep itself pointed toward justice, but he also knew that the struggle for justice was threatened by the power of religion. Fighting for the poor, the unemployed, or the disadvantaged requires broad coalition building, and religiously motivated politicians too often put sectarian beliefs and interests ahead of practical consensus.

Cuomo and Souder mirror Niebuhr's conviction that it is perfectly proper, indeed necessary, for Christians or Jews or Muslims to bring their religion into politics. They also appear to concur with Niebuhr's sense that the Jewish and Christian idea of sin offers an essential safeguard against fanaticism. But for all the ground they share, Cuomo and Souder ultimately embrace very different ideas about how to make love real in the world. The format of the October 2002 discussion—and of this volume—tends to paper over these differences between Cuomo and Souder. They never engage one another directly but only through answers to questions from third parties. In the end, the gap between Cuomo's liberal vision and Souder's conservative perspective is so vast as to be unbridgeable.

Thankfully, they both say they cherish continued dialogue. The importance of that dialogue cannot be overestimated. Political evangelicalism of the Souder variety and political liberalism of the Cuomo stamp are going to have to coexist for a long time to come, and both sides will benefit from clarity about what they do and do not have in common. What is so refreshing about Cuomo's and Souder's presentations is that they both seem willing to respect their opponents' intelligence and good faith, while also trying to persuade their adversaries to change their minds.

Mario Cuomo wants to bring his Christian beliefs into the public arena, but the Christianity he wants to bring with him is not a set of doctrines distinctive to Christians. It is a conviction shared, in his view, by all religious traditions and some secular ones: Human beings deserve respect and dignity. According to Cuomo, this religious common denominator—love your neighbor as you love God and as God loves you—can be deduced from reason alone. Like the good Thomist that Catholics of Cuomo's generation were taught to be, Cuomo knows that reason and faith are mutually supportive. Christ's love commands can inform the political deliberations of a religiously pluralist nation without being sectarian.

In Cuomo's vision, Catholics, Jews, Protestants, Muslims, Buddhists, Hindus, and others can work together to improve a society that too often favors rich over poor and denies too many people their dignity. Cuomo's opposition to the death penalty, like his support for public education, health care, and progressive taxation, stems from his entire outlook on life, not from a prescribed list of moral prohibitions supplied by his religion. Yet his outlook is religious since it is based on his belief that God, a power bigger than he is, loves him and models for him how to love the least of his brethren.

The kind of religion that Cuomo wants to bring into politics is unifying and harmonizing across religious and secular lines. And it is progressive: It sparks action to change a world that arbitrarily punishes some people while rewarding others. Cuomo does not explicitly call the world sinful, but in a general way the world is sinful in his estimation because individuals put themselves ahead of others and disregard their obligation to treat their fellow human beings with justice. One aspect of treating other people fairly is to respect their distinctive beliefs, indeed, to explore those beliefs for the illumination they can offer even to a person from another tradition. Cuomo notes how much religious insight he has gained from Jewish teachings. He makes an elegant case for not pushing the particulars of your religious tradition on anyone else but instead examining your neighbors' spiritual inheritance to spark new insight into your own.

The politician's responsibility, according to Cuomo, is to bring love to bear on real social problems, to try to solve those problems—education and health care are two of his examples—through collective action (that is, governmental as well as nongovernmental initiatives). Some problems can be adequately addressed privately, but others cannot. Politicians, like their constituents, will disagree about which problems require collective action. Since politicians must answer to constituents, they must make prudent choices about which issues to push. Being too insistent about a favorite issue can mean defeat at the next election.

Implicit in Cuomo's presentation is a second type of prudence, which applies to every issue. Cuomo wants politicians to center their efforts on practical results rather than ideological imperatives. He wants politicians to calculate how much improvement of what sort can be expected from a particular debate or piece of legislation. Faith gets in the way of effective politics when it puts moralistic preaching ahead of practical benefits. For Cuomo, making love real in a sinful world means, in effect, erecting a wall of separation between what you most wish for and what you can realistically make happen. Politics at its best means getting things done, with the aid of rational deliberation across religious, ethnic, and party lines. His desire to engage in rational deliberation is driven by religious faith, but the discussion itself is conducted according to the best lights of reason and expertise.

To judge from his remarks, Mark Souder diverges dramatically from Cuomo at precisely this point. He does not conceive of the public arena as a place of deliberation according to the lights either of reason or of some broad Judeo-Christian consensus. The idea of such a consensus was invented, in his view, by liberals who had no use for edgy Evangelical faiths committed to an uncompromising biblical Christianity. Souder sees the public sphere as a place of peaceable but monumental struggle among discrete moral worldviews. Those viewpoints are so divergent that one cannot seek compromises among them. You either see abortion as the taking of a life or you do not. You either see gay coupling as an assault on divine purpose or you do not. You either see "evolution across species" as an attack on God's "intelligent design" or you do not. Souder looks forward to the day when his side will have the power to eliminate abortion on demand. He looks forward to the day when his side will have the power to make the teaching of intelligent design (an updated version of creationism) as common as the teaching of evolution.

Where Cuomo posits an interpenetration of faith and reason, each reinforcing the other, Souder sees an identity of faith and reason. He knows his intelligent design theory is reasonable because he knows by faith that it is true. Reason, in his conception, is inseparable from and subordinate to revelation. For Souder there can be no compelling appeal to the authority of a religiously neutral science. I infer from Cuomo's remarks that he would take evolution as the most reasonable explanation for the facts of the fossil record because it is the explanation overwhelmingly endorsed by the best scientists in the world. For Cuomo science has its own proper sphere, and none of its rationally driven inquiry poses the slightest danger to religious faith or to God's purpose.

The importance of the essays by Cuomo and Souder is that exponents of two deeply divergent approaches to religion and politics, and to faith and reason, have aired their differences in an atmosphere of respect. That atmosphere is crucial for permitting an Evangelical Christian such as Souder (who labels himself a member of an aggrieved minority) and a liberal Catholic such as Cuomo (who may now regard himself as a member of an extinct species of liberal Progressives) to try to make their views comprehensible to their opponents. Dialogue of this sort is not likely to change minds, but participants are pushed to clarify and justify their positions in the light of sympathetic criticism. That kind of candor is a small but essential victory in the campaign to prevent the culture wars from blocking constructive collaboration on urgent issues—preventing nuclear war, halting the spread of AIDS, addressing global warming, and others—that many liberals and conservatives could agree upon even as they keep jousting elsewhere.

CUOMOLOGICAL FALLACIES

ROBERT P. GEORGE

Mario Cuomo is widely admired as one of our nation's most intelligent and thoughtful public servants. Indeed, the former governor, who is also a former law professor, is regarded as an intellectual as well as a statesman. He is a student of history, philosophy, and theology. His speeches and writings reflect an impressive range of intellectual interests. So what happened to Mario Cuomo at the forum on Politics and Faith in America on October 2, 2002?

Something went wrong. Indeed, things began going wrong almost right off the bat. In setting up his analysis of the question of religious faith in politics, Cuomo evidently forgot about the elementary principle of logical argumentation that forbids employing as a premise the very proposition one is marshaling an argument to prove. In his essay in this volume, which is based on his presentation at that forum, Cuomo asserts that holders of public office who happen to be Catholic have a responsibility "to create conditions under which all citizens are reasonably free to act according to their own religious beliefs, even when those acts conflict with Roman Catholic dogma regarding divorce, birth control, abortion, stem cell research, and even the existence of God." According to Cuomo, Catholics should support legalized abortion and embryo-destructive research, as he himself does, because in guaranteeing these rights to others, they guarantee their own right "to reject abortions, and to refuse to participate in or contribute to removing stem cells from embryos." But Cuomo's idea that the right "to reject" abortion and embryo-destructive experimentation entails a right of others, as a matter of religious liberty, to engage in these practices is fallacious. The fallacy comes into focus immediately if one considers whether the right of a Catholic (or Baptist, or Jew, or member of any other faith) to reject infanticide, slavery, and the exploitation of labor entails a right of others who happen not to share these "religious" convictions to kill, enslave, and exploit.

By the expedient of classifying prolife convictions about abortion and embryo-destructive experimentation as "Roman Catholic dogmas," Cuomo smuggles into the premises of his argument the controversial conclusion he is trying to prove. If prolife principles were indeed merely dogmatic teachings—such as the teaching that Jesus of Nazareth is the only begotten Son of God—then according to the church itself (not to mention American constitutional law) they could not legitimately be enforced by the coercive power of the state. The trouble for Cuomo is that prolife principles are not mere matters of dogma nor are they understood as such by the Catholic Church, whose beliefs Cuomo claims to affirm, or by prolife citizens, whether they happen to be Catholics, Protestants, Jews, Muslims, Hindus, Buddhists, agnostics, or atheists. Rather, prolife citizens understand these principles and propose them to their fellow citizens as fundamental norms of justice and human rights that can be understood and affirmed even apart from claims of revelation and religious authority.

If Cuomo would like to persuade us to adopt his view that people have a right to destroy nascent human life by abortion or in embryo-destructive research, it is incumbent upon him to provide a rational argument in defense of his position. It will not do to suggest, as Cuomo seems to suggest, that the sheer fact that the Catholic Church (or some other religious body) has a teaching against these practices, and that some or even many people reject this teaching, means that laws prohibiting the killing of human beings in the embryonic and fetal stages violate the right to freedom of religion of those who do not accept the teaching. If that were anything other than a fallacy, then laws against killing infants, owning slaves, exploiting workers, and many other grave forms of injustice really would be violations of religious freedom. Surely Cuomo would not wish to endorse that conclusion.

Yet he provides no reason to distinguish those acts and practices putatively falling within the category of religious freedom from those falling outside it. So we must ask: If abortion is immunized against legal restriction on the ground that it is a matter of religious belief, how can it be that slavery is not similarly immunized? If today abortion cannot be prohibited without violating the right to religious freedom of people whose religions do not object to abortion, how can Cuomo say that the Thirteenth Amendment's prohibition of slavery did not violate the right to religious freedom of those in the nineteenth century whose religions did not condemn slaveholding? Cuomo cannot respond to this challenge by asserting that, religious teachings aside, slaveholding really is an unjust practice and abortion is not. Cuomo takes pains to assure us that he believes what the Catholic Church teaches about abortion: that is to say, that it is nothing less than the unjust taking of innocent human life. Nor, I hope, would Cuomo wish to retreat to the position that those nineteenth-century politicians who recognized the profound injustice of slavery should have supported a "right" to own slaves, on the "prudential" ground that no social consensus existed at the time on the question of slaveholding. Surely this is not what Cuomo means in mentioning "an American Catholic tradition of political realism" in connection with the slavery question "in the late nineteenth century." Cuomo says that the Catholic Church "understands that our public morality depends on a consensus view of right and wrong," but it would be scandalous to argue that Catholics should have opposed a constitutional amendment abolishing slavery in the nineteenth century, or legislation protecting the civil rights of the oppressed descendants of slaves in the mid-twentieth century, on the ground that "prudence" or "realism" requires respect for "moral pluralism" where there is no social "consensus" on questions of right and wrong.

At one point at the forum on Politics and Faith, Cuomo suggested that laws against abortion and embryo-destructive research would force people who do not object to such things to practice the religion of people who do. But this another fallacy. No one imagines that the constitutional prohibition of slavery forced those who believed in slaveholding to practice the religion of those who did not. Would Cuomo have us suppose that laws protecting workers against what he, in line with the solemn teaching of every pope from Leo XIII to John Paul II, considers to be exploitation and abuse have the effect of forcing non-Catholic factory owners to practice Catholicism?

At another point, in denying that there was any inconsistency between his willingness as governor to act on his anti–death penalty views but not on his antiabortion views, Cuomo denies ever having spoken against the death penalty as "a moral issue." He claims, in fact, that he "seldom talk[s] in terms of moral issues" and that, when he speaks of the death penalty, he never suggests that he considers it a moral issue. Then, in the very next sentence, he condemns the death penalty in the most explicitly, indeed flamboyantly, moralistic terms: "I am against the death penalty because I think it is bad and unfair. It is debasing. It is degenerate. It kills innocent people." He does not consider that these are precisely the claims made by prolife citizens against the policy of legal abortion and its public funding— a policy that Cuomo defends in the name of religious liberty.

After more than two decades of bobbing and weaving on the subject of prenatal homicide, it is time for Mario Cuomo to face up to the fact that people who oppose abortion and embryo-destructive research oppose these practices for the same reason they oppose postnatal homicide. Catholics and other prolife citizens oppose these practices because they involve the deliberate killing of innocent human beings. Their ground for supporting the legal prohibition of abortion and embryo-destructive research is the same ground on which they support the legal prohibition of infanticide, for example, or the principle of noncombatant immunity even in justified wars. They subscribe to the proposition that all human beings are equal in worth and dignity and cannot be denied the right to protection against killing on the basis of age, size, stage of development, or condition of dependency.

If Cuomo is indeed the faithful Catholic he claims to be, then he too believes this. But if he does believe it, then he has no rational warrant for denying that the unborn, like the newly born, are entitled to the equal protection of the laws—above all, the laws against homicide. His claim that one can be "personally opposed" to abortion yet support its legal permission and even its public funding collapses. But things are worse for Cuomo, for by supporting the right to abortion and embryo-destructive research he is implicating himself in the injustice of these practices.

As governor of New York and as an influential figure in national Democratic Party politics, Cuomo has actively defended legal abortion and its public funding. From his own perspective, he was protecting not abortion as such but, rather, a woman's right to choose an abortion. The resulting abortions, he no doubt told himself, were in no way his responsibility. If they were wrong, unjust, even homicidal (as the Catholic Church teaches, and as Cuomo presumably believes—after all, why otherwise would he profess to be opposed to abortion and to believe what the church teaches about its wrongfulness?), they were not burdens on his conscience. While defending others' right to choose what he himself "personally opposed," he did not encourage them to exercise that right. Indeed, Cuomo might contend that he actually reduced the number of abortions by advancing social and economic policies that helped women to avoid unwanted pregnancy and enabled women who did become pregnant to afford to carry their babies to term. In any event, I assume that Cuomo's sincere hope was that fewer, rather than more, women would choose abortion, despite his belief that the choice was their right.

Of course, it is possible for a person wielding public power to use that power to establish or preserve a legal right to abortion and even to provide public money for it while at the same time not wanting or willing anyone to exercise the right. But this does not get Cuomo off the hook. For someone who acts to protect legal abortion necessarily wills that abortion's unborn victims be denied the elementary legal protections against deliberate homicide that one favors for oneself and those whom one considers to be worthy of the law's protection. Thus one violates the most basic precept of normative social and political theory, the Golden Rule. One divides humanity into two classes: those whom one is willing to admit to the community of the commonly protected and those whom one wills to be excluded from it. By exposing members of the disfavored class to lethal violence, one deeply implicates oneself in the injustice of killing them—even if one sincerely hopes that no woman will act on her right to choose abortion. The goodness of what one *hopes* for does not redeem the evil of what one *wills*. To suppose otherwise is to commit yet another fallacy.

THE PURITANS
AND AMERICAN POLITICS

ANDREW GREELEY

The most dangerous intrusion of religion into American politics in the last hundred years was the effort of a largely southern, largely Evangelical, largely Calvinist cabal to cancel the election of an American president by a gross intrusion into the private life of that president. It may not have been a mammoth right-wing conspiracy as Senator Hillary Clinton suggests. The various groups and individuals who set out to drive President Bill Clinton from office may not have been formally joined to one another. There may not have been any master conspirator. But there did not have to be. The results were the same as if the various participants in the plots to destroy the president were cooperating formally with one another. The attempt to burn Bill Clinton did not need a John Winthrop to light the fire.

Nor was the cooperation of the elite national media with the various conspirators deliberate. But the *New York Times* demanded investigations and a reprimand of the president. By what right did the *Times* ask for an extraconstitutional punishment of a president for actions that had nothing to do with his exercise of the office of the president? As for the Whitewater investigations, several had already cleared the president before the *Times* and the other national media remained silent when a group of southern senators and southern judges decided that yet another special prosecutor should be appointed. Regarding the *Washington Post,* did not its reporter Susan Schmidt become a virtual flack for Kenneth Starr? Nor was there any outcry from the alleged liberal media when Starr's failed prosecution for Whitewater became an exercise in prurient prying into the personal sexual behavior of the president? Although it may seem strange to claim that the *Times* and the *Post* cooperated in an Evangelical assault against the president, it must be remembered that Calvinism is a major energy in American culture and that both newspapers have consistently through the years pursued scandal with puritanical energy.

I take it as self-evident that the noncriminal personal behavior of a public figure is not a justification for removing him or her from public office save in a country in which Calvinist Puritanism (with the accompanying hypocrisy) equates sin (especially sexual sin) with crime. And if alleged sexual sin is a crime (indeed a high crime) for a president, how much lower on the political ladder does it cease to be criminal? Surely the marital infidelity of a Speaker of the House of Representatives and of a chairman of the House Judiciary Committee ought to mandate their removal.

I am not defending sin. Nor is it my responsibility to throw the first stone (although millions of Americans, being sinless, were prepared to throw stones). Some argued that the sin became a high crime because it took place in the Oval Office. Ah, perhaps a sacrilege in a holy place. Yet the Constitution gives no grounds for contending that adultery in the Oval Office is a high crime but that adultery in the presidential bedroom is not. The alleged sin was considered by some even worse because the partner was a White House intern. In fact, the young woman was patently a consenting adult. Ah, it is said, but the president obstructed justice and committed perjury, both felonies. Yet it is most unlikely that in an ordinary court of law these particular allegations would have led to an indictment.

The truth of the matter is that the whole charade (there was never going to be a conviction anyway) was the result of a cynical manipulation of that substantial minority of the American people who are unable to distinguish between sin and crime. Those who were determined to destroy Clinton launched a religio-moral crusade to oust from office a man whom they determined in 1992 was not a legitimate president. To the people in their base (which is also George Bush's base) this made sense: A sinner could not be a good president. A more modest statement of the same sentiment was that the president ought to be a moral example to the people. Again one has to ask where it is written in the constitutional history of America that moral failures that are not crimes may nonetheless be grounds for removing someone from public office. They may be grounds for voters refusing to reelect him, but that is an entirely different matter.

To miss the religious twist—the Calvinist Puritan dimension—in the attempt to destroy Clinton is to misunderstand it completely. But to see the Calvinist twist one merely needs to note that it was Protestant divines, Protestant professors (such as Jean Bethke Elshtain), and Protestant prayer breakfasters who rose up to demand that the adulterer be thrown out of office. It was seventeenth-century Massachusetts all over again.

I would seldom be inclined to praise the American Catholic hierarchy. However I was proud of the Catholic bishops for keeping their mouths shut when the religio-moral card was being played against Clinton. They understood—perhaps some of them despite themselves—the difference between sin and crime and between private and public life.

I was in Ireland during some of the impeachment proceedings. The Irish of course greatly admire President Clinton, despite what one might have thought to be their Jansenist moral leanings. At that time, the prime minister of Ireland was living in notorious and public concubinage. What about that? I demanded of my Irish friends. Sure, doesn't the poor man need someone to take care of him? they would answer. The Irish are, however, not Calvinists but Pelagians.

The Calvinist crusade against sin is a major component of American culture; crusades against witchcraft and for abolition, prohibition, the Comstock laws, and racial segregation have been an important part of American life. Some of these holy wars have been beneficial, some have not. However, the Prohibition movement shows how a clever leadership can activate the Calvinist Puritan base to do great harm to the country.[1]

It is disappointing to realize how few observers of contemporary American life seem aware how much the attack on President Clinton was shaped by a highly peculiar—and highly American—perception of the role of religious morality in public life. Perhaps the reason for this is that many members of the national press corps do not understand who their allies were in their campaign to get rid of Clinton.[2] Hence their bafflement that the public did not see the overriding moral issue the way reporters inside the Beltway saw it—men and women (as we all know) of impeccable moral lives.

I am astonished that in this examination of religion in American political life the only mention of the religious crusade against Clinton is Mark Souder's self-serving and Puritanical description of his agony over his vote on impeachment.

The American public voted in the 1998 congressional election against those who would have dismissed Clinton from public office. Support for the president rarely varied from a 60 percent favorable rating, no matter how much filth Kenneth Starr put in the public domain. In fact, support for the president went up, not down, when Starr released his notorious report, doubtless much to the surprise of that Calvinist inquisitor.

The good news, then, is that in the end it did not work. The bad news is that same minority of self-righteous Puritans is running the country now, heaven save us all.

Notes

1. For an excellent history on this subject, see James Morone, *Hellfire Nation: The Politics of Sin in American Life* (Yale University Press, 2003).

2. Colin Kidd, in a review of Morone's book in the *London Review of Books*, suggests another explanation: "A focus on the Puritan provenance of American moral politics might well obscure a more profound horror at the heart of the liberal tradition. Was it Puritanism alone which perverted American liberalism? In certain respects, the Enlightenment and the redneck fringe are more closely aligned than we imagine. After all, even John Locke, the acknowledged grandfather of Anglo-American liberalism, excluded two obnoxious groups from his broad scheme of religious toleration: Roman Catholics, whose allegiance was suspect, and atheists, who could not be trusted to observe oaths and promises. Morone's story ends with the war on terror, but it might have led just as plausibly to the ultraliberal fad of political correctness."

TWO FACES OF RELIGIOUS PLURALISM
IN AMERICAN POLITICS

JOHN C. GREEN

Mario Cuomo and Mark Souder describe two different faces of religious pluralism in American politics. At the risk of oversimplification, one might label these faces *universalist* and *particularist*. Both tendencies are common among the American public and have important implications for the role of religion in public affairs.

Democrat Mario Cuomo, a liberal Roman Catholic, offers an eloquent description of the universalist impulse in a pluralist democracy—that is, the desire for politics to be rooted in values common to diverse faith communities, including secular people. Much admired for his sophisticated examination of the tensions between personal faith and public service, Cuomo summarizes his approach this way: "I conclude that religious convictions . . . are not a serious impediment to efficient and proper service by a public official in today's America. In fact I am convinced that some of the fundamental propositions common to all religious convictions actually enrich, instead of inhibit, public service, and they make public service especially inviting to people who are trying to be religious."

Cuomo is uncomfortable with moral appeals in politics. Instead, he argues, appeals should be based on a concept of the common good. Such appeals are proper and possible because, in his view, there are two principles at the core of all the world's major religions: "What our religious principles urge upon us comes down to this: We need to love one another, to come together to create a good society, and to use that mutuality discretely in order to gain the benefits of community without sacrificing individual freedom and responsibility." These principles, love and charity, can be found in natural law, which Cuomo defines as follows: "Natural law is derived from human nature and human reason without the benefit of revelation or a willing suspension of disbelief. It is the law . . . that would occur to us if we were only 500,000 people on an island without books, without education, without rabbis or priests or history, and we had to figure out who and what we were."

It is through the application of such universal values that diverse religious people can cooperate and compete in the democratic process, preserving freedom and avoiding violence. Public officials must "create conditions under which all citizens are reasonably free to act according to their own religious beliefs, even when those acts conflict with Roman Catholic dogma regarding divorce, birth control, abortion, stem cell research, and even the existence of God." Cuomo's descriptions of his struggles with two of the preeminent moral issues of our time, abortion and capital punishment, powerfully illustrate his application of these universal values in his political career.

In contrast, Republican Mark Souder, a conservative Evangelical Protestant, provides a vivid description of the particularist impulse in a pluralist democracy—that is, the desire to root politics in a special vision of moral truth arising from the unique experience of a religious community. Known for his political independence, Souder describes his perspective this way: "Conservative Christians as individuals do not separate their lives into a private sphere and a public sphere. . . . To ask me to check my Christian beliefs at the public door is to ask me to expel the Holy Spirit from my life when I serve as a congressman, and that I will not do. Either I am a Christian or I am not. Either I reflect His glory or I do not."

In place of Cuomo's universal principles, Souder argues for the imperative of moral judgments based on specific religious values: "Some time ago, a trendy Evangelical expression was WWJD—What would Jesus do? A better question, given that we are not God, would be: To the best of my limited capability to understand, what do I believe Jesus would have me, as a humble sinner, do?" Indeed, it was just this kind of questioning that led Souder to oppose three of the four articles of impeachment directed against President Clinton.

Souder answers Cuomo's view of natural law this way: "The notion of a natural law common to all religions is in fact a worldview and a moral view that is different from a Christian worldview and moral view—and is unacceptable to me. . . . I believe that the Holy Trinity is nature's God, since I believe the Trinity is the God who created nature." And he is skeptical about the existence of common moral principles in the major world religions: "If you ask, What is common to all religions? Well, what if child abuse is? What if date rape is? What if religions allow twelve-year-olds to have sex with adults? Does the law have to be common to all religions? Or just to major religions? And what if major religions disagree on the role of women? What is nature's God? I do not believe there is a common denominator that is workable in the American political system." In fact, Souder believes that people of faith, especially Evangelicals, are discriminated against in the public square precisely because of their religious values.

How common are Cuomo's and Souder's perspectives in the American public? The following survey data offer a first step in answering the question.[1] First, the universalist impulse can be tapped by agreement or disagreement with the statement, "All the great religions of the world are equally true and good." Overall, 42 percent of the public agreed and 40 percent disagreed, with the remaining 18 percent undecided.

Capturing religious particularism is more difficult, since by definition each religious community has its own distinctive beliefs. However, a good proxy is the strength of preference for the respondent's own religious affiliation. Indeed, this measure is strongly correlated with the core beliefs of the major religious traditions. Overall, 64 percent of the public expressed a strong preference for their own affiliation, 29 percent a moderate preference, and 7 percent a weak one.

There is considerable overlap between these measures of religious universalism and particularism. This overlap can be illustrated by dividing the survey respondents into four categories.

First, the largest of these categories might be called "particular faith," made up of respondents who do not agree that all the great religions are equally true and good and who also claim a strong religious preference. Souder's Evangelicalism would fall within this category, but at 36 percent of the population, it includes many different kinds of religious people.

Second, the next largest category might be called "general faith," made up of those who agree that all the great religions are equally true and good but who also claim a strong religious preference. Cuomo would probably fit within this category due to his combination of univeralism and Catholicism. Accounting for 25 percent of the public, this category is also quite diverse.

Third, the next category might be called "universal faith" and includes those who agree that all the great religions are true and good but who do not claim a strong religious preference. In a sense, this category represents the logical extensions of Cuomo's perspective. At 20 percent of the population, this third category is slightly larger than the fourth and final group.

Fourth, this category is made up of those who disagree that the great religions are equally true and who also lack a strong preference; this last category might be called "other faith," for lack of a better term. Accounting for

TABLE 1. *Major Religious Traditions and Type of Faith*
Percent

Religion tradition[a]	Particular	General	Universal	Other
Evangelical Protestant	54	16	14	17
Other Christian	54	23	11	12
Black Protestant	49	32	11	8
Other non-Christian	34	26	25	15
Secular	26	15	30	29
Mainline Protestant	26	30	21	23
Roman Catholic	24	37	22	17
Judaism	18	25	33	24
All	36	25	20	19

Source: Third National Survey of Religion and Politics, University of Akron, 1996.
a. Religious traditions are based on denominational affiliation. Other Christian traditions include small denominations such as the Latter Day Saints, Eastern Orthodox, and Unitarian-Universalist; other non-Christian traditions include Islam, Hinduism, and Buddhism. For details see Lyman A. Kellstedt and others, "Grasping the Essentials: The Social Embodiment of Religion and Political Behavior," in John C. Green and others, *Religion and the Culture Wars* (Lanham, Md.: Rowman and Littlefield, 1996), pp. 174–92.

19 percent of the public, this category includes many people who are nominally religious or secular.

How are these four categories of faith distributed across the major religious traditions in the American public? Table 1 reveals a complex picture. For example, more than half of Evangelical Protestants have a particular faith, but roughly a sixth are found in each of the general, universal, and other faith categories. In partial contrast, a quarter of Catholics have a particular faith, more than a third a general faith, and about a fifth each are in the universal and other faith categories. Thus Cuomo is right to stress the enormous diversity of American religion, but Souder is right to regard universalism as just one piece of this mosaic.

Does this typology of faith matter politically? Table 2 suggests that the effects may be profound. Three-fifths of those with a particular faith claim that their religion is important to their political thinking, a figure that drops to less than half in the general faith category and to a quarter or less in the universal and other faith categories. This change is striking, given the internal diversity of each of these broad categories. This pattern strongly suggests

TABLE 2. *Type of Faith and the Relationship between Religion and Politics*
Percent agreeing

Relationship	Particular	General	Universal	Other	All
Religion important to political thinking	60	45	22	25	42
Laws should be view of religious majority	41	38	28	28	36
Special protection for rights of religious people	47	45	32	32	41

Source: Third National Survey of Religion and Politics, University of Akron, 1996.

that it is a particular faith (whatever that might be) that directly connects religion to politics at the individual level. In contrast, a universal faith (however persuasive it may be) has the opposite effect, tending to disconnect individuals' religion from their politics.

It is just this personal connection between religion and politics that allows for the kind of moral responsibility that Souder demands of politics and that Cuomo finds inherent in all the great religions. But such connections can also produce a politics of discrimination, which Cuomo fears and Souder complains about. Other survey evidence offers some encouraging news in this regard. Respondents were asked if the law should be based on the religious values of the majority, and in no case did a majority agree with this proposition. This finding was reinforced by support for protecting religious minorities, to which nearly half of the particular faith agreed.

These figures suggest that most religious communities in America sense their minority status in a pluralist society. The public appears to sense that majority rule cannot be a direct translation of special religious values, a point argued by Cuomo. And Souder's concern about protecting the rights of religious communities is also widely shared.

Of course, in a democracy many issues must be settled by majority rule, even when minority rights are adequately protected. Here Cuomo's and Souder's positions are less contradictory than they might at first appear. Indeed, they are in important respects complementary: Cuomo's universalism is a good model for the *results* of the democratic process, while Souder's particularism is a good model for the *beginning* of the democratic process.

Thus it is fitting that these eloquent spokesmen for the two faces of religious pluralism in American politics have the last word:

Mario Cuomo says, "My Church understands that our public morality depends on a consensus view of right and wrong. Religious values will not be accepted as part of the public morality unless they are shared by the community at large. The plausibility of achieving that consensus is a relevant consideration in deciding whether or not to make the effort to impose those values officially."

Mark Souder says, "Faith institutions are the key to developing a moral foundation. The government may foster these institutions, encourage them, nurture them, or it may discriminate against them, harass them, or undermine them. But it is not the job of government to replace these institutions as the primary moral agents of society."

Note

1. These data come from the Third National Survey of Religion and Politics, conducted at the University of Akron in the spring of 1996 ($N = 4,037$; margin of error plus or minus 2 percent). This study was supported by a grant from the Pew Charitable Trusts.

RELIGION, POLITICS, AND A CHANGING AMERICA

ANNA GREENBERG

In election year 2004 the political agenda will be dominated by Iraq and the economy. The politics of values and character that consumed the 1990s and the 2000 presidential contest are diminished in the face of economic uncertainty and troubles abroad, which threaten our international and domestic security. But this has not stopped the discussion about the continuing potency of religion in American politics. In fact developments around issues such as gay marriage and late-term abortion only give increased attention to the persistence and divisiveness of religion in electoral politics. All of these developments have led to anguished calls for Democrats to deal with their "religion" problem. Whether Democrats can do this or not, in the short term, will be evident in the 2004 elections, as the nominee battles with a religiously defined president. In many ways, however, the long-term answer to this question is much more interesting.

Religiosity has been associated more strongly with Republicans than with Democrats for a number of election cycles. To be clear, most Americans are religious if the term is defined broadly enough. According to the Pew Research Center, 81 percent of Americans say that prayer in an important part of their daily life, and 87 percent say they never doubt the existence of God. What matters is the intensity of the religious commitment (measured by such behavior as attending church or reading the Bible) and denomination affiliation. People with a high level of religious commitment or a conservative religious worldview identify with the Republicans—Republicans have a fourteen-point identification advantage among people who attend worship services every week—while Democrats have an advantage with everyone else.

The movement of religious voters to the Republican Party began during the late 1970s and the Reagan years but accelerated during President Clinton's two terms in office. In 2000, 62 percent of voters who attend church every week voted for George W. Bush, while 62 percent of voters who never attend church voted for Al Gore.[1] These trends are persistent and are likely to emerge in 2004 as well. According to data collected by Democracy Corps

TABLE 1. *Religious Attendance and Generic Presidential Vote*
Percent responding

Candidate	Every week	Once or twice a month	A few times a year	Hardly ever	Never
Bush	57	45	42	38	25
Generic Democrat	35	48	50	54	65
Net	−22	3	8	16	40
Percentage of the electorate	40	17	13	21	7

Source: Democracy Corps, August–November 2003.

between August and November 2003, President Bush leads a generic Democratic candidate by twenty-two points (57 to 35 percent) among voters who attend worship services every week and trails by forty points (65 to 25 percent) among voters who never attend services (see table 1). These trends are even more pronounced among white voters—64 percent of white voters who attend church every week say they will support President Bush's reelection bid. All of these sentiments are more intense among the most religiously committed and conservative group in the electorate—white, Evangelical voters. In 2000, 70 percent of these voters supported President Bush, and 80 percent of them intend to do so again in 2004.

The political impact of these religious divisions are felt most powerfully around the so-called values agenda, in which the parties fundamentally take opposite positions. Intense religiosity is strongly associated with holding politically conservative views about issues ranging from abortion to gay rights to sex education, while secular Americans invariably take the more progressive view. For example, in a poll conducted in October 2003 for the Pew Forum on Religion and Public Life, 80 percent of people who expressed a high religious commitment oppose gay marriage, compared to 57 percent who express an average religious commitment and 39 percent who express a low religious commitment.[2] Fifty-eight percent of white Evangelicals favor stricter laws against abortion, compared to only 37 percent of white Catholics, 25 percent of white mainline Protestants, and 18 percent of seculars. According to Democracy Corps, positive feelings toward prolife groups measure 70 percent among white devout Evangelicals, 56 percent among voters who attend religious services every week,

36 percent among voters who attend services monthly, 29 percent who attend a few times a year, 21 percent who hardly ever attend, and 16 percent who never attend religious services.

These cleavages may lead many to forcefully make the case that Democrats have a religion problem. Amy Sullivan wrote an impassioned plea to Democrats to speak authentically to religious Americans in the pages of the *Washington Monthly*.[3] In particular, she focuses on swing religious voters—the "free floating" Evangelicals, "Cadillac" Catholics, and Hispanics who are not solidly in the Republican camp but who clearly hold socially conservative worldviews. And in fact many of the Democratic candidates made their faith and religious values a prominent part of how they talked about themselves in the Democratic primaries. Joe Lieberman was the most vocal about his faith commitment and how it affected his political views, but Wesley Clark and Dick Gephardt weighed in with a discussion of the evolution of their religious views and how their faith helped them during particular important moments in their lives.

There is no question that it is important for Democrats to speak without embarrassment, or fear of alienating base Democratic voters, about their faith if for no other reason than to counter the assumption that the Republican Party is the party of the faithful and the Democratic Party is the party of the godless. This construction is patently untrue—just look at African Americans, the most reliably Democratic voters in the electorate and possibly the most faithful people in the country.

But this debate about how Democrats approach questions of faith raises a much larger question about the enduring nature of religious divisions and their association with values in politics. The differences between the parties on social issues emerged over a period of thirty years and will not diminish merely if a candidate talks about his or her religious commitment. Throughout the 1960s and 1970s the Democratic and Republican Parties have taken differing positions on civil rights, women's rights, abortion, and more recently gay rights. These positions were not preordained. In fact, given the Republican Party's historic attachment to civil rights and civil liberties, it is entirely possible that it might have gone the other way.

The growing division between these parties was reinforced by organizational efforts, primarily on the Right. Since the 1970s religiously conservative groups have been systematically working to dominate the airways with a broad network of Evangelical church networks. Groups such as Focus on the Family and Concerned Women for America rely on these networks to disseminate information on public policy issues and to mobilize activists when necessary.

In other words, the role that religion and values play in American politics is deeply entrenched, rooted in the historical evolution of the parties' positions and supported by broad organizational networks. Merely talking about religious faith neither alters these structural differences between the parties nor overcomes the fundamental sticking point, which is that no matter what Democratic candidates say about their faith, the Democratic Party is associated with a more socially progressive agenda.

To reiterate: Democrats should not cede God to the Republicans; in recent memory, the most successful Democratic candidates (Jimmy Carter and Bill Clinton) have been authentically religious. But it is also entirely possible that the Right will go too far. Values such as tolerance are highly valued in our society, and as Alan Wolfe persuasively argues, America is fundamentally moderate.[4] We are seeing fairly dramatic movement on such issues as gay rights and interracial relationships. For example, according to the Pew Research Center, since the late 1980s the percentage of people who say we should fire teachers who are known homosexuals has declined from 51 percent to 33 percent. There is a reason that President Bush avoids engaging the issues of abortion and gay marriage directly, even going so far as to say that the country does not support making abortion illegal.

The country is changing, too, in ways that will profoundly affect the influence of religion and values in politics: The number of secular voters in the electorate is increasing, so that people who never or hardly ever go to worship services now make up a third of the electorate. This evolution stems from real social change in American society, including increasing educational attainment, the participation of women in the work force, and the rise of unmarried households. Ruy Teixeira and John Judis argue that a more socially progressive majority will emerge as minority voters and single, working, and highly educated women who are "products of a new postindustrial capitalism, rooted in diversity and social equality" make up a larger portion of the electorate.[5]

Although it is too early to predict the death knell of religion and values in politics, Generation X (people born between 1964 and 1975) and Generation Y (people born between 1975 and 1995) are significantly more progressive on a range of social issues (except abortion) than older generations. For instance 72 percent of those between ages eighteen and twenty-four agree that there should be "laws that provide gay and lesbian couples who form civil unions the same legal rights as married couples when it comes to things like inheritance, employer-provided health insurance, and hospital visits."[6] More than half of adults under the age of thirty think that gays and lesbians should have a legal right to get married, compared with 37 percent of baby boomers, and 20 percent of seniors. For young people, it is simply perplexing that as a society we would worry about whom people pick for a partner.

The conclusion to draw here is not that Democrats should dismiss religious values in politics—most Democratic candidates and Democratic voters have a genuine religious commitment that they value and that informs their commitment to pursue social change—but that we should not treat this as a simple matter of talking about faith. It is a complex situation, tied up in the evolution of the parties since the 1960s and the organizational structures of the Left and the Right. And it is not static; patterns of religious commitment and values in politics will change as our society itself very profoundly changes.

Notes

1. Author's analysis of Voting News Service (VNS) exit poll data, November 7, 2000.

2. Pew Research Center for the People and the Press and the Pew Forum on Religion and Public Life, "Religious Beliefs Underpin Opposition to Homosexuality: Republicans Unified, Democrats Split on Gay Marriage" (//people-press. org/reports/display.php3?reportid=197 [November 18, 2003]).

3. Amy Sullivan, "Do Democrats Have a Prayer? To Win in '04 the Next Nominee Will Need to Get Religion," *Washington Monthly*, June 2003.

4. Alan Wolfe, *One Nation, After All: What Middle-Class Americans Really Think about God, Country, Family, Racism, Welfare, Immigration, Homosexuality, Work, the Right, the Left, and Each Other* (Viking, 1998).

5. John B. Judis and Ruy Teixeira, *The Emerging Democratic Majority* (Scribner's, 2002), p. 35.

6. Henry J. Kaiser Family Foundation and MTV Choose or Lose 2000, "Sex Laws: Youth Opinion on Sexual Health Issues in the 2000 Election," October 10, 2000.

PROTECTING RELIGION
FROM POLITICS

SUSANNAH HESCHEL

It is hard to be a person of faith in secular America. I sympathize with Mark Souder: As an Orthodox Jew attending a secular private high school in New York City, I found it was hard not to be able to attend the class parties, held on Friday nights (my Sabbath), not to be able to eat the school lunches (which were not kosher), and to hear teachers mock the Hebrew Bible while extolling classical Greece. And then there was Hebrew School, which taught texts by rote memorization, using tactics of intimidation to scare the kids into studying. My faith was attacked by both sides.

It was the work of Martin Luther King Jr. and my father, Abraham Joshua Heschel, that rescued me from despair. In their words the Bible became the most vivid and powerful way to challenge the status quo. Martin Luther King changed the social and political fabric of America, just as my father changed the religious fabric of American Jewish life. Through the speeches and writings of these two men, Amos and Isaiah became perhaps the most important figures of the past, demanding social justice and purity of intention and, most of all, insisting that there is no room for complacency in a religious life. A religious person, my father said, can never say, "I am a good person." And that it is the goal of prayer to be subversive—subversive of our conventional values and of our self-righteousness. The words of Amos unsettle all of us, the pious as well as the cheaters, kings, priests, and merchants. Perfection belongs to God alone.

I try to understand why I am uncomfortable with Mark Souder's remarks. I certainly share his desire to have my personal religious commitments honored by schools; his school took the children to a movie, against his religious faith, while my school thought I should abandon my religious observances for the "privilege" of attending an elite institution. I, too, like the idea of schools reciting a psalm, teaching religious values, and talking about faith as an important dimension to human life. Why should religion be banned, when psychology and economics are standard parts of the curriculum, honored tools for understanding the nature of human life?

My hesitation derives, in large measure, from the dangers I have uncovered as a historian of the Protestant church in Nazi Germany. My research has uncovered the archives of a church-sponsored institute that sought to de-Judaize Christianity by removing the Old Testament from the canon, all positive statements about Judaism from the gospels, and Hebrew words from the hymnal. To become a Germanic faith, Christianity was to be cleansed of all Jewish accretions and Jesus declared an Aryan. Hundreds of thousands of de-Judaized hymnals and New Testaments were purchased by churches through the Reich. Swastikas were placed next to crosses on church altars, and Hitler was viewed as part of Christian salvation history. It was a theological deformity, a defamation of Christianity, to be sure, but a church-sponsored effort nonetheless, carried out by bishops, theologians, pastors, and religion teachers, with widespread public support.

In calling for an increased religious presence in the public sphere of America, my first fear is that, if religion can be brought into the public sphere, then the public sphere will more easily infiltrate the realm of religion. What is to protect our religion when we bring it into the public sphere from a comparable political corruption of our faith? In hindsight, the Nazi church sounds outrageous or perhaps absurd. But in its day some highly distinguished theologians supported with enthusiasm and scholarly justification the transformation of the church through National Socialist principles as well as the presence of the church within the realm of the Nazi regime, in its political arena as well as in its schools and other societal institutions. Remember that it was the goal of the Nazis to secularize German society, removing church figures from positions of institutional and symbolic prominence in the public realm. The churches protested, corrupting their teachings to show their sympathy with Nazi values. The Sermon on the Mount was changed to show a Jesus who was not meek but a fighter, in accord with a militarized Germany.

The Nazis wanted a *Judenrein* Germany (a Germany free of Jews), and the churches complied, creating a *Judenrein* Christianity. In some cases, the churches actually took the lead, anticipating Nazi policy: In 1932 the German Christian movement called for an end to marriages between Jews and Germans, something the Nazis did not implement officially until 1935. Naturally, some religious leaders protested, calling for support for non-Aryan Christians (Jews who had been baptized), but very few stood up in the name of Christianity in support of Jews. Mark Souder may urge a Bible in every classroom, but what if, in the future, some teachers bring an Aryanized New Testament into their classroom? Who will adjudicate religious claims to authenticity?

We as religious people often want greater involvement in our society's seats of power. My father, for example, was appalled that the My Lai massacre was revealed to the world by journalists: Where were the chaplains? he demanded. He called for a religious authority to be present in all military institutions and also in banks and corporate headquarters. Yet the moral authority and spiritual inspiration of such figures can be effective only if they stand outside our political institutions, as untainted as possible by political commitments. Had the prophets been receiving subsidies from the kings or priests, would they have criticized them? If American faith-based charities receive funding from the federal government, how will they dare to criticize that government? How will they be able to take a prophetic stance, speaking truth to power, if by so doing they jeopardize the monetary grants that make possible the charity they undertake? Will their faith become Americanized, their scriptures revised, in accord with the prevailing political winds? Strict separation of religion and politics may be essential to preserving the sanctity of religious teachings. The quickest way to compromise freedom is to cede moral authority to the state; that is a central lesson of the Nazi churches.

Both Mario Cuomo and Mark Souder call for the infusion of religious values into the work of political leaders (and, I imagine, all of us), and I applaud that. The classic difficulty, of course, is determining what our religious values actually demand of us. Cuomo believes that the death penalty is wrong; other Christians, even Catholics, arrive at opposing conclusions. Elsewhere, in discussing abortion, he has said that he cannot call a crime what other people do not consider a sin. For Cuomo, both individuality and community are central to religious concerns. The problem is that it is not always easy to define the position of one's religion.

Within the Jewish community some claim that Greater Israel is holy land and that keeping it in Jewish hands is a divine obligation and is central to Judaism. For other Jews ending the occupation of the West Bank and supporting a Palestinian state alongside a Jewish state represents the highest religious values of Judaism. Both groups can easily cite scripture to prove their points, both have wide support among other Jews, and each side feels the other is the enemy. How do we adjudicate two opposing interpretations that have led in recent years to extraordinary hostilities between Jews?

A major difference in the articulation of their positions by Souder and Cuomo is that the former speaks of his own faith and struggles to gain recognition for his convictions while the latter speaks far more inclusively, defining religion in language that can encompass nearly all faith traditions alive in America today. As an observant Jew, I have often stood on the margins and felt excluded, yet this quintessentially Jewish position has also created a sense of Jewish community and stimulated in Jews a remarkable intellectual creativity. It is a sacrifice with enormous benefits.

By contrast, Cuomo stands in the tradition of Abraham Lincoln and Martin Luther King, whose religious language is never exclusive. That King spoke of the civil rights movement as an exodus rather than a cross to bear (and quoting the prophets far more often than he did Jesus) was intended to create a religious language that could inspire all of us. The creation of a nonsectarian, public religious discourse gives us a chance to come together and experience an affirmation of ourselves as religious people without elevating one religion over another.

Precisely that unity of spirit in the public realm dramatically changed the nature of race in this country. The prophets were public religious figures during the 1960s, and it was their spirit, through King, that transformed the hearts of Americans. My father, whose book about the prophets was widely read by leaders of the civil rights movement, calls on us to focus not only on the words of the prophets but also on their religious consciousness: the nature of their experience of divine revelation. He speaks of that revelation as a divine pathos, God's identification with human beings and resonance to their suffering. In speaking of divine pathos, my father drew from a rabbinic concept, *zoreh gavoha*, a higher, divine need. God is not the detached, unmoved mover of the Aristotelian tradition, he insists, but is "the most moved" mover, deeply affected by human deeds. Divine pathos indicates a constant involvement of God in human history but insists that the involvement is an emotional engagement: God suffers when human beings are hurt, so that when I hurt another person, I injure God. The prophets' response is their passionate identification with the divine consciousness.

What manner of man is the prophet? asks my father in the opening pages of *The Prophets*. He answers that a prophet is a person of agony, whose "life and soul are at stake in what he says" and who is able to perceive "the silent sigh" of human anguish. Hence the prophet is not a messenger, an oracle, a seer, or an ecstatic but a witness to the divine pathos, bearing testimony to God's concern for human beings. God is not simply a topic of human interest but is also concerned with humans. Being gripped by the anguish experienced by God in response to human affliction leaves the prophet overwhelmed and tormented. Facing callousness and indifference, the prophet does not present God as a source of comfort and reassurance but as an incessant demand: "While the world is at ease and asleep, the prophet feels the blast from heaven." "God is raging in the prophet's words." While we may all criticize injustices in our society, they remain tolerable; to the prophet, however, "injustice assumes almost cosmic proportions." We may be troubled by social injustice and war crimes, but to the prophet these are unbearable. To the prophet Amos justice is not simply an idea or a moral norm but also a divine passion. The opposite of good is not evil; the opposite of good is indifference.[1]

In promoting the preferences of our own religious faith, perhaps we all have to remember that the greatest value is not to speak out for oneself but to speak out on behalf of others. Indeed, our very humanity depends upon our compassion. In speaking out against the war in Vietnam, against the killing of thousands of innocent civilians, my father warned, "Remember that the blood of the innocent cries forever. Should that blood stop to cry, humanity would cease to be." Hearing the silent anguish is not limited to the prophets but devolves upon all of us: "Few are guilty, but all are responsible."

If there is a role for religion in the public sphere, let it be an expression in which all may participate, and let us, as religious people, demonstrate what it means to be religious: a passion for justice, an assumption of responsibility, and a cultivation of our humanity so that we never lose our ability to hear the silent anguish of this world.

Note

1. See Abraham Joshua Heschel, *The Prophets* (Harper and Row, 1965), pp. 16, 5.

FAITH AND POLITICS

AMORY HOUGHTON JR.

"Liberty and duty, freedom and responsibility. That's the deal," wrote one of America's heroes, John Gardner, several years ago.[1] I believe that because it makes sense and because John Gardner wrote it. We all had a one out of twenty chance of being born in this country. Thousands try to immigrate each year. Few want to leave. We are blessed beyond belief. John Gardner's greatest fear was that "America would be a great nation full of talented people with enormous energy—who forgot they needed each other."[2]

I am a member of the Faith and Politics Institute. It is not a religious and public policy institute; it is about faith and politics in its rawest and most beautiful form. It is run by an extraordinary minister whose main objective is to provide occasions for reflection as well as to encourage civility. It "strives to strengthen political leadership that contributes to healing the wounds that divide our nation." We who meet and at times travel to places such as Selma, Alabama, even Johannesburg, South Africa, are in this setting neither liberals nor conservatives, Republicans nor Democrats. We merely appreciate each other's values and commitment in searching for our faith in the messy, high-powered world of the United States House of Representatives.

When partisan pressure forces certain actions or votes, our bond in a faith-based group enables each of us to reach down and engage a gear others might not possess. We try to resist dishonesty. This dishonesty is not to be confused with stealing or lying; political dishonesty takes the form of rationalization. No one of us claims total integrity; we are all subject to the same constituent calls and e-mails and faxes and letters. But somehow our group and its outlook help in a strange way to set our political thermostats at the right temperature.

I have just returned from Iraq as part of a congressional delegation. Our purpose was to get a better feel for the struggle that was about to require another $87 billion in U.S. citizens' credit. We met with hundreds of soldiers—tired, underpaid, away from their families, but with extraordinary conviction and a powerful, positive attitude. We also met with Polish troops. "Why are you here?" we asked. "It is very simple," one of the officers replied. "We were released from the iron hand of dictatorship in 1989. We know what it is to have your spirit crushed. We wanted to help."

When we peeled back a layer or two, we found the troops to be ordinary people doing extraordinary work with a willingness to take huge personal risks, care for each other, and smile. They get up in the morning, don their uniforms, shoulder their weapons, and go out into a debilitating, crushing heat. They are the true life-givers and, as E. M. Forster says, there is a special bond between them.[3]

But this is true not just in Iraq but also—in a less dangerous way—in all of our lives. My mother and father had a special bond. They provided the glue that kept us all together, and it stemmed from a deep faith plus a screaming sense of humor. We just had fun together and could not wait to get home. As the years went on, their faith mutated to us. My sister is one of the stalwarts of her parish; one of my brothers is active in our home church in Corning, New York, and sings in the choir; another is a priest. We all plugged into the faith game.

So it was no surprise when I ran for office that the first thing I did was to pray for strength in a field dramatically opposite to the one in which I had been engaged for over thirty-five years. I soon learned that the Founding Fathers had pointed us in the direction of a system of government with the essential element of self-correction. Benjamin Franklin, one of the wise men, had this special idea. It put a stamp on a different type of nation, one that could draw strength from its religious pluralism. It required not only free expression but also a willingness to compromise.

I remember Peter Gomes, a professor of theology at Harvard, talking about the absolutists in religion or government who draw that proverbial line in the sand, willing to lose virtually anything rather than compromise a principle. His answer to this dilemma was that "the essence of Christianity as with any religion is love. But a subessence is a willingness to say, 'I may be wrong.'" In the House of Representatives we have to vote possibly a thousand times a year. At least four or five times a day we are asked to vote for this measure, oppose that one, cosponsor another. I am an older man, and I have a reasonably clear set of benchmarks that anchor by life. The most important one came fifty-one years ago when I first joined the Corning Glass Works fresh out of graduate school. My boss said to me, "Your life here will be set in a ring of two concentric circles; the outer circle is the law of the land. You must live within that. The second and inner circle is your own set of values, what you believe. I want you always to operate inside that inner circle."

Another benchmark is the willingness to reach out to others, help them as they help you. Share your values, open the dialogue. We need this.

I remember hearing an extraordinary Catholic priest at the funeral of a friend of mine talk about Robert Fulghum, the man who mused that everything he ever needed to know in life he learned in kindergarten. Robert Fulghum remembered a day in his college philosophy class. As the class was ending, his professor, an immigrant from Greece, wondered if there were any more questions. Fulghum raised his hand and asked the professor, tongue in cheek: "Dr. Papaderos, what is the meaning of life?" Everyone burst out laughing knowing that there was no answer to this unanswerable question.

But the professor took the question quite seriously, and he answered by telling a story of his childhood in World War II. He related how one day he came upon a wrecked German motorcycle. He took a piece of the shattered rearview mirror and began to scrape the shard on a rock in order to remove the sharp edges from it. He spent days scraping the mirror on rocks until finally it was a perfectly round mirror. He had no toys to play with and very little with which to amuse himself and so became fascinated with the mirror. It became a game for him to reflect light into the most inaccessible places. And as he grew into adulthood, he came to see that this was no child's game but a perfect metaphor for what one should do with one's life. He came to understand that he was not the light nor the source of light. But the light was there, and it would only shine in many dark places if he reflected it.

The battles of the twenty-first century will most likely be between the forces of fanaticism and the forces of tolerance. To be tolerant we must have a sound footing, and that means faith. Faith within the circle of politics in which I live is not faith if it is not used to help others. That is the light and that is "the deal."

Notes

1. John Gardner, *Living, Leading, and the American Dream* (Jossey-Bass, 2003), flap copy.
2. Ibid., p. xiv.
3. E. M. Forster, *Two Cheers for Democracy* (Harmondsworth: Penguin, 1965).

THE FATE OF THE CHRISTIAN LEFT

MICHAEL KAZIN

When you hear a good democratic speech it is so much like a sermon that you can hardly tell the difference between them.

—WILLIAM JENNINGS BRYAN, 1904

Once upon a time there was a mass Christian Left. It included both ministers and the unfrocked, optimistic liberals and chiliastic radicals, learned theologians and vitriolic stump speakers, the well-heeled and the working class, blacks and whites. They did much to generate the wave of diverse, far-reaching changes that gave the Progressive Era its name: the income tax, workplace safety laws, woman suffrage, a ban on child labor, the regulation of trusts, and the outlawing of both prostitution and the manufacture and sale of alcoholic beverages.

Of course, the Christian Left was never a unified movement. Devout activists worked on dozens of campaigns and sometimes clashed over competing moral claims. Should striking workers restore civic harmony by submitting to binding arbitration or should they fight on to teach arrogant employers a lesson in the Golden Rule? Christian insurgents flocked to no one political party. They stumped for Democrats and Republicans, Prohibitionists and the short-lived Progressive Party, and even for Socialists. Eugene Debs, the latter's perennial candidate for president, adored Jesus Christ as "a pure communist" and pinned his portrait to the otherwise bare walls of the Atlanta prison cell where he was sent for speaking out against World War I. But the idea that "applied Christianity" could solve the nation's problems and bring America closer to the Kingdom of God was common to all.

The most continuously popular leader of the Christian Left was William Jennings Bryan. That may come as a surprise. Most Americans who recognize Bryan's name identify him with two events that took place almost thirty years apart—his delivery of the Cross of Gold speech at the 1896 Democratic convention and his prosecution of John Scopes in 1925. Disapproving accounts of these episodes at either end of his career leave the deathless image of a blowhard and a censorious fundamentalist, grimly seeking to pull the nation back toward a simpler, agrarian world.

But Bryan enjoyed immense popularity and influence during his three decades in the spotlight. Rather than being a last-ditch defender of rural America, he was actually a forerunner of modern liberalism. As the leading Democrat from 1896 until Woodrow Wilson's election in 1912, Bryan transformed his party from a bulwark of conservatism—the defender of states' rights and laissez-faire economics—into a bastion of anticorporate Progressivism that favored federal intervention to help workers and small businesses. Herbert Hoover once snapped that the New Deal was "Bryanism under new words and methods," proving that bitterness need not impair one's historical acumen.

Bryan's oratorical magnetism and crusading pietism won him a following of remarkable size and intensity. The historian Richard Hofstadter wrote that other reform politicians such as Theodore Roosevelt and Woodrow Wilson "only sensed popular feelings, Bryan embodied them."[1] That image helped win Bryan the durable allegiance of millions of working and middle-class Protestants and a respectable number of Catholics, who viewed him as the only politician who understood their plight and embodied their hopes for a more egalitarian and more godly America.

They expressed their feelings in a volume of correspondence: During and just after the 1896 campaign Bryan received approximately 250,000 letters and telegrams, far exceeding the quantity sent to any president until Franklin D. Roosevelt. The torrent slowed only slightly during his next two campaigns for president, in 1900 and 1908. Most messages were marked by melodramatic devotion, suffused with biblical citations and metaphors. Hundreds of Americans sent laudatory poems or anecdotes about hearing Bryan speak; thousands named their newborn sons after him, an honor normally reserved for presidents and generals.

Bryan used his celebrated status to promote the entire program of the Christian Left, from protection for union organizers to the peaceful arbitration of disputes between nations. Undergirding each stand was a simple, pragmatic gospel: Only mobilized citizens, imbued with Christian morality, could save the nation from "predatory" interests and the individuals who did their bidding.

Mario Cuomo's caveat, "I seldom talk in terms of moral issues," would seem illogical to Bryan and to the other Social Gospelers of his day. What was the use of religion if not to guide people's thoughts and behavior, both in private and in public? They probably would have agreed with Mark Souder that "it is not the job of government to replace [faith] institutions as the primary moral agents of society." After all, that is merely a restatement of the hallowed separation between church and state. Yet Christian Progressives did cheer officeholders who acknowledged their debt to biblical sources as they crusaded to rid the nation of cupidity, corruption, and violence.

Most Americans first glimpsed Bryan's hard-charging faith in the final sentences of his Cross of Gold speech, which his opponents scorned as blasphemous. It was a gospel that the preacher-politician would amend continuously in subsequent battles with powerful men whose personal piety, ironically, often matched his own. After the heyday of free silver, Bryan blasted President William McKinley, a faithful Methodist, for trying to convert the Filipinos to democracy with bayonets and artillery shells. Next he trained his wrath on churchgoing captains of industry, whom he accused of cheating the public, destroying competition, and exploiting their workers. Bryan argued that no private or public institution—colleges, YMCAs, or boards of missionaries—should accept donations from John D. Rockefeller. The fact that the aging baron of Standard Oil was a faithful Baptist made his lucre all the filthier. How could this multimillionaire "preach so much religion while he practices so much sin?" Bryan even turned down a request to join the board of trustees of his underfunded alma mater until the small Illinois college agreed to cut its ties with Rockfeller's affluent University of Chicago. "It is not necessary," Bryan instructed, "that all Christian people shall sanction the Rockefeller method of making money merely because Rockefeller prays."[2]

This gospel of good works made it almost superfluous to debate particulars of the faith. Though Bryan was a Presbyterian he never accepted a central tenet of his Calvinist church—the doctrine of election, which holds that God chooses which individuals he will save, independent of human will. What is more, Bryan never took an explicit stand in the dispute between pre- and postmillennialists, which then preoccupied some of the best minds in Protestant seminaries. "There are so many people who do not believe in the first coming of Christ," Bryan told a church official in 1923, "that we ought not to worry them about the second coming until we can get them to accept the first."

However, both his personality and his politics usually made him a tacit ally of the liberal optimists, for whom Jesus was a benevolent figure and hell an anachronistic abstraction. Faith in God's word, Bryan wrote in 1906, would allow ordinary Americans to envision "a government brought into harmony with divine will" and then to get busy realizing that lofty goal.

Applied Christianity was as simple to understand, and as difficult to achieve, as that.[3]

Only after World War I did Bryan become pessimistic and link his Social Gospel to what we would now regard as a conservative purpose. He believed agnostic intellectuals were seeking to substitute a cruel belief in the "survival of the fittest" for faith in a loving God—the only basis for moral and altruistic conduct that most ordinary people had. Bryan, like many other Americans at the time, assumed that Darwinism implied social Darwinism, particularly a belief in eugenics, promoted by scientists in the 1920s as the quickest way to improve the human race. The consequence, the Evangelical populist predicted, would be "a system under which a few supposedly superior intellects, self-appointed, would direct the mating and the movements of the mass of mankind—an impossible system!" Hitler's embrace of eugenics just a decade later suggests that Bryan's fear was not entirely unfounded.

The Christian Left declined rapidly in the 1920s and has never recovered. There were abundant reasons: The bitter conflict over "fundamentalism" pitted former allies against one another (and Bryan's death days after the Scopes trial fixed his image at that point). The World War burst the bubble of Evangelical optimism. And African Americans began to exercise their cultural power, which exposed the paternalist racism that Bryan shared with most older Progressives. Subsequently, most liberals and radicals would proudly declare their secular motivations and seek to quarantine talk of the sacred from infecting the political arena. In the 1960s even the public religiosity of Martin Luther King Jr., Cesar Chavez, and the Berrigan brothers did little to alter the dominant image of an agnostic Left.

The obvious problem is that most Americans do not think that way. Whether Christian or not, they believe in a God and an afterlife and, like William Jennings Bryan, derive their sense of morality from spiritual sources and prefer that others do the same. As Mario Cuomo puts it, "I do desperately want to believe in something better than I am. If all there is is me in this society, then I have wasted an awful lot of time, because I am not worth it." Any revival of a religious Left would have to begin from that premise—the need to regard one's fellow Americans as brothers and sisters whose welfare and happiness ought to be the goals of public policy.

Sadly, the rhetoric of collective responsibility sounds hollow to many people today, unless it is tethered to a war of self-defense against terrorists. And the born-again Christian who currently sits in the Oval Office appears to own the franchise on that one. How many Americans are even aware that, in the winter of 2003, both the National Council of Churches and the National Conference of Catholic Bishops took strong stands against a unilateral invasion of Iraq?

But those who insist on collective sin and collective redemption did find public acceptance a century ago. And they took their place in a long narrative of reform that already included the abolitionists, early temperance agitators (who battled poverty as much as saloons), and the populist insurgency, all led by men and women whose piety motivated their activism. From William Lloyd Garrison to King and Chavez, the Left has never advanced without a moral awakening entangled with notions about what the Lord would have us do. It is enough to make a secular leftist gag, before reluctantly acknowledging the power of prayer.

Notes

1. Richard Hofstadter, *The American Political Tradition and the Men Who Made It* (Knopf, 1948), p. 187.

2. Quoted in Willard H. Smith, *The Social and Religious Thought of William Jennings Bryan* (Lawrence, Kans.: Coronado Press, 1975), pp. 33–34; *The Commoner,* July 19, 1903, p. 3.

3. Clarence True Wilson to Bryan, November 3, 1923, Box 38, William Jennings Bryan Papers, Library of Congress. Quoted in Paolo Coletta, *William Jennings Bryan*, vol. 1 (University of Nebraska Press, 1964), p. 385. James H. Moorhead comments that the great debate about millennialism probably failed to grip rank-and-file Protestants at the time: "Most persons probably had not sorted out their views clearly but lived with a mental hodgepodge of images of the last things, which they had not ordered into a distinct or coherent theory." Moorhead, *World without End: Mainstream Protestant Visions of the Last Things, 1880–1925* (Indiana University Press, 1999), p. 17.

THE MYTH OF SECULARISM

M. A. MUQTEDAR KHAN

*Had Allah willed He could have made you all one community. But He made
you as you are [diverse] as a test. So vie one with another in good works.
Unto Allah you will all return, and He will then inform you of the meaning of differences within you.*

—QURAN 5:48

Identity and Politics

As a Muslim intellectual living in the West, researching and teaching political theory and political philosophy, I have always marveled at the durabil-
ity of the idea of secularism. For a civilization that boasts considerable
sophistication in most areas to assume that politics and religion constitute
two separate realms or that the two can be separated is uncharacteristically
naive. This belief, not in separation of church and state but in the separa-
bility of church and state, in my opinion is one of the enduring myths of
modernity. This myth rests on the false assumptions of pure politics and
pure religion. Secularism is a device that seeks to protect religion from the
corruption of politics and politics from becoming usurped by religion.

All core issues not only are normative in nature but also impinge on individual and collective identities. Neither the conception of the individual
self nor the construction of the collective self is free from political or religious considerations. Even in societies that were antireligious, such as the
former Soviet Union, or more secular than the United States, such as
Turkey, religion remained an important political issue and politics shaped
the way religion was practiced. Christianity played a significant role in the
collapse of communism in Eastern Europe, and Islamists found a way to
come to power in secular, fundamentalist Turkey. The place of religious
symbols in the public sphere, whether it is *hijaab* (the Muslim head scarf)
in French public schools or the Ten Commandments in American courts,
remains contested primarily because there is no consensus anywhere on the
exclusion of religion from the public sphere.

Not only does religion play a role in politics, but the politicization of religion is also a common occurrence. Notice how some Republicans are relish-
ing the idea of trouncing Howard Dean, if he becomes the Democratic

nominee in the coming presidential elections, by painting him as an advocate of gay marriage. This would be a clear case of exploiting religious sentiments (that marriage is a divine institution) for political gain. I notice that often American politicians couch their religious motivations in secular terms while advocating specific policies. A good example is the unyielding support for Israel and Israel's occupation of the West Bank and Gaza among certain Republican politicians with Evangelical connections. Although they support it for biblical reasons, they justify it by arguing that Israel is the "only democracy in the Middle East." I often wonder if their support for Israel would stop if Israel became less democratic or if it could be shown that some people within its borders do not enjoy basic democratic rights.

In the Muslim world, on the contrary, legitimacy comes from Islam, and therefore many politicians justify material motivations using Islamic cover. Religious politicians in the West often use secular discourse to gain legitimacy; Muslim politicians deliberately Islamize mundane issues for the same reason. Notice the Islamization of Saddam Hussein's rhetoric in the first Gulf War. While religion in the West lacks legitimacy in the public sphere and must therefore be concealed, in the Muslim world all legitimacy derives from Islam and hence Islam is used as a justification for politics.

There are two reasons that religion and politics are intertwined. The first is the increasing use of complex discourses for the purpose of legitimization. Today all politicians seem to follow the Machiavellian dictum that it is not important to be just, it is important to be seen to be just. Therefore politicians and political parties and regimes produce discourses to legitimize their goals and strategies. It is in the production of these discourses that religion either underpins political logic or camouflages politic motivations, depending upon the cultural context.

The second and perhaps the most important reason that religion will always play a role in crucial issues is the important role that religion plays in identity formation. All political issues that are important eventually affect individual and collective identity and in the process trigger religious sentiments. As long as religion plays a role in the identities of people, it will play a role in politics.

Self-Restraint or Constitutional Limits

Both Mario Cuomo and Mark Souder link religion with private and public morality. They both agree that it is difficult for believers to divest themselves of their religious values while also serving in a public capacity. However, it is interesting to see how each uses separate mechanisms to limit the impact of religion on public policy. Cuomo argues that politicians must exercise self-restraint and allow only those religious values that are universal in nature to influence their politics—and abstain from allowing particularist values to shape their agendas. Souder rejects the notion of a natural law and common religious values by suggesting that the uncommon is more important than common ground among religions. This is an interesting contrast between identity and difference. Cuomo seeks to overcome differences by seeking the identity of all faiths, while Souder celebrates difference in search of identity.

As a member of a religious minority in America, I feel very uneasy with Souder's response to the question about the fears of non-Christian religious minorities. To put it bluntly, his response that because Christianity is so diverse Christians will never manage enough consensus to impose their religious values over others seems evasive. What if they do agree upon some basic issues? What if the Christian coalition does manage to construct a broad coalition to deprive Islam, Hinduism, and Buddhism of the same legal protections as Christianity (for example, in England blasphemy laws protect Jesus but not Muhammad)? When Muslims repeatedly asked President Bush to condemn the anti-Islam (Islamophobia) bigotry of prominent Christian figures such as Pat Robertson, Franklin Graham, and Jerry Falwell, the president hedged for weeks, because these individuals have a large following that translates directly into political power at the ballot box and in campaign fund-raising.[1]

In an era when religious minorities in America are becoming extremely nervous about the relations between the Christian Right and the Republican establishment, which controls both the White House and the Congress, a plain, unequivocal statement (such as, We will not impose Christian beliefs on non-Christians) would go a long way to allay fears. Souder makes the point that as a Christian politician he is conscientious enough to fulfill his constitutional obligations. He will abide by the U.S. Constitution since he has sworn to protect it and abide by it. After listening to Cuomo's eloquent argument for self-restraint, I wish someone had asked Souder whether he would promise to abstain from advocating an amendment to the Constitution to make his religious beliefs the law of the land. In a democracy, what stands between minority rights and majority domination are constitutional guarantees, which are themselves at the mercy of the good intentions of the majority.

The Muslim world today is experiencing a deeply divisive and traumatic religious resurgence. This is not a venue to discuss this phenomenon, but it is important to draw a parallel prompted by Souder's claim that his faith is a worldview. The Islamists too make this claim. They argue that Islam is not a religion, it is a worldview, and they even compare it to other ideologies and worldviews such as capitalism and communism. Islamists have penned tons of books comparing Islam with communism, socialism, capitalism, liberalism, and democracy to prove not only that Islam has something to say about every aspect of life but also that whatever it may say is necessarily superior to what other ideologies say on the same subject. This for them is an article of faith. Claims about religious creeds as an all-encompassing worldview have the potential to blossom into totalitarian ideologies.

The two politicians demonstrate contrasting models. Cuomo's is a model of statesmanship, as he chooses wisdom over parochialism and seeks to exercise self-restraint on personal beliefs in search of common public values. In doing so he chooses to become a generic religious politician and not just a Catholic politician. Souder's, on the other hand, is a model of citizenship in which his commitment to the Constitution proscribes the role of his religion in politics. But his view that his faith is a worldview and the true worldview, including those elements that question the authenticity of other faiths, places the Constitution in jeopardy. His citizenship will prompt him to uphold the Constitution, but I fear that his Christianity will compel him to change the Constitution whenever possible to accommodate his beliefs. The statesman will always be the ally of religious minorities in pluralist democracies, but the Christian citizen is an imminent threat to constitutional guarantees of freedom from religions.

Islam and the Political Sphere

Two verses from the Quran are apt here: "O humanity! We have indeed created you from one man and one woman, and have made you into various nations and tribes so that you may know one another" (Quran 49:13). "And let there be amongst you a group of people who invite to goodness, encouraging that which is right and forbidding that which is wrong; it is they who are the successful" (Quran 3:104). These verses and the one with which I begin this essay make two important points: that diversity is a consequence of divine designs and that Muslims have an ethical role to play in the public sphere. Verse 3:104 in the opinion of some Muslims scholars is a

Quranic call for political parties to emerge and play a normative role in the public sphere. I argue that the mission of Islam and Muslims in the West can be to become the moral conscience of free societies.[2] The objective of Muslim participation in Western, particularly American, politics should be to encourage what is right and forbid what is wrong rather than seeking to advance the geopolitical agendas of the Muslim world.

Islamic sources recognize racial and ethnic and even religious differences and advocate a culture of inclusion and equality. However, there are also sources that lend themselves to exclusivist politics. Consider the following verses: "Those who believe [in the Quran], and those who follow the Jewish [scriptures], and the Christians and the Sabians, any who believe in God and the Last Day, and do good deeds, shall have their reward with their Lord; on them shall be no fear, nor shall they grieve" (Quran 2:62 and 5:69). "And if one seeks a religion other than Islam, it will never be accepted from him; and he is among the losers in the Hereafter" (Quran 3:85).

Today liberal and radical Muslims are divided over which of the above two verses should determine Muslim relations with other faith communities. The first verse is inclusive and clearly indicates that those who are good people have nothing to worry about. And if one treats the word *and* as joining sets of people ("any who believe in God") "and [any who] do good deeds," one could even argue that atheists who do good deeds, such as stand up for justice or help the poor, may have nothing to fear. This status of fundamental moral equality of all people can become the basis for political equality in a multicultural, multireligious society.

But radical Muslims who believe that only Islam has the truth and that only good Muslims are good people, rely on verse 3:85 exclusively, arguing that it is not only the ultimate source for defining Muslim and non-Muslim relations but also abrogates both verse 2:62 and verse 5:69. Some Muslim leaders in Dallas, Texas, now object to my speaking there because I once rejected the idea of abrogation of Quranic sources that radicals do not like; I argued that the only reason God repeated verse 2:62 in verse 5:69 was to ensure that bigots did not use verse 3:85 to annul verse 2:62. How can one verse abrogate two verses from the same sources? was my point. Muslims must realize that not only does Islam influence politics, but politics too shapes what Islam is.

Today Islam has once again become the ethical language of the Muslim world. Islam will not only guide Muslim public discourse but also the Muslim conception of what is ethical politics. The Iraqis today have managed to make President Bush an advocate of Islamic democracy. European Muslims are making sure that Europe's foreign policy balances the pro-Israeli stance of the United States in the Middle East. As Muslims become a political force in America, they will most certainly seek to redefine the role of religion in American politics. I only hope that an inclusivist rather than an exclusivist understanding of Islam shapes American Muslim politics. I hope verse 2:62 prevails over verse 3:85 and that Muslims seek to emulate Mario Cuomo and not Mark Souder.

Final Thoughts

The reason that the myth of secularism is so precious to modernity is not its potential to separate religion and politics but its potential to advance a framework for dealing with religious diversity under conditions of unequal power. In perfectly homogeneous societies, it does not matter if the state is influenced by religion or not. It is only when there are other faith communities, or other interpretations of the same faith, that the state can become an instrument of religious oppression in the hands of the majority. But religion disguised as national interest or secular reason can play havoc with minority rights. As religion becomes more assertive and religious zealots become more adept at "playing the system," then constitutional guarantees become meaningless if even the Supreme Court can be rigged. In the modern West, the best examples of freedom and protection of religious minorities has come under the reign of secular democracies; in the Muslim experience the same has happened under the reign of Islam.

Today, as all religions experience revivals, we must find ways to guarantee religious freedom without proscribing the scope of religion. Ultimately the plight of minorities is at the mercy of those who are enlightened among the majority and who are willing to break ranks with their kind and stand up for equality and justice for all. Systems are safe only as long as we strive everyday to keep them safe.

Notes

1. Muslims hope that one day this word will become as powerful as the term *anti-Semitism* in calling attention to prejudice.
2. See M. A. Muqtedar Khan, *American Muslims: Bridging Faith and Freedom* (Beltsville, Md.: Amana Publications, 2002).

THE SPIRITUAL DIMENSION
OF SOCIETAL LIFE

GLENN C. LOURY

I once heard a twenty-two-year-old former gang member, who had had quite a few scuffles with the law, say, "You know, there's some stuff wrong with us only the Lord can fix." He was in church, trying to find his way back to a life of dignity and responsibility. Although he was talking about his friends and his peers in the world he had been a part of, it occurred to me that his observation is true for most of us.

I spent some time one summer reading the nonfiction writings of the great Russian novelist Leo Tolstoy, who argues that the core of Christianity lies in the Sermon on the Mount. Unless we take this teaching of Jesus to heart, he claims, we can be self-righteous, legalistic, ungenerous, stiff-necked, and hypocritical. We will neglect to raise questions of social justice. We will fail to ask, for instance, how the pathology of the underclass is related to systemic factors—to our private, gain-driven economy, our culture of materialism, and our vacuous political discourses.

It is not enough simply to decry the decline of morality, to lament our "slouching toward Gomorrah." When there is a breakdown in the moral fabric of society, it is necessary to ask, Who has the authority to reconstruct it? And more important, What is the source of that authority? In my view, human relationships of trust are essential to the establishment of authoritative moral criticism. Consequently the building of respectful human relationships is basic to mending the social fabric—to forestalling the corrosive effects of modernity. I cry out as a Christian to see that compassionate posture more explicitly reflected in the public political witness of the religious Right. Of course, there will always be problems of implementation. But the spirit that ought to animate a critical appraisal in public and political life of the behavior of our fellow citizens should be a spirit of charity, a spirit of love.

More than a quarter of a century ago the National Advisory Commission on Civil Disorders, popularly known as the Kerner Commission, issued its report on the urban riots of the 1960s.[1] This report declared that the rage, alienation, and hopelessness of the ghetto were the inevitable consequence of racial isolation, inferior education, limited economic opportunity, and an attitude of indifference, if not hostility, toward blacks from the white majority.

Although much has changed in American social history since this landmark document, America continues to confront the profound problem of integrating the inner-city minority poor more fully into the economic and social mainstream. We cannot make progress unless we face this reality—that black ghettos still today reveal the disintegration of urban black society and the indifference, hostility, or racism of white society. Institutional barriers to black participation in American life still exist. Although these barriers have come down considerably, other barriers have grown up. The effects of these barriers are sometimes manifest in behaviors by blacks themselves that prevent a person from seizing existing opportunity; these behaviors include criminal offending, early and unwed childbearing, low academic achievement, drug use, gratuitous violence, and gun use. These behaviors have to be changed if progress is to be made.

Social analysts have failed to provide us with an adequate analysis of these behavioral problems. Liberals like the sociologist William J. Wilson of Harvard University acknowledge that behavioral difficulties are fundamental but argue that these problems derive ultimately from lack of economic opportunities and believe they will abate only when good jobs at good wages are at hand. Conservatives like Charles Murray of the American Enterprise Institute argue that these behaviors are the unintended legacy of a misconceived welfare state and that poor people will discover the virtues of self-restraint only if the government stops underwriting irresponsible behavior with its various transfer programs.

Both of these perspectives are missing something. They overlook the importance of spiritual matters. Fortunately, in every community there are agencies of moral and cultural development that seek to shape the ways in which individuals conceive of their duties to themselves, their obligations to each other, and their responsibilities before God. The family and the church are primary among these. These institutions have too often broken down in the inner city, overwhelmed by forces from within and without; yet they are the natural sources of legitimate moral teaching—indeed, the only sources. If these institutions are not restored, the behavioral problems of the ghetto will not be overcome. Such a restoration obviously cannot be the object of programmatic intervention by public agencies. Rather, it must be led from within the communities in question, by the moral and political leaders of those communities.

Let me extend this line of thought about the importance of spiritual concerns in a slightly different direction. First, a confession: I am a Christian and an economist. I became an economist many years before I became a Christian, so my methodological commitments were forged long before I began to raise questions about how my work might be connected to my faith. Nevertheless, since I have become a Christian, the way I do economics has changed. Economists study markets, the behavior of consumers and firms, the art and science of buying and selling, the theory of rational choice, and so on. This is important work, to be sure. It is, for example, prudent to think carefully about incentives when creating social programs. We should try to conceptualize and to measure the costs and benefits of alternative public policies. Doing so is a technical enterprise, with respect to which economics has considerable power.

As a Christian, however, I find this analytical perspective inadequate to the task of social prescription: A single-minded focus on benefits and costs is an impoverished way of thinking about how we should live together in society. Let me give an example drawn from the problem of racial profiling. When screening resources are limited, there is a statistical argument that an agent seeking to detect an unobserved hazard can do so more efficiently by making use of any readily observable information that correlates with the presence of the hazard. If one happens to know that dangerous people are drawn disproportionately from a group whose members look a certain way, then using that knowledge in the design of a screening process will, as a statistical matter, ease the monitoring problem. But when we classify people categorically and treat them differently based on this categorization, we do more than simply solve a resource allocation problem. We also make a statement about how we relate to one another.

When we build racial categorization into the bureaucratic practice of law enforcement or of antiterrorism defense, we give a face to our enemy, saying in effect: "Our enemy, those whom we rightly fear and despise, look more or less like this." When this face we paint on our enemy is also the face of a great many of our neighbors and friends, our pursuit of efficiency through profiling has the effect of sundering our community and debasing our values. Now, does it make any sense to talk of the benefits and the costs of doing, or not doing, something like this? I think not. Because our value commitments (What manner of people are we and how then must we comport ourselves?) can transcend our economic concerns (How much do we have and how might we get even more?), we are often moved to eschew what would otherwise appear to be the most efficient course of action. As a result, the cost-benefit calculus is, in general, insufficient to prescribe a course of action.

More generally, I am of the view that social science can capture only a part of the human subject. Of necessity social science methods project the full person onto those material and deterministic dimensions that we think we understand. As an object of scientific inquiry, the human subject must ultimately be reduced to a mechanism. Yet in so doing social scientists leave out that which most makes a person human: the soul. My fundamental conviction is that human beings are not defined by our desires at a point and time or indeed by our biological inheritance. God is not finished with us when he deals us our genetic hand. As spiritual beings, what we are in the fullness of our humanity transcends that which can be grasped with the particular vision that an economist, a sociologist, or psychologist might bring.

Questions of incentives and efficiency are of a fundamentally different order than questions of spiritual identity, which are of a higher order than the former. Economics cannot finally resolve questions at the center of our struggles as individuals, as families, and as a nation: Who are we? What must we do? How shall we live? What is right? Absent the spiritual grounding that permits us to pose such questions, the rest of our intellectual efforts amount to so much puzzle solving.

In the end, we are spiritual creatures, generators of meaning, beings who must not and cannot live by bread alone. My conviction, as a Christian who happens also to be an economist, is that until social science views this aspect of the human drama with the utmost seriousness it will do justice neither to the subject of its study nor to the national communities that look to it for useful advice about a host of social ills.

Note

1. Some of this discussion is drawn from "God and the Ghetto," in Charles K. Wilber, ed., *Economics, Ethics, and Public Policy* (Lanham, Md.: Rowman and Littlefield, 1998), pp. 107–10.

GOVERNING RELIGION

MARTHA MINOW

What divides Senator Joseph Lieberman and Chief Justice William Rehnquist? I assume many things do, not the least important being the street running between the Capitol and the Supreme Court.

Yet it is also striking that Democratic and Jewish Senator Lieberman has argued that individuals' religious beliefs and practices should guide their professional conduct, while Republican and Lutheran Rehnquist has disagreed. Attorney General John Ashcroft offers still another position, or positions, on the subject: He certainly turned to his religious views to guide his policies as a legislator, but he explained at his confirmation hearing that his professional duties at the Department of Justice would require enforcement of laws with which he has personal religious objections. He also instituted prayer meetings on site at the Justice Department before the workday starts. How should a religious individual holding public office adhere to both religious commitments and the duties of public services in a secular and diverse state? Even more generally, how should a diverse society treat the place of religion in politics?

Committed to protecting freedom and equal respect for all individuals and groups, the society surely should allow and foster expression and association that may well combine religion and politics—as people affiliate in religious terms to address political issues. But to ensure that these basic commitments to freedom and equal respect endure, society (through its laws, politics, and mores) should guard against use of public power to implement—or to suppress—particular religious views. This kind of abstract formulation may not, however, fully capture the reasons that religious issues and language increasingly inform political debate and deliberations.

That religious ideas infuse political debate would not surprise the Founders of the nation, though public leaders twenty years ago acted as though this were not the case. Thomas Jefferson may have tried to institutionalize John Locke's call to separate church and state, but Jefferson still assumed far greater scope and influence for religion as a feature of public life than the courts and legislatures of the late twentieth century permitted. If eighteenth- and nineteenth-century policies aspired to distinguish church and state in this country at all, the aspiration applied only to the federal government, not to states or localities. No responsible historian denies that publicly funded schools throughout the nineteenth and early twentieth centuries taught the Bible and presided over prayers without much opposition—that is, without much mainstream opposition. The integration of religion into public life in the United States largely meant mainline Protestantism. The common school movement in particular confirmed a Protestant culture.

Public schools seemed to fail the Catholic community, at least in the eyes of Catholic leaders in the nineteenth century. Anti-Catholic sentiment worked its way in cultural and political conflicts, and arguments for compulsory school laws were pressed in large measure to block parochial Catholic schools. Only when the Supreme Court decision rejected compulsory public schooling as a violation of parents' rights to influence their children's upbringing did such laws end. Increasing waves of Jewish and Catholic immigrants encountered hostility and pressure to assimilate. Many immigrant Jews held onto orthodoxy and thereby surprised both well-established German Reform Jews and other Americans. The Catholic leadership decided to preserve the ethnic and national traditions of new Catholic immigrants and structured parishes with imported priests to reinforce religious and ethnic particularities rather than combine all Catholics in a melting pot. Struggles between these groups and the Protestant majority generated political battles as well as federal and state court decisions that increasingly challenged the assumption that this was a Protestant nation. Combined with pragmatic cooperation among religious groups during and after World War I, these political and legal developments challenged the implicit hegemony of Protestantism.

Between the 1920s and the 1980s, the emerging public solution required explicit secularization. Both the process and the effects of secularization probably occurred more at the level of legal doctrine—inconsistent as it was—than in practice. Often over religious objections, courts approved public school teaching of evolution, rejected public school instruction in "creation science," prohibited prayer in public schools, recognized nonreligious conscientious objection to military service, and legalized abortion—but local practices continued often to integrate religion and public life.

After 9/11, references to Islamic terrorists by public officials and media injected divisive religious stereotypes even while prompting an unprecedented level of interest among non-Muslims in learning about Islam. Immediately after the catastrophe and since, elected officials joined members of the broader community to express, through prayer and religious ritual, public concern for victims. The collective responses have been led by political leaders, often using explicitly religious language even while displaying public ecumenicism.

Public events after 9/11 mix rituals from Christianity with gestures of religious inclusion. President George W. Bush talks openly about being "saved" but also defers to the politically correct multiculturalism of the age. A superficial multicultural tone governs with allusions to the civil rights movement and identity politics. Political leaders (or their handlers) create photo opportunities to display cordial relations across racial and religious lines and among Christians, Jews, Muslims, Hindus, and members of other religions. Whether due to commitment or to advice by pollsters, Republicans as well as Democrats adopt these symbols of inclusion. That members of religious minorities participate in public events and political debate suggests some degree of comfort and sense of safety in a world that has not always provided much reassurance on these scores.

When operating at a deeper level of idea and argument, multiculturalism demands respect for diverse identities not only at public events but also in policy and practice. Multiculturalists question different treatment of any group as suspicious discrimination and argue for equality and accommodation for groups excluded in the past. Leaders of the religious Christian Right increasingly take advantage of this framework, an obvious example being the equal access movement, which convinced Congress and the Supreme Court to ensure to religious student groups the same rights to hold meetings and events accorded to other student organizations on the premises of public schools. The framework also represents a middle position between those who would ban religion from public places and those who would integrate it fully. It is not at all clear whether the religious groups triumph in using a secular framework of pluralism with an equal right to be heard or whether, instead, this represents a deep victory for the secular. Under either view, by the 1990s the growing search for religious values and "God talk" in many settings followed the resurgence of an Evangelical Christian religious Right and the dominance of the secular framework of tolerance and equal respect across identity groups.

In the past decade repeated public scandals and profound collective global and national political problems have led many people to draw upon spiritual and religious resources and to bring them into public debate and public policy. Examples range from the moment when President Clinton asked pastors not only for forgiveness but also for their public relations assistance to the partnerships joining local, state, and federal government with religious institutions to deliver human services, educational programs, health care, day care—and even prison management.

Difficulties arise if government actions cross over from reflecting religious sources of vision and energy to preferring one kind of religion over others. The historic origins and continuing purposes of the establishment clause of the Constitution reflect concerns about government intrusions into religion as much as worries about religion moving into the government realm. Both concerns press against public preferences even as individuals' religious views and practices warrant deep respect and protection. And both concerns caution against activities that would lead members of different religions to bring theological and institutional conflicts into the public sphere or to involve the government in monitoring or regulating religious belief or practice.

Yet religiously inflected arguments and perspectives bring critical and prophetic insight and energy to politics and public affairs. The civil rights movement depended upon the ideas and social networks of the African American churches and on the congregations of the many religions that joined the cause. Michael Harrington's *The Other America*, drawing inspiration from Dorothy Day's Catholic Worker movement, helped jump-start the War on Poverty.[1] Religious leaders and ideas animate movements against the death penalty, against abortion, and against war—movements that improve democratic deliberation even for those, like me, who may disagree with particular policy proposals or particular theological traditions. Religious beliefs and practices give people bases for criticizing their circumstances and for working, by their own lights, to improve them. Thus there is something woefully lacking in any view that excludes religion entirely from the public sphere.

It remains difficult, however, to draw the line between respecting the religious commitments of voters and politicians that help animate their arguments and their work—for peace, for relieving suffering, for pursuing justice—and elevating one or more religious views in politics in ways that risk excluding, devaluing, or coercing people who do not share those views. What might seem from the outside to be undue psychological sensitivity to exclusion by, for example, repeated references to Jesus Christ in the inaugural address of a U.S. president must be understood as concern precisely about this line. Guarding that line requires vigilance against divisiveness or mobilization against "others." For religion in politics can produce intergroup distrust, hatred, and violence. Religious conflict in places as varied as Bosnia, Israel, Northern Ireland, Pakistan, and Sri Lanka reminds us that our Constitution's framers rightly warned against too much religion in government and politics.

So if religions offer rich resources for envisioning a better world and motivating people to strive for it, they also generate divisions, hatreds, and barriers to communication and a sense of commonality. A liberal democracy should enable people to draw on their distinctive religious traditions without letting them either render communication across group differences difficult or unravel the already fragile sense of commonality in a diverse polity. Pursuing precisely these goals, philosopher John Rawls argues that religious motivations may be appropriate but that contributions to political debate must be expressed in a public language, devoid of the particularities of any religious tradition.[2] He also argues that the value of religious views to political debate should be tested by asking how well those views advance values recognized by reasonable liberal conceptions of justice, conceived as the overlapping consensus of varied comprehensive views. Yet these conceptions risk neglecting the way that the overlapping consensus—the very boundaries of reasonable liberal conceptions of justice—does and must change over time as people criticize, argue, and struggle with one another, informed by life experiences and multiple sources of values and beliefs.

Some may try to use the instruments of government to impose their views on others rather than to work for a world that can be held in common. Increasing the religious content of political argument can make communication, trust, and coalition building across groups more difficult. Both dangers could be reduced if people who are tempted to use religious ideas and language in politics act with humility and acknowledge that they do not have an exclusive hold on the truth. Humility itself is a concept with deep and multiple religious roots. Yet so often its opposite seems to come with the territory of religious practice and expression.

Jokes, so often repositories of collective wisdom, make the point better than logical arguments. So one Christian minister is alleged to have said to another at the conclusion of an ecumenical conference where they had shared respectful discussions of their denominational differences: "I now see that we both worship God, you in your way, and me in His."

And then there is the story about the rabbi, the cantor (singer), and the *shammas* (custodian) in the sanctuary preparing the synagogue for Yom Kippur. Suddenly overcome with religious fervor, the rabbi throws himself down before the Ark, containing the Torah, and says, "Before you, Almighty One, I am nothing, I am less than a speck of dust, please bless me, please forgive me." Seeing the rabbi on the floor, the cantor throws himself down and says, "Before you, Almighty God, I am nothing. I am less than a squeak of the door, I am nothing, please bless me, forgive me." The *shammas,* mopping up in the back of the sanctuary, sees the rabbi and the cantor on the floor and throws himself down too, saying, "Almighty God, I am nothing, I am nothing, I am nothing." At that point the cantor nudges the rabbi, points to the *shammas,* and says, "Look who thinks he's nothing!"

Resisting the implication that your own religious convictions give all the answers—for you and others—may be the most critical challenge for those who would bring religion to political life.

Notes

1. Michael Harrington, *The Other America* (Macmillan, 1962).
2. John Rawls, *Political Liberalism* (Columbia University Press, 1996).

PARTICULARIST RELIGION
IN A PLURALIST POLITICAL ARENA

STEPHEN V. MONSMA

Religion and politics mix. For better or for worse this basic fact characterizes American politics and public policymaking and has done so throughout American history. After all, Thomas Jefferson's religious beliefs—and his alleged heterodox views—were an issue in the 1800 presidential campaign, and many nineteenth-century abolitionists firmly rooted their policy positions on slavery in their Christian faith. This mixing of religion and politics is no less true in present-day American political campaigns and public policymaking debates. This raises the twin questions of whether or not it is appropriate for religion to be included in political campaigns and public policy debates and—if its appropriateness is accepted—what the correct nature and terms of its inclusion are. These are the questions I address here.

At the outset, I reject the position that religion and religiously rooted perspectives have no place in public discourse. This contention is typically put forward on the basis that democratic public discourse must involve free discussion, openness to new ideas, negotiation, and compromise. And, it is argued, religion involves absolute truth claims rooted in faith and thus by nature is not open to rational discussion and negotiation. This means that religion and claims based on religion offer no room for the discussing and searching for common ground at the heart of the democratic process. In a healthy democracy, therefore, religion must be kept out of the public square and be consigned to the purely private realm, one of personal opinion and private rituals.

This position, I submit, is based on two patently false assumptions. One is that persons who take policy positions and advance their candidacies for public office on purely secular grounds do so only with basic predispositions that are subject to factual, rational proof or disproof. This assumption is, of course, untenable. Every person enters the public realm as a product of life experiences and deeply ingrained ways of looking at the world that have shaped his or her politically relevant predispositions. These are no more subject to empirical proof than are revealed religious truths.

The second false assumption is that a person's religiously rooted beliefs—because of their revealed nature—are not subject to rational discussion and debate. There is a grain of truth and a mountain of error in this assumption. Deeply religious persons do hold to certain fundamental truths on the basis of divine revelation or religious authorities; for a Christian these include such truths as the existence of one God in three persons, the compulsion to show care for the poor and needy, the belief in the fallen nature of human beings, and the common worth and dignity of all persons. But the mountain of error lies in the fact that these are fundamental beliefs, not a concrete political program. These fundamental beliefs need to be applied in concrete situations, specific to a certain time and place, and that is anything but an automatic, preordained matter.

For example, one may believe as a Christian—or as a believer in any number of other religions—that public policies should show special concern for the poor. But does that mean one should support a strong free market system? Or should one support more generous welfare programs? Does this mean one should support greater free trade? Should globalization be opposed? Merely posing these questions demonstrates that different persons who hold to the same basic religious beliefs may nevertheless come to widely different applications of those beliefs in concrete political situations. Holding deeply felt religious beliefs does not lock one into fixed public policy positions. Gathering relevant facts, making prudent judgments, and participating in open discussion are all needed.

Even if one grants me my position that religion can properly be introduced into political campaigns and public policy discussions, the question still remains of the appropriate manner in which this should be done. There are, I would argue, proper and improper uses of religion in the public realm. In the rest of this essay I suggest two improper uses of religion in the public realm and then suggest what I see as the proper role of religion in the public square.

One way that religion is sometimes improperly used in the public realm is as a symbol to garner votes. I am thinking here of politicians out on the stump who sprinkle their speeches—especially before audiences they view as being especially religious—with a little "God talk." Or they give lip service to policy positions calculated to appeal to religious folks. I am thinking here of politicians who close their speeches with "God bless America!" who make references to the religious faith of the nation's Founders (with a quotation usually taken out of context), or who indicate support for such policy positions as prayers before high school football games (when campaigning in the South) or the public posting of the Ten Commandments. Yet those same politicians show no real evidence of God playing a controlling role in their lives and have not worked out a rationale for supporting prayers at high school football games or the public display of the Ten Commandments.

If these politicians are elected they will at the most make a few symbolic efforts—but no real push—to act on the policy positions they espoused during the election campaign to appeal to religious voters. Such politicians thus treat deeply religious voters like a special interest group: They try to corral their votes while not alienating other, opposing groups. They engage in a few symbolic gestures while making no substantive commitments. This is using religion in the most negative sense of the word.

Another improper use of religion is to seek a preeminent place for one's own religion in the public policy realm. Here the politician or the policy-maker has a substantive goal rooted in his or her religious faith, but it is an improper goal in a religiously pluralist society. Public policymakers fall into this error when they try to reintroduce spoken prayers into the nation's classrooms and when they support public displays of symbols of their religion without giving equal recognition to other religious or secular systems of belief. In both cases they are seeking public preferment of their religious beliefs or of religion more broadly.

Some Christians try to recreate nineteenth- and early twentieth-century America, when there was an informal Protestant establishment. Public school then reflected a consensual, genial Protestantism, and Christian symbols and references (usually Protestant) abounded in the public realm. Nonbelievers and religious minorities such as Catholics and Jews were reminded, subtly and not so subtly, that they were outsiders, not a part of mainstream American society. This was wrong, and any attempt to recreate such a situation is wrong.

It is equally wrong, of course, for a secular system of belief or a more genial secular ethos to be given preferment in the public realm, with the result that deeply religious believers are made to feel that they are outsiders. Giving public preferment to either religious or secular belief systems is wrong.

There is, however, a way to bring religious beliefs and perspectives into public discourse rooted in our nation's traditions of pluralism, openness, and competition. *Principled pluralism*, as it has been called, derives from the fact that religious faith serves for many adherents as a basis for their political thinking. As a Christian in the Evangelical tradition, I am thinking now especially of traditional Christianity. Many Christians see their faith as speaking to issues of poverty, racial discrimination, overweening government power, tax structures, abortion, the death penalty, environmental degradation, gay rights, war and peace, international trade, and much, much more.

The United States today is marked by an increasing religious pluralism. The day when the public scene was dominated by the large, mainline Protestant churches and the Catholic Church is long gone. The mainline Protestant churches are declining in numbers and influence, while Evangelical Protestants are increasing in numbers and influence. The Catholic Church is probably even less of a monolith than it was in the past. Due largely to immigration, Muslims, Buddhists, and Hindus constitute distinct religious groupings. Meanwhile, New Age and other intensely personal religions are on the rise. The number of Mormons is growing. In addition, studies are showing that the percentage of the American population that espouses no religious beliefs is on the rise. I see this increasing religious diversity not as leading to doom but as potentially adding to the richness of public life.

Although the question of how a variety of belief systems is to be accommodated in the public square has always been present in the United States, this increasing religious diversity makes that question even more urgent. Those who see religion in the public realm as being illegitimate and dangerous would say that all points of view explicitly rooted in religion should be ruled out of the public realm, that all persons should behave in the public square as though they were secularists. But we have already seen the problems in this. On the other hand, those who long for the reinstatement of a Christian America would say that, although we should tolerate all religions and religious points of view, since America has been marked by more Christians than any by other religious adherents, Christians should occupy a favored position in the public realm. This too is wrong.

The answer that principled pluralists give is that adherents to all religious and all secular points of view should be welcomed to the table of public policy debate and discussion. They should be able—openly and freely—to discuss their differences and similarities. These should include their fundamental religiously or secularly rooted beliefs and assumptions as well as the ways in which they would apply them to the contentious issues of today.

This means that persons running for public office should be able to freely discuss their religious views. But they should not stop there. They should link their religious views to the approach to governing they would follow and to the public policies they advocate. My concern with candidate George W. Bush in 2000 in citing Jesus Christ as the most influential political philosopher in his life was not his listing of a religious figure but his failing to spell out how Jesus Christ shaped his approach to governing his public policy positions. Similarly, candidates for public office holding secular systems of belief should explain the concepts and ideals that animate their governing philosophies and policy positions. Officeholders, such as members of Congress and cabinet members, should also explain their underlying religious or secular beliefs and how they inform their political philosophies and policy positions.

Under principled pluralism our public life and discussion would be enriched and clarified, not limited and stifled. Now too often public officials and candidates for public office feel they must not appear "too religious." Or they are tempted to use religion in only a symbolic, superficial manner. The public as a result ends up not fully understanding what shapes and motivates candidates and public officials. The application of a principled pluralism approach to religion in the public square would result in freer and more open discussion and debate and, ultimately, a richer democracy.

VOTING NOT TO VOTE

MARK A. NOLL

As has been the case for the last few presidential elections, on November 2, 2004, I will almost certainly cast my vote once again for none of the above. For candidates seeking office in the state of Illinois, in DuPage County, and in the city of Wheaton, I will try to cast an intelligent ballot. But unless something unexpected happens, I will not be voting for the presidential nominee of either major party. Here is why.

Seven issues seem to me to be paramount at the national level: race, life, taxes, trade, medicine, religious freedom, and international rule of law. In my mind, each of these issues has a strong moral dimension. My position on each is related to how I understand the traditional Christian faith that grounds my existence. Yet neither of the major parties is making a serious effort to consider this particular combination of concerns or even something remotely resembling this combination.

In searching for a party that is working for something close to my convictions, I am not necessarily looking for a platform supported by overtly expressed religious beliefs. It would be enough to find candidates promoting such positions by reference to broad social goals and general patterns of American democratic tradition. In fact, because each of these issues is of vital national concern for people of all faiths (and none), I am eager to find public voices willing to defend convictions similar to my own in generic social terms rather than with specifically religious arguments. My disillusionment with the major parties and their candidates comes from the fact that I do not see them willing to consider the political coherence of this combination of convictions, much less willing to reason about why their positions should be accepted—much less willing to break away from narrow partisanship to act for the public good. Broad principles and particular interests have never in the history of the Republic been more confusedly mixed as they are today. Sketching reasons for my political convictions will make my electoral dilemma clear.

Regarding race: From 1619, when the first African indentured servants were offloaded in the American colonies, until the 1960s, American political institutions wavered in deciding whether African Americans could be full and equal citizens of a democratic nation. A general principle of American democracy demands that members of every race and ethnic group be treated equally before the law, but a general fact of history demands that sustained, accumulated wrongs must be addressed by sustained, ongoing remediation. The most chilling words ever spoken about the fruits of American inequality were part of the second inaugural of Abraham Lincoln, in March 1865: "Yet if God wills that it [the Civil War] continue, until all the wealth piled by the bond-man's two hundred and fifty years of unrequited toil shall be sunk, and until every drop of blood drawn with the lash, shall be paid with another drawn with the sword, as was said three thousands years ago, so still it must be said 'the judgments of the Lord are true and righteous altogether.'"

Shortly after Lincoln made this speech, the Civil War did come to an end. Yet the "scourge," the "offense," of race-defined social inequality did not end until much later, if in fact it has actually come to an end. The United States pays a heavy price, and it pays it daily, for its history of injustice to African American citizens—African Americans who wait for redress, who do not take into their own hands the challenge of shaping their own future, compound this larger difficulty. But full attention to the racially infested plight of impacted urban areas—a Marshall Plan in some shape or form— is certainly the least that could be asked of the major political parties as recompense for America's longest lasting and most debilitating political crime.

Regarding life: I am militantly prolife because I do not want the United States to commit the social suicide that results when nations allow personal preference to trump human life. Through the long course of the ages, a personal preference to disregard life has been mostly exercised by male authority at the top of society. Today it is exercised by different actors because of the spread of egalitarian values. But whether exercised from above or below, personal preference is mortally dangerous if it operates without reasonable restraint. Assumptions that are nearly universal in human history testify that, without compelling reasons to the contrary, life should be favored over death.

To be sure, free societies need to defend the prerogatives of citizens to bring life into existence or not. And free societies, especially those that claim to hold life as a supreme value, should offer all possible support to the mothers who bring new life into the world and to the intact families that young lives so desperately need in order to become useful, productive citizens. In addition, since prenatal life is closely bound up with maternal life, it is necessary to legislate with nuance and sensitivity when acting to preserve life. All necessary qualifications having been made, however, it is imperative for nations that want to promote liberty and justice for all to stand behind the principle of life and against any effort, however well intentioned, to compromise that fundamental principle.

Regarding taxes: The United States needs to base its income tax policy on broad views of justice and equity—that is, it needs sharply progressive income taxes. The ability to create wealth does depend on personal initiative, personal intelligence, personal work, and personal luck. It depends also upon a social infrastructure that allows initiative, intelligence, hard work, and luck to result in the creation of wealth. If you live in Bangladesh, Haiti, Zimbabwe, or many places in Russia, your chances of becoming wealthy are nugatory, regardless of how smart you are, how hard you work, or how much initiative you take.

It is a matter of justice that those who benefit most from the social infrastructure of the United States—from its traditions of liberty as well as its traditions of entrepreneurial creativity, its provisions for making business work as well as its culture of personal consumption—should pay the most to maintain that infrastructure. What I earn is in some real sense "mine," but in another equally valid sense it is "ours," since what "we" provide is the kind of political and social environment in which money can be made.

Regarding trade: The United States should continue to defend principles of free trade and, wherever possible, expand the operations of free trade. Free trade, admittedly, can be painful for individual segments of advanced economies like the United States, and so there needs to be temporary assistance for segments hurt by the expansion of free trade (which assistance could be adequately funded if tax revenues were being raised from segments of the population benefiting from the expansion of free trade).

But in broader terms free trade opens up opportunities for the kind of entrepreneurial activity that creates jobs and expands markets. It binds nations with cords of commerce. It makes the necessities of life more widely available. It provides long-term solutions for problems exacerbated by poverty and the failures of education. It shows citizens of dictatorships and statist regimes the economic advantages of free economic activity. And it makes the United States safer from international resentment or attack by promoting new jobs in poverty-stricken regions of the world.

Regarding medicine: Basic medical coverage, supplied at minimal cost and with minimal hassle, should be offered to all. The wisdom of this argument does not require that such coverage be considered a basic human right. Prudent self-interest should be all that is needed: Those whom illness or disability incapacitates become a drain on the public purse and are kept from functioning as productive workers. Those who live in constant fear of being pauperized by illness or disability do not function productively or contribute to the institutions of political and civil society. America's history of free competition has contributed to the splendors of American medicine. But locking those splendors away from a growing portion of the American populace is a problem of the first order.

A problem of nearly equal magnitude is the skyrocketing expense of medical coverage that results when individual parts of the medical system act only from their own perceived short-term interests. Timorous solutions are not the answer. Political leaders must find the courage to propose comprehensive programs, the perseverance to push them along, and the commitment to make things change.

Regarding religious freedom: All of modern world history reinforces the proposition that people must be allowed to exercise the basic human right of worshiping God, or not worshiping God, as they choose. The violation of this right has proven destructive of social well-being, corrosive of social harmony, and stultifying to human flourishing. That religious freedom is almost certainly the most basic human right has been demonstrated by the repeated social constriction and economic regression where it has been abridged.

Regarding international rule of law: In an increasingly complex and riven world, the United States must act with scrupulous justice in its actions overseas. U.S. policies based on unilateralism—whether in trade, diplomacy, or war—can only make the international arena more dangerous for all. Since the United States is by far the strongest nation in the world—the new Rome of the early twenty-first century—it should ponder the overextension, the shortsighted presumption, the failures of imagination, and the unilateral use of force that caused such difficulties in the latter phases of the Roman Empire. Warfare remains the most explosive instrument of international policy. Self-interest is a legitimate reason for the use of force but only where the strictest standards of *jus ad bellum* and *jus in bello* are observed.

I have arrived at these seven political convictions as a result of my Christian faith. Yet each can be advanced in terms of the public good without reliance on a particular faith. Of course, I may be mistaken either in what traditional Christianity should mean politically for an American citizen in the early twenty-first century or in how best to argue for these positions with reasoning not demanding a commitment to traditional Christianity. But as long as I hold these positions, I am a citizen without a political home.

RELIGION, FAITH, AND ELECTIONS

DAVID NOVAK

I served as a rabbi to a congregation in New York City in 1982, the year Mario Cuomo was first elected governor of New York State. During that campaign I was impressed by the way Cuomo incorporated his Catholic religious convictions into the overall program he advocated. I envied New York Catholics for having Mario Cuomo in their community, since I did not know a Jewish politician who could incorporate Judaism in a comparable way into his or her espousal of a public program.

My admiration for Mario Cuomo, more specifically, is because of his principled stand on the question of capital punishment, a stand I did not accept then but that I do now. The fact that Pope John Paul II has now adopted that stand makes Mario Cuomo a very prescient Catholic. (It is also worth noting that the pope's opposition to capital punishment creates a considerable conflict for Supreme Court justice Antonin Scalia—certainly as faithful a Catholic as Cuomo—between his religious commitments and his civic commitments.)

Since I agree with just about everything Mario Cuomo says in these pages, I only want to recast his informal argument into, for me anyway, a more rationally persuasive form. (Following that, I attempt the same for the remarks of Mark Souder.)

Mario Cuomo makes four points of reference: religious conviction, moral opinion, political prudence, and natural law. Let us take his paradigm case of capital punishment and see how he employs all four points of reference in his opposition to this public practice and, simultaneously, rework those points.

Religiously, Cuomo seems to be opposed to capital punishment because human life, even the human life of a murderer (the usual candidate for capital punishment), has a sanctity that no other human being has a right to violate, even if that violation is in response to the most heinous crime possible. Morally, Cuomo seems to be opposed to capital punishment because it offends the dignity of human life, even the dignity of the life of someone who has destroyed the equally dignified life of another human being. I assume that by *natural law* Cuomo means universal morality, hence I cannot see why he did not conflate natural law and morality. So I will be presumptuous enough to do that for him. (Perhaps Cuomo feels that the term *natural law* has a specifically Catholic connotation, even though other religious and legal traditions have similar doctrines.) Finally, political prudence would seem to indicate that enough citizens are sympathetic to Cuomo's religious or moral opposition to capital punishment to accept his proposal for its abolition.

All that being said, though, I do not understand why Cuomo calls his public stand *religious* rather than *moral*. A religious stand is based on a person's relationship with God, and indeed human life is sacred because of its innate capacity for a relationship with God. But many people in our society do not share Cuomo's Catholic relationship with his God; in fact, not a few people in our society claim to have no relationship with any god, and even if they do, that relationship has no bearing on their relationship with their fellow human beings. Conversely, no one can claim to have no relationship with their fellow human beings; hence a moral claim cannot be as easily rejected as a religious claim. By the logic of Ockham's razor, since a moral claim requires the acceptance of fewer assumptions than does a religious claim, a moral claim seems preferable.

But Cuomo's secularist opponents could retort that his moral claims stem from his religious convictions; hence calling them *moral* is disingenuous. In fact are not these so-called moral claims only rationalizations for Mario Cuomo's Catholicism, which he, like all other religious believers (especially believers in one law-giving God, such as Christians, Muslims, and Jews), is attempting to foist on nonbelievers in our society, a society whose government is supposed to protect everyone from the imposition of anyone's religion?

The answer that Cuomo (or Cuomo admirers like me) should give to this charge—one heard all the time in debates about public morality—is as follows: You assume that the public morality I am advocating for everyone in our society stems from my religion, that is, that my religion entails a system of moral norms to be enforced for everybody. However, it is the other way around. My morality does not stem from my religion; rather, my religion presupposes the system of moral norms I advocate. Furthermore, since my religion did not invent this system of moral norms, it is easy for me to accept the fact that religions other than my own—and even some philosophically formulated systems of ethics—accept similar norms. That is why, for example, Jews, Christians, Muslims, and even secularly inclined people can come to remarkable agreement on what constitutes natural law—that is, the law required by human nature.

The reason that Mario Cuomo as a Catholic Christian and I as a traditional Jew need religion over and above universal morality is because there is more to human life in the world than the presence of other human creatures. People like us need a relationship with the one who created human life, who directs humans in their attempt to make the world our dwelling, and who will reconcile us with himself in the end. All of this—what might be called the transcendent dimension of human existence—is beyond universal morality. Nevertheless, we would have never been able to coherently seek our God if we were not first committed to living in a just peace with our fellow human beings. That is because even in our most exalted religious moments we are still social beings. Our religious commitment is to sanctify this world, not escape it. The dignity of our fellow human beings needs to be constantly affirmed—as public policy, whenever that is politically prudent (that is, politically doable)—because they are also striving toward transcendence, whether or not they are aware of that striving. That striving has immediate and constant social implications. Thus what is immanent points to what is transcendent, and what is transcendent can never remove our feet from the earth and all the finite beings who are immanent therein.

It is more *for the sake of God* than *because of God* that a person of faith can make moral claims in secular public space. Indeed, we can make these claims even to people who affirm different origins and different ends for humans on earth. Therefore, these moral claims can be made in public neither because of our religious convictions nor in spite of them. These religious convictions and the God whom they ultimately intend always surround believers. Yet they need not, indeed they ought not, be imposed, politically or even rhetorically, on anyone who does not want to hear them. Our religious convictions are about our origin and our end. Our moral concerns are about what transpires in between.

Since I am also sympathetic to the basic thrust of Mark Souder's remarks, I would like to reformulate a key sentence of his in order to turn my sympathy into rational agreement: "But it is not the job of government to replace these institutions [the church and its people] as the primary moral agents of society." Taken at face value, this sentence cannot be true about society in the United States. In fact, this sentence could only be true about a premodern European society that considered itself part of "Christendom."

At that time, society as a whole was considered to be a Christian society divided into two parts: the state, which dealt with political, economic, and military matters; and the church, which dealt with religious and moral matters. To be subject to the state and enjoy the privileges of membership therein, one had to be a member of the church. In this way, the state derived its moral legitimacy from the religious authority of the church. Those who were not members of the established church, like Anabaptists and Jews, were at best tolerated by—and at worst persecuted by or expelled from—society. Needless to say, this is not the case in the United States, due to the nonestablishment clause of the First Amendment to the Constitution.

However, what ought to happen in a secular constitutional democracy like ours is that people bring to society moral convictions already formulated by their religious communities (churches). The state should be the beneficiary of these prior moral convictions, not their benefactor nor their origin. In that way, Souder can be the Christian he wants to be in church, at home, and in his life as a public official. Nevertheless, there is an intermediary step he must take before he brings his Christian (specifically, Anabaptist Christian) convictions into the public square for the sake of making public policy proposals. He cannot simply advocate that the rest of us, who are not Anabaptist Christians (or Christians at all), do what he proposes for us in society because this is what his church teaches.

Instead, Souder must identify the moral teachings of his church that are held in common with other worldviews, because these teachings are true to human nature conceived of as having an inherent dignity, if not yet an inherent sanctity. He can believe that the ultimate source of these moral teachings is the revelation his own community accepts as its existential foundation, but he must first identify a more immediate moral source. Thus his public argument should not be made in the name of revelation, even though he need not personally deny it. His public argument ought to be made by moral reason, the reason he shares with all other rational persons who recognize that human dignity is irreducible and inalienable.

To do this, Souder—and all those who share his specific faith or have an Evangelical faith similar to it—must appropriate earlier Protestant efforts to affirm natural law, or universal morality, and not regard such law as a Roman Catholic doctrine repudiated by the Reformation, especially the radical Reformation that produced the Anabaptist churches. (Similarly, traditional Jews need to retrieve natural law thinking and not regard it as a Christian innovation.) In this way, there would be powerful moral agreement among diverse Christians, Jews, and even members of faith communities farther removed from that of Mark Souder. Such an agreement could include every-body who is not a militant atheist. At the same time, natural law could, in the name of religious liberty, defend the civil right of persons who are non-religious—even antireligious—to follow their own moral convictions.

REASONING TOGETHER

RAMESH PONNURU

Mark Souder rejects Mario Cuomo's idea that there is a natural law of things common to all religions. He describes that idea as a non-Christian "worldview." He suggests that as a factual matter religions do not unanimously agree on any moral principles. He argues that the concept of natural law is not useful because too many people interpret it to mean different things. Religious believers, in Souder's view, should not have to settle for a watered-down, least-common-denominator set of transreligious truths in their public lives. They should instead be able to bring their entire faith, in all its integrity, to the public square.

Souder is correct to say that politicians and voters may make political decisions on the basis of their religious beliefs, whether or not those beliefs can be defended purely as a matter of reason, and that they do not offend the U.S. Constitution merely because they have done so. He may also be correct to deny the existence of moral truths that are affirmed by all the world's great religions; I doubt it, but I do not begin to know enough to answer that question.

But Souder goes further in two ways. First, he implicitly denies the power of reason to reach moral truths. That denial cannot be taken on faith; it must itself be proven by reason. For reasons that I do not have space to go into here but that have been explored by many bookshelves' worth of authors, I do not believe that it can. Second, Souder denies the usefulness of natural law. But that criticism can hardly conclude comfortably in a call for purely religious argument. It is true that asking people of varying religious backgrounds to use reason to settle public questions does not by itself settle those questions. (Who ever said it would?) It does, however, provide a common idiom or at least constrain modes of argument. Religious arguments for public policy, on the other hand, cannot even in principle be useful in persuading people who do not share the religion from which the arguments spring.

If we are convinced that God has told us to vote against a particular bill, that revelation is an indefeasible reason for us to act accordingly. Most of us, however, have not received such specific guidance. We are left, along with Mario Cuomo, trying to think our way through what constitutes justice and (therefore) what God would have us do.

But—to circle back to what Souder gets right—we will not always agree on the answers. Reason (or what I think is reason) leads me to disagree with certain of Cuomo's conclusions. He argues in quick succession for several propositions:

—That Catholic government officials are obligated to protect the rights to divorce, to procure abortion, to use birth control, to remove stem cells from embryos, and to deny the existence of God.

—That these rights are aspects of religious freedom and as such are protected by the Constitution.

—That these rights are thus bound up with the rights of Catholics *not* to procure abortions, *not* to remove stem cells from embryos, and so on.

—That there is also a legal right for officials to argue for prohibitions on divorce, abortion, and so on, on the grounds that such prohibitions would promote the common good.

—And that whether an official should try to advance such an argument is a complex prudential determination.

Only the last two of these propositions strike me as sound, and they are in serious tension with the others. How can someone be simultaneously obligated to protect the right to abortion and allowed to call for its elimination? One possible escape route from this dilemma can be immediately cut off. The obligation cannot be understood simply as a matter of a public official's duty to follow Supreme Court decisions. The obligation arises because the rights in question really are (on Cuomo's account) aspects of religious liberty. (The Supreme Court, by the way, has never held that the right to divorce or to harvest stem cells from embryos is connected to religious liberty.) How can the decision to advocate a narrowing of religious liberty be a prudent calculation?

Cuomo's third proposition is an echo of the Supreme Court's declaration in *Casey* that even opponents of abortion must support reproductive freedom since otherwise they would have no defense against a policy of forced abortions. The argument's distinguished pedigree does not, however, render it valid. To see why, Cuomo should consider how he would react to the suggestion that the only way to protect citizens from being forced to own automatic weapons is to protect the right of citizens to own them.

I conclude that the way to resolve the dilemma is to jettison most of the content of Cuomo's first three propositions. (The qualifier is necessary, since public officials are obligated legally and morally to protect the right to deny the existence of God.)

How to make the prudent decisions about what to advocate for public policy? Here again I think Cuomo wanders off course. He asserts that he seldom talks about issues in moral terms. ("When I speak against the death penalty I never suggest that I consider it a moral issue. I seldom talk in terms of moral issues.") Instead, he says, he makes other kinds of arguments: "I am against the death penalty because I think it is bad and unfair. It is debasing. It is degenerate. It kills innocent people." The description of the death penalty as unfair, degenerate, and so on is a moral evaluation even if the *m*-word is not explicitly used—a point that I would have thought obvious. The proposition that it is immoral to kill (or to risk killing) innocent people is equally a moral proposition. Souder is much closer to the mark when he suggests that public officials cannot reach a conclusion about what they ought to do—a loaded word, that *ought*—without making moral judgments, whether or not they recognize those judgments as moral in nature.

Cuomo maintains that a Catholic official's position and rhetoric on embryonic stem cells and abortion must be constrained by what the public can be expected to understand. He says that such religious values "will not be accepted as part of the public morality unless they are shared by the community at large. The plausibility of achieving that consensus is a relevant consideration in deciding whether or not to make the effort to impose those values officially." This makes sense, to a point. It must be added, however, that it is part of a conscientious public official's duty to make the public understand moral truths to the extent he or she can. (A Southern politician circa 1852 who knew that slavery was immoral could not rightly have excused his silence by saying that his public would not understand.) Cuomo's remarks do not succeed in this task for three reasons.

First, he sets the standard too high. He does not allow public officials to divide subjects the way political systems necessarily divide them. He notes, for example, that the logic of the argument against federal funding for embryonic stem cell research pushes in the direction of a ban on privately funded research. That claim is correct. The leading argument against federal funding for such research, and the one that Cuomo mentions, is that the human embryo is a member of the human species—a truth, by the way, that requires no religious revelation to establish, as the Catholic Church itself recognizes—and that all members of the human species have a right not to be killed. For the same reason that we do not federally fund research that destroys teenage humans, we do not allow anyone to perform such research, period.

But does it follow from the extreme difficulty of getting a political majority to go along with a complete ban that a public official should support federal funding? Not if the elimination of federal funding limits the amount of embryo destruction, keeps the government from putting its imprimatur on an evil practice, and helps to educate the public about its wrongness. You achieve what consensus you can and then move on from there—in the direction of justice and truth.

Second, Cuomo's ability to get other people to understand the issues involved is impaired by his own flawed framing of them. Among the arguments he has put forward for embryo-destructive research is the claim that the Catholic Church at one point dated the beginning of life at forty days after conception. But what that church's doctrine was or is should not be relevant to the discussion. Cuomo says that public policy has to be made on the basis of truths that are accessible to all people, whatever their religion. As it happens, the Catholic Church has had no trouble coming to the conclusion that embryos are living human beings from conception onward; and it has done so for reasons that are in principle accessible to non-Catholics and, indeed, atheists: Embryos are not dead or inanimate, and they are not some species other than human.

Third, Cuomo suggests that Catholics can "convert this community to our point of view" by refraining from having abortions themselves. As the bumper sticker puts it, "Don't like abortions? Don't have one." But this is to assume what is at issue. Opponents of abortion consider it to be a public evil and a dual injustice. It is unjust both to take the life of a young human and, crucially, to allow the taking of this life as though it were not a life at all. A person cannot mitigate this second injustice by not participating in abortion. As a citizen of a polity that maintains an unjust legal standard, he or she has an obligation to change the law.

All of this is a way of saying that Cuomo, in rightly saying that we must make public policy by reasoning together from our very different perspectives, has chosen a hard road. It obliges him to say what he thinks the content of (what I describe as) the moral law, or that portion of it applicable to government officials, is. It obliges him to provide reasons for thinking that way. It obliges others, such as me, to respond with our own reasons for thinking otherwise. In other words, we have to make arguments in public, and we have to continue them until (dare I say, at this point, providentially?) we reach the truth.

FAITH IN PUBLIC OFFICE

DAVID E. PRICE

The conversation among Mario Cuomo, Mark Souder, and their interlocutors provides a useful basis for further exploration of the proper role of faith in public office. Lord Melbourne, whom Souder quotes regarding the danger of allowing religion "to invade public life," seems a straw man in this context: All participants understand the centrality of religious faith to the motivations drawing many people into politics and to the shape their political advocacy and practice assume. Both Cuomo and Souder also express a commitment to religious pluralism, avoiding state sponsorship of "sectarian religion" (Souder), and protecting the rights of all to express their beliefs both privately and in the public arena. But there the agreement ends.

My reflections focus on a major point of disagreement: when (or whether) it is appropriate to attempt to embody religiously grounded precepts in civil law. I then turn to a critical matter that the discussion—with the exception of a question from J. Brent Walker of the Baptist Joint Committee—largely bypasses: the theological grounding of humility in political practice.

The U.S. Constitution, Cuomo acknowledges, "guarantees my right to try to convince you to adopt my religion's tenet as public law." The question, however, is, "Should I try?" "As I understood my own religion," he says of his Catholicism, "it required me to accept the restraints it imposed on my own life, but it did not require that I seek to impose all of them on all New Yorkers." Souder bridles at such counsels of restraint, warning against a compromise of Christianity as a faith that encompasses "all reality." "To ask me to check my Christian beliefs at the public door is to ask me to expel the Holy Spirit from my life when I serve as a congressman." Souder lists a number of areas of religious belief—"homosexual marriage, pornography, abortion, gambling, evolution across species"—which he specifically refuses to "check . . . at the public door." But he does not attempt any analysis of where the line should be drawn, if at all. He professes opposition to "state-sponsored religion" while ridiculing what he takes to be absurd interpretations of that notion (for example, "a Bible on a teacher's desk"). But what would a *defensible* interpretation entail, and what limits should it place on public advocacy? Souder does not say. Cuomo makes a more serious effort. His key criterion is the coincidence of the religious precept with broader public values. In determining whether and when to take an issue into the public arena, one should consider the presence of consensus—or the "plausibility of achieving that consensus"—on the basis of shared convictions that transcend the specific religious tradition.

If common ground does not exist or cannot be found, that is often a good reason for stopping short of embodying our religious and moral precepts in civil law and for leaving the individual and communal expression of conscience free. Other criteria may also apply: For example, should religiously inspired disapproval of certain behaviors be translated into laws that violate the principles of civil liberty, nondiscrimination, and equal opportunity—or into opposition to laws that would implement these fundamental and broadly shared democratic values? These are partly prudential judgments based on how a pluralistic society functions. But they are also theologically based judgments, based on an understanding of religious freedom and of the limits and dangers of putting the authority of the state behind any group's moral agenda.

This leads to what strikes me as the Cuomo-Souder discussion's most glaring omission: the need for a kind of religious humility, rooted in the sense that our own will and striving are always subject to God's judgment. No policy or program, even the most well-intentioned, can be assumed to be free of the taint of self-interest and self-seeking. Consequently, as Reinhold Niebuhr taught, the task of democracy is not only to realize our positive aspirations but also to provide a check against inevitable miscarriages of justice and abuses of power. James Madison employed a similar rationale for the Constitution's checks and balances: "It may be a reflection on human nature that such devices should be necessary to control the abuses of government. But what is government itself but the greatest of all reflections on human nature? If men were angels, no government would be necessary. If angels were to govern men, neither external nor internal controls on government would be necessary."[1]

Questioned by Brent Walker, Souder acknowledges that humility is counseled by the difficulty of interpreting the Bible's implications for a specific political situation. But the question runs deeper than that. The problem is not fallibility but sinfulness. Integral to the Jewish and Christian traditions is the understanding that people are inclined to a kind of idolatry whereby they identify their own interest or ideology with God's sovereign will. But God's will remains transcendent, imperfectly reflected in human endeavors, which are subject to the taint of self-seeking and the will to power.

The American statesman who best understood this was Abraham Lincoln. Recall the words of his Second Inaugural Address, all the more remarkable for being uttered after almost four years of civil war: "Both [sides] read the same Bible, and pray to the same God; and each invokes His aid against the other. It may seem strange that any men should dare to ask a just God's assistance in wringing their bread from the sweat of other men's faces; but let us judge not, that we not be judged. The prayers of both could not be answered—that of neither has been answered fully."

Niebuhr once wrote that this passage "puts the relation of our moral commitments in history to our religious reservations about the partiality of our own moral commitments more precisely than, I think, any statesman or theologian has put them."[2] Lincoln expresses the moral commitment against slavery in uncompromising terms, along with the determination to "finish the work we are in." But there follows the religious reservation, the recognition that ultimate judgment belongs to God alone, the refusal, even in this extreme instance, to presume an absolute identification between his own cause and God's will.

A second theological foundation for political humility is the voluntary character of Christian obedience. Souder might well take more seriously the insights of his Anabaptist tradition in this regard. The instrumentalities of law and government, after all, are fundamentally limited in their ability to compel the good will and "clean heart" from which morality springs. Who are we to think that we can compel something that Christians regard as a gift of God? The scriptures portray the temptation of Christ to worldly dominion as the work of Satan. Instead, Christ took his place among the poor and humble and taught by inspiration and example. Nowhere in that teaching do we find the slightest hint of using political instrumentalities to compel religious faithfulness or obedience.

These then are the ultimate reasons for rejecting the political pretensions of those who would claim divine sanction for their own political program. Not only does that kind of religious arrogance violate the tenets of American pluralism and American democracy: It also violates the deepest insights of our religious traditions themselves. There are compelling reasons, rooted in the theology of divine transcendence, human freedom and responsibility, and the pervasiveness of sin and pride, for refusing to identify any particular ideology or political agenda with the will of God and for rebuking those who presume to do so. "For my thoughts are not your thoughts, neither are your ways my ways, says the Lord" (Isaiah 55:8).

Notes

1. Madison, *The Federalist,* no. 51. See the discussion in David E. Price, *The Congressional Experience,* 2d ed. (Boulder, Colo.: Westview Press, 2000), pp. 215–18.

2. Quoted in William Lee Miller, "Lincoln's Second Inaugural: A Study in Political Ethics" (Bloomington, Ind.: Poynter Center, 1980), p. 8. I am drawing here on Miller's insightful exegesis.

THE PERSONALIZATION OF POLITICS

JEFFREY ROSEN

Mario Cuomo argues that politicians should be free to bring their religious commitments into the public square as long as they try to persuade their fellow citizens with rational moral arguments that all citizens, religious and secular, can understand. The one thing that religiously devout politicians should not do, he says, is appeal to transcendent sources of authority that command obedience because of their divine truth. But Cuomo is missing a broader and unsettling truth about the role of religion in politics today. At the beginning of the twenty-first century, the progressive majority of Americans, which includes religious and secular people, is far more likely to vilify or marginalize the religiously orthodox minority than the orthodox are to impose their beliefs on an unwilling nation.

In distinguishing between the orthodox minority and the progressive majority in America, I am borrowing the terminology of James Davidson Hunter.[1] More than a decade ago, in *Culture Wars,* Hunter wrote of the battles over abortion, homosexuality, and religion that were being waged between the orthodox, who define morality as adherence to external and transcendent sources of traditional authority, and the progressives, who define morality in the spirit of rationalism, subjectivism, and individual choice. Both camps include religious and secular people; but the progressives increasingly have gained the upper hand. As the expansion of higher education and gender equality made Americans increasingly libertarian in the postwar era, conservatives as well as liberals began to embrace what the sociologist Alan Wolfe calls an ethos of "moral freedom," based on the laissez-faire belief that individuals should decide for themselves what it means to lead a good life.[2] In a world of moral freedom, where the only sin is to judge the choices of others, the vocabulary of progressivism is the only one in which religious politicians can address their fellow citizens in moral terms that the majority can accept.

Cuomo celebrates this constraint instead of exploring the ways that it forces the religiously devout to treat their faith as just another aspect of identity politics, like a disability or a history of overcoming alcoholism. Religion has to be presented as a lifestyle choice rather than a commitment to God's will, in order to be democratically intelligible. We saw the apotheosis of this in the presidential campaign of 2000. George W. Bush set the tone by declaring that his favorite political philosopher was "Christ, because he changed my heart." Not to be outdone, Al Gore boasted that he decided important questions using the religious shorthand WWJD for a saying, he explained, "that's popular now in my faith: What would Jesus do?" Both Bush and Gore were offering their faith as a signal of their personal authenticity rather than their public policy commitments. It was something to be confessed rather than aspired to or imposed.

One danger of the rampant subjectivism of progressive rhetoric is that it cannot be debated. When Bush says that Christ changed his heart, he is not inviting follow-up questions from Buddhists or Hindus; he is asking to be accepted for who he is rather than for the policies he proposes to enact. No personal confession in our therapeutic culture is open for debate. But in an era when all politics is identity politics, it would seem like discrimination—the only unforgivable sin in a multicultural age—to prevent politicians from brandishing the religious aspects of their identity in the same ways that they brandish their race or sex or history of personal adversity. Because religious progressives are seeking to establish forms of personal connection with their fellow citizens rather than challenging them to live up to higher ideals, the personalization of religion represents a distracting sideshow in public life instead of illuminating the complicated policy choices we face.

Nevertheless, the personalization of religion threatens the religiously orthodox far more than it threatens secularists. What are politicians to do if they believe in good faith that the Bible condemns abortion or homosexuality as a violation of God's will? They might, as Cuomo suggests, try to recast their beliefs in terms of rational appeals to abstract ideas of natural law. But this would be a misrepresentation of those beliefs, a form of pandering to the individualistic ethos of American democracy rather than a candid acknowledgment of deeply held principles. The most successful religiously orthodox politicians, such as Attorney General John Ashcroft, are able to separate their religious commitments from their public duties: Ashcroft has enforced laws that he disagrees with (such as those mandating access to abortion clinics) because he believes that his oath of office requires no less. But Ashcroft, because of his Pentecostal upbringing, has been subject to vilification by secularists that no progressive religious politician has ever had to endure: Leading presidential candidates, for example, have called him a racist and a bigot, even though his leadership, as senator and attorney general, in opposing racial profiling has been one of his most prominent achievements.

Progressives feel at liberty to denigrate and vilify the religiously orthodox because a commitment to moral freedom is the only nonnegotiable commitment in an individualistic age. These progressives do not merely want to prevent the orthodox from making their case in the public square; they are also uncomfortable with the very fact that the orthodox exist. They are unable to conceive of the fact that many religiously orthodox politicians have no trouble separating their personal moral beliefs from their public positions and, indeed, are forced to do so by an individualistic majority that refuses to accept the legitimacy of their moral universe. This leaves orthodox politicians in an uncomfortable spot, and Cuomo's suggestion that they reinvent themselves as progressives is not exactly helpful.

It is now obvious that the party of orthodoxy, both religious and secular, has decisively lost the culture wars that inflamed America in the 1980s and 1990s. The orthodox sought to resurrect school prayer, to ban abortion, and to discourage homosexuality on moral grounds. They lost all of these battles because their position clashed with the ethos of individual choice and moral freedom that a majority of the country has adopted. Although many orthodox conservatives acknowledge their defeat in the culture wars—as Paul Weyrich did after the Clinton impeachment in 1998—many progressive liberals refuse to acknowledge their victory. They persist in claiming, apocalyptically, that the Supreme Court is one vote away from overturning *Roe* v. *Wade* (in fact, it is two votes); or that moralistic religious conservatives are rampant in the Bush administration (in fact, Bush has kept them at bay).

The result of all this alarmism is to distort the debate about the appropriate role of religion in public life. There is little danger that a religious minority will impose its orthodox beliefs on an unwilling secular majority, because we live in a society ruled by public opinion: The will of the majority is the ultimate authority. The greater danger is that all politicians, religious and secular, orthodox and progressive, will be forced to address the public in therapeutic and individualistic terms, which will contribute little to our understanding of the public policies these politicians are likely to enact. In short, the personalization of politics is the problem, of which the personalization of religion is a symptom, not a cause.

Notes

1. James Davison Hunter, *Culture Wars: The Struggle to Define America* (Basic Books, 1991).

2. Alan Wolfe, *Moral Freedom: The Search for Virtue in a World of Choice* (Norton, 2001).

THE ROLE OF RELIGION
IN ELECTORAL POLITICS

CHERYL J. SANDERS

Notwithstanding the very different positions taken by Mario Cuomo and Mark Souder with respect to the role of religion in politics, I experienced the October 2002 conference—from which this volume springs—as a congenial exchange of ideas rather than an argumentative debate.

Mario Cuomo's anecdotal, analytical approach, grounded in a penchant for natural law, lifts up the dual principles of individuality and community: "We need to love one another, to come together to create a good society, and to use that mutuality discretely in order to gain the benefits of community without sacrificing individual freedom and responsibility." Mark Souder, speaking from the vantage point of a dissenting conservative Christian, acknowledges two problems that have to be worked through, namely, the peaceful resolution of moral disputes and the protection of the rights of the religious sector, including personal beliefs and the rights of churches. These two views are not incompatible; indeed, love would require the peaceful resolution of moral disputes, and religious rights ought not be sacrificed in the pursuit of the good society.

Emergent from the conversation, however, are divergent views of religious responsibility. Cuomo's sense of religious responsibility finds validation in the ethical humanism that resonates for him among Catholics, Protestants, Jews, and others. On the other hand, religious responsibility for Souder signifies the moral agency of religious people, especially those identified as fundamentalists of various faiths, in keeping with his high regard for religious diversity and dissent: "A significant percentage of this country is Evangelical, charismatic, fundamentalist, or conservative Catholic, or conservative Lutheran, or Orthodox Jewish, or fundamentalist Muslim, and these people hold passionate views, views that are essential to their very being. These believers will not—and it is unfair to ask them to—check those beliefs at the public door. It is not going to happen."

In the course of his defense of the rights of religious conservatives giving moral voice in the public sphere, Souder mentions a number of issues in which these moral views come to prominence, such as homosexual marriage, pornography, abortion, and gambling. Same-sex marriage is the one issue from his list that will likely be raised in the upcoming presidential elections, drawing attention to the question of how faith informs one's understanding of public policy.

Let me say from the outset that as I reflect upon the debate I resonate with Cuomo's politics and with Souder's religion. Cuomo's notion of ethical humanism appeals to me as an ethicist teaching in a university-related divinity school because of its focus on the implementation of love and justice in community. Although this ethical humanism is rooted in a variety of religious traditions by way of natural law, it finds strength in its application to politics and in its articulation in the public sphere as humanism rather than theism. I am pastor of an urban congregation in Washington and an ordained minister of the Church of God, a holiness church with agency offices in Anderson, Indiana. Firmly entrenched in the distinctive dissenting posture of a people self-identified as in the world but not of it, I approve of Souder's refusal to either "check" his Christian beliefs at the "public door" or to "expel the Holy Spirit" from his life as a congressman, however far removed I may be from his conservative partisan politics.

According to a recent Pew Forum report, "Religious Beliefs Underpin Opposition to Homosexuality," survey data show that Democratic candidates for the presidency appear more likely to support same-sex marriages or civil unions than President George W. Bush and other Republican leaders, and opposition to these initiatives is much higher among Republican voters than Democratic voters.[1] The data also indicate that Evangelical Christians are especially likely to reject same-sex marriage for religious reasons. Thus this issue has potential as a wedge issue for voters in the 2004 election.

To be more specific, the issue may motivate voters to make a political decision based upon religious grounds, that is, to vote for a particular candidate based on whether he or she holds positions deemed to be consistent with religious teachings. Persons of faith who object to same-sex unions are most likely to base their position on personal or denominational interpretations of biblical texts condemning homosexual relations. To the extent that their point of view is grounded in biblical faith, they are unlikely to be amenable to political appeals to justice and fairness as criteria for supporting the public normalization of same-sex unions. Faith may trump politics and philosophy in this public policy debate but not to the extent that this one issue becomes the sole measure of any one candidate's suitability for public office. I cannot imagine that many voters will base their final decision solely or primarily upon a particular candidate's view of same-sex unions, whether they are otherwise impressed or unmoved by that individual's expressions of religious faith.

What might be instructive for people of faith participating in the debate over same-sex marriage is to observe the broader perspective put forth by the prophet Ezekiel when commenting upon the sin of Sodom in comparison with the sins of Jerusalem: "This was the guilt of your sister Sodom: she and her daughters had pride, excess of food, and prosperous ease, but did not aid the poor and needy" (Ezekiel 16:49).

As significant as the matter of legalizing same-sex unions may be, from a biblical perspective it would seem undesirable for a nation to be preoccupied with such matters in a presidential election to the exclusion of weightier matters, such as disparities in wealth and income and the need for a coherent and comprehensive public policy response to poverty. While I affirm along with Mark Souder the right to vote my conscience with respect to social issues and political candidates, I maintain as my deeper conviction Mario Cuomo's reconciling vision of a people coming together in genuine mutuality to create a good society for the benefit of all, regardless of sexual orientation or income.

Note

1. Pew Forum on Religion and Public Life, "Religious Beliefs Underpin Opposition to Homosexuality" (//pewforum.org/docs/index.php?DocID=37).

MOBILIZING
POLITICAL PARTICIPATION

JULIE A. SEGAL

Religious people turn out to vote more than nonreligious people.[1] Despite the much-publicized appearance that this is a liberal-versus-conservative phenomenon, all practicing religious people, regardless of their political beliefs, tend to participate more in their government and society than non-adherents. Even a brief discussion of one of the necessary ingredients for sustainable civic engagement illuminates the connection between religious participation and political participation. Any examination of the appropriate role of religion in the electoral process, therefore, must occur in the context of religion and civic participation generally.

Mario Cuomo recognizes the source of civic participation in the origin of society and government. Just as John Adams described the need for government, Cuomo describes politics in terms of "individuality and community."[2] Cuomo contends that community encompasses a coming together of people through government "to do for one another collectively what they could not do as well or at all individually." Individuality, according to Cuomo, is contrasted with community but nevertheless still includes personal responsibility.

Religion comes into play, Cuomo asserts, by creating the "need to love one another, to come together to create a good society and . . . gain the benefits of community without sacrificing individual freedom and responsibility." Cuomo's communitarian view of religion and the resulting impact on civic engagement is consistent with decades of research of citizen participation, voting trends, and the proposition that religious people are more involved in both civic and political activities. People who define themselves as religious—especially those who are religiously active—are more likely to volunteer, join community associations, and socialize and entertain friends in their home. They are also more likely to join political clubs and vote in presidential and local elections than nonreligious citizens.[3]

Even when broken down by denomination, the fact remains true. According to Robert Wuthnow, the director of the Princeton University Center for the Study of American Religion, "to the extent that one would expect this mobilization to be more characteristic of evangelicals than of mainline Protestants, it does not appear to be particularly profound."[4] Further, while much research focuses on Christian denominations, the considerable evidence of the civic participation of religious people generally points to the same conclusion for other faith groups. The key appears to be actual participation rather than simply membership in a religious organization; nor does it appear to be the denomination or fundamentalism of the religion involved.[5]

Religious participation connects strongly to political participation for reasons that are varied and likely include indefinable factors of faith. Even with the debate over the appropriateness of religious beliefs motivating public policy positions, there is little doubt that a correlation exists. Apart from the possible religious motivators, however, there is a valuable lesson about civic engagement in the relationship between involvement in a house of worship and involvement in the political process. This lesson—that there are elements of religious participation that lead to increased political participation—should be emulated but has been obscured by media and scholars' attention to the rise of groups like the Christian Coalition and the link between partisan alignment and election outcome.

The formula is simple. In order to participate in the political process, citizens need as a foundation three characteristics: to care about something, to have the confidence to take action, and to have the skills to know how. According to the Harvard professor Robert Putnam, "religiously active men and women learn to give speeches, run meetings, manage disagreements, and bear administrative responsibility."[6] This civic experience leads naturally to political participation skills. Learning how to attract others to attend meetings is community organizing. Creating and working together on committees is useful for building coalitions. Writing letters to the local newspaper teaches the impact of utilizing the media. These activities, combined with specialized training in meeting with elected officials and working with the media, give citizens the necessary encouragement and political participation skills to take action on public policies and, of course, to vote. As long as the activity remains nonpartisan, participation in religious organizations is "beneficial to the functioning of American democracy because it generates civic skills."[7]

These benefits need not be limited to participation in houses of worship. Historically, participation in labor unions yielded the same results. Diminished participation in unions and lower attendance at meetings, however, has hindered labor's ability to mobilize political action to the same degree.[8]

Even large corporations have emulated the religious organization method. They have recognized the natural constituency made up by their employees to serve as a voice on political issues in the corporate interest and have committed resources to outreach and advocacy training of their staff.

For nonprofit, issue-based organizations the lesson should be clear. As with religious groups, other nonprofit organizations can give their members the confidence and the skills to take action. If citizens care enough about an issue—such as the environment, civil rights, or the separation of church and state—to pay a membership fee to support the mission of the organization, the organization should build the political capacity of its membership. With a focus on the process rather than on partisanship, they could build a sustainable sense of community, teach people how to participate in the political process, and spawn the sense of power citizens develop when they become active participants in their civic life. This in turn would mobilize all citizens, in addition to religious individuals, to take action on political issues.

The appropriateness of building civic skills among citizens, however, does not extend to political activity by religious organizations and institutions themselves. Political participation among churchgoers should not be replicated by the church. Houses of worship, as institutions, should remain neutral about partisan politics, and involvement in electoral activity is different from involvement in issues of public policy. Religious organizations have always taken stands on social and political issues—the civil rights movement led by Martin Luther King Jr. and other clergy stands out as the most obvious example. People of faith who stimulate a movement or debate over issues, however, are different from houses of worship that turn themselves into dens of political vote gathering, as well as from partisan political organizations that cloak themselves in religion to claim the moral high ground.

Religious institutions, like all not-for-profit organizations, are prohibited by federal tax law from partisan political activity such as supporting or opposing a candidate for public office, distributing campaign fliers, or endorsing candidates from the pulpit. There are, however, ample opportunities for houses of worship to participate legally in the political process. They are allowed to register voters, arrange to transport people to the polls, encourage voting as a civic duty, and invite all candidates to a "meet the candidates" night. Churches and other houses of worship can even take stands on ballot referendums.[9]

The United States is a pluralistic democracy and, as Alexis de Tocqueville noted, one of America's unique attributes is that organized religion remains apart from politics.[10] The U.S. Constitution guarantees religious freedom and a democracy with liberties we should all hold dear. Yet the separation of church and state is one of the most maligned and least understood concepts in today's political discourse. Many people forget that church-state separation is a two-way street: protecting government from the improper influence of religion and, at the same time, defending religion against the intrusive control of government.

Mark Souder, however, appears more comfortable with a closer link between religious organizations and politics. One of his opinions is that the First Amendment merely prohibits the establishment of a state-sponsored church and that any contrary view of the separation of church and state is a fabrication. According to Souder, some religious liberty complaints move from "extrapolations from [certain] practices to accusations of government-sponsored religion [that] are downright ridiculous, particularly when these accusations are anchored in the so-called wall-of-separation argument."

Unfortunately, these views are also often implied in presidential campaigns and congressional debates as well. During the last presidential election cycle, the Democratic vice presidential candidate Joseph Lieberman said that Americans "need to reaffirm our faith and renew the dedication of our nation and ourselves to God."[11] Similarly, on the Republican side of the 2000 election, presidential candidate George W. Bush said that, in his opinion, Jesus Christ was history's most important philosopher-thinker because Christ changed his heart. When asked to explain how Christ changed his heart, Bush replied, "Well, if [people] don't know, it's going to be hard to explain. When you turn your heart and your life over to Christ, when you accept Christ as the savior, it changes your heart. It changes your life."[12]

What effect does the magnitude of religious talk among politicians have on a pluralistic society? How much is religion damaged by its association with political wrangling? How much will the 2004 presidential candidates use religion as a talking point and a sound bite? How many people will decide that both Democrats and Republicans are pandering to religious conservatives? How many people decided in 2000 to vote for Ralph Nader as a result of religious alienation? How many people decided as a result not to vote at all?

Maintaining our pluralistic democracy requires space for believers, regardless of their belief, and nonbelievers to participate equally in the political process. The natural and proper relationship between religion and politics must not be exploited for partisan aim. The risk to both religious autonomy and civic engagement is too serious and enduring. We can hope that the lessons of past elections and unsustained attempts to mobilize citizen participation will be learned soon.

Notes

1. "Social Capital Community Benchmark Survey," Kennedy School of Government, Harvard University (March 1, 2001).

2. Preamble of the Constitution of the Commonwealth of Massachusetts, 1780.

3. Robert D. Putnam, *Bowling Alone: The Collapse and Revival of American Community* (Simon and Schuster 2000), p. 67.

4. Robert Wuthnow, "Mobilizing Civic Engagement: The Changing Impact of Religious Involvement," in Theda Skocpol and Morris P. Fiorina, eds., *Civic Engagement in American Democracy* (Brookings, 1999), p. 354.

5. See "Social Capital Community Benchmark Survey."

6. Putnam, *Bowling Alone*, p. 66.

7. Wuthnow, "Mobilizing Civic Engagement," p. 346.

8. Kay Lehman Schlozman, Sidney Verba, and Henry E. Brady, "Civic Participation and the Equality Problem," in Theda Skocpol and Morris P. Fiorina, eds., *Civic Engagement in American Democracy* (Brookings, 1999), pp. 455–56.

9. Internal Revenue Service, *Tax Guide for Churches and Religious Organizations*, publication 1828 (rev. 9-2003).

10. Alexis de Tocqueville, *Democracy in America*, vol. 2, pt. 1 (1835).

11. Joseph Lieberman, speech to the Fellowship Chapel, Detroit, August 27, 2000.

12. George Bush, Iowa Republican primary candidate debate, December 13, 1999.

RELIGIONS AND THE
AMERICAN RELIGION

JAMES W. SKILLEN

The intriguing discussion of religion and politics between Mario Cuomo and Mark Souder opens the way to further questioning. The most important question, it seems to me, is not whether candidates may or should voice *personal* religious convictions in the course of political campaigning but rather whether they are able and willing to articulate their *politically* religious convictions. Let me explain.

In the course of campaigning, candidates invariably say things that may not be directly related to the responsibility of filling the public office they seek. Proud comments about spouse or children, about past military or business service, or about their interest in the arts, sciences, or sports—all of these are expressed to reveal their personality, their identification with particular groups, or their talents and capabilities. In the same way and for the same reason some candidates choose to reveal something about their religious affiliations as an indirect reason for voters to support them.

What is most important for voters to know, however, are the religious convictions of candidates that directly undergird or define politics from their point of view. If a candidate really believes that America is God's specially chosen nation, then the candidate should tell us that and be asked to explain how his or her policy stances on (for example) defense, taxes, the environment, and the Israel-Palestine issue flow from that conviction. If a candidate believes that the Republic has no relation to God whatever, then he or she should be asked to explain the source of that conviction and its implications for policy conclusions.

When Mario Cuomo comments that his Catholic faith commits him to certain dogmas but that as governor of New York he felt constrained to act in ways that guaranteed to others the same religious freedom he enjoyed, he is ambiguous and somewhat obfuscating in this *politically* religious comment. Consider, for example, his statement that all citizens should be "free to act according to their own religious beliefs, even when those acts conflict with Roman Catholic dogma, such as divorce, birth control, abortion, stem cell research, and even arguing against the existence of God." The ambiguity here is that the Catholic Church holds abortion and embryo destruction to be more than merely personal religious beliefs. They are, from a Catholic point of view, actions that *governments* ought not to permit.

Cuomo could say that on the basis of his Catholic faith he was committed to doing everything possible as an officeholder to try to bring an end to abortion and embryo destruction. That would be compatible with his Catholic faith. Moreover, he could at the same time say that if abortion and embryo destruction were the law of the land, despite his public opposition to them, he would have upheld the law, as would be his obligation as New York's chief executive.

That stance would also be compatible with Catholic recognition of the legitimacy of democratic government. Instead, what Cuomo actually does, in my view, is to use the language of religious freedom as a generalized cover for privatizing certain Catholic public commitments and thereby making room for his own public support of abortion. Something deeper than Catholic faith and commitment to religious freedom is operative here—in a politically religious way. Cuomo explains some of that with an interpretation of natural law, which for him clearly trumps Catholic social teaching in politics and government.

Mark Souder is ambiguous in a similar way. He is explicit about his fundamentalist Christian convictions, articulating his faith in the saving and judging work of Jesus Christ. He is also forthright in saying that a Christian worldview is different from a natural law worldview. Nevertheless, his religious declarations do not have a direct bearing on his political views. He insists that conservative Christians "as individuals do not separate their lives into a private sphere and a public sphere," yet the phrase "as individuals" already locates the supposed unity of private and public in the individual, not in the public order. His view of government and the Constitution is, in fact, very close to Cuomo's, which is the view held by President John Adams (and other Founders) that this country was made for a moral and religious people. But whereas for Cuomo public respect for the dignity of each person should mean allowing women to choose abortion, Souder is convinced that the moral and religious people who make up America should protect the life of the unborn with the same public laws that protect any other citizen's life. Souder no more than Cuomo, however, shows how his religious convictions about human dignity, morality, and religion lead to his particular policy conclusion.

If we judge only from the comments made herein by these two elected officials, we would conclude that personal religious convictions articulated by candidates may, indirectly, tell us something about them, just as their statements about family, work, and other interests tell us something about them. But most talk about religion does not reveal much that is relevant in a politically religious way. This is why Ron Sider's comment about Cuomo's two principles—righteousness and repairing the world—(Sider claims that they do not work "at all") seems relevant here. Contrary to Sider, I would say that the two principles do work for Cuomo—but only and precisely because they are unobjectionable moral generalizations and not politically significant guides to action. Cuomo and Souder both express strong convictions, whether moral or religious, but we do not learn how their policy conclusions flow from these convictions.

Now one might say that, in a quintessentially American way, this is precisely as it should be. Candidates should be free to tell us about their private faith, as they tell us about their other nongovernment experiences, personal talents, and interests. But the real reasons for their political stances should be uncovered or discovered by looking carefully at their actions in government, their party affiliations, the demands of their voting constituents, and the aims of the interest groups that contribute to their campaigns.

It seems to me, however, that in this day Americans need more, not less, politically religious articulation from candidates. When Cuomo responds to Margaret Steinfels by saying that government ought to respect the consciences of medical practitioners by making room for Catholics not to perform abortions or distribute contraceptive devices, he says that her question is really about accommodating religious liberty. But is there anything more to be said about this? Does the governor believe that government support of medical care should be grounded in respect for the *independent* responsibilities of hospitals? And if there is room for conscience and associational diversity in at least one aspect of medical care, should there not also be equal treatment for conscience and associational diversity in publicly supported social service organizations and schools? The latter questions arise from Catholic social teaching about "subsidiarity," which implies a way of thinking about government recognition of, and relation to, God-given responsibilities that do not originate with government. It is about much more than just accommodating religious liberty. Does Cuomo rely on Catholic tradition in this respect? If so, what might be the policy implications of such reliance? If not, why not?

Closely related to this is the good question from Robert Edgar about what he believes is the obvious injustice of growing economic inequality in the

United States and tax breaks for the wealthy. Why is this obviously unjust? And what does it have to do with religion? I would like the hear Edgar (and public officials who share his convictions) dig deeper into his professed biblical tradition to show how it leads to this particular economic judgment. What distinguishes his religious conviction from the equally fundamental conviction of a social egalitarian or a communist in this regard? The principle of economic justice goes back at least as far as God's laws for Israel about Sabbath-year land redistribution to ensure that no family was left without access to the means of production or left permanently in poverty. This is highly relevant, politically religious speech, and it is urgently needed (even though many Americans might think that such talk should be kept out of public discussion because it seems religiously imposing). Similarly, I would like to hear Souder explain how his belief in individual responsibility and his views of government's taxing responsibilities arise from Christian teaching about government and social responsibility and how his views are different from those of a non-Christian economic conservative or libertarian.

I daresay that Jimmy Carter's piety and Sunday School teaching did not bother Democratic moderates and liberals as much as Souder's fundamentalist piety and talk about Jesus Christ's lordship. But the reason for this, I think, is not so much the piety but the different political stances and ideologies of the two men. And this again raises the question of whether a candidate's private religious convictions have any relevance at all to political discourse and action. Why could Cuomo appeal without hesitancy to two Jewish principles of faith (*tzedakkah* and *tikkun olam)* without seeming to impose religion illegitimately on politics? Because what he does with the principles is to disconnect them from any particular faith and turn them into moral generalities that supposedly satisfy everyone and leave open the political conclusions. Cuomo is then free to be the kind of Democrat he wants to be, just as Souder, doing what he does with his Christian confession, is free to be the kind of Republican he wants to be.

None of this seems particularly helpful as a way of illuminating politics by means of religious talk. The press and the people had best just ignore the chatter and look to policy stances, funding sources, and public opinion to learn what candidates really believe about politics. Yet if this is all that voters and the media do, it will leave many of us wondering why the candidates—who all love America, believe in its Constitution, and support religious freedom, human dignity, and repairing the world—seem to come out at such different points on so many policy issues.

My hunch about the conundrum here is that the typical questions about faith and politics are misdirected. Asking about the private faiths of candidates does not yield much. Instead, we should go in a different direction and look for the source of many important political differences in the growing crisis of the American *civil* religion, which dominates all other religions in public life. This religion—the glue of the Republic for almost two hundred years—is now in trouble because its nineteenth-century tenets no longer grip a large majority of Americans.

This country's increasingly diverse society, culturally speaking, can live comfortably enough with religious diversity in private. What Americans do not yet accept or know how to establish, however, is religious diversity in public—in politics and in government—because the old-time civil religion demands an America whole and undivided. Consequently, the real political fights and culture wars are not over differences among private faiths but over the principles of political faith that should define the American way of life as a whole. The contest over the right to define those principles is the contest for majority control of Congress, the White House, and the courts—and the winner takes all. Those who disagree with the majority will still have every right to hold their private convictions and to worship and protest in private, but they will not have authority to exert any public control.

What would be most helpful, then, in political campaigns and media analysis is a probing examination of where candidates stand with respect to the American civil religion, which would require dealing with the really serious and truly relevant questions of political religion.

RELIGIOUS LIBERTY
AND THE AMERICAN FOUNDING

MATTHEW SPALDING

The story of religious liberty in America begins with religious persecution in the Old World. At root, of course, is the much deeper controversy of divided loyalty between the City of God and the City of Man—what philosophers call the theological-political problem. The dueling claims—revelation and reason—undermined political authority and obligation and led to religious battles and the civil coercion of faith.

The basic parameters of the American Founders' arrangement in the New World are well known: They addressed the problem—and sought to prevent the resulting religious battles that had bloodied the European continent—by removing entirely the authority of the church from the authority of the government. Instead, they sought to secure the basis for political obligation in the consent of the governed, premised on individual freedom and equality, grounded in the doctrine of natural rights. Religious liberty was secured by the limited nature of the social contract.

George Washington in a letter of 1790—all the more powerful because it is written by the first president to a Jewish synagogue—declares that "the Government of the United States . . . gives to bigotry no sanction, to persecution no assistance" but "requires only that they who live under its protection should demean themselves as good citizens."[1] Toleration, he continues, is no longer "spoken of as if it were the indulgence of one class of people that another enjoyed the exercise of their inherent natural rights."

How are we to understand the Founders' argument? One line of interpretation is that an emphasis on equal rights sets aside the claims of religious faith in favor of unaided reason and individual choice. There are fundamental principles common to all religions, as Mario Cuomo points out, but the principle of individual rights—and the government's responsibility to uphold those rights—trumps religious truth claims. This is essentially the position of the United States Supreme Court. In 1944 the Court (in *United States* v. *Ballard*) decided that it would not question the sincerity and reasonableness of any claims of religious belief; the religious views espoused by individual respondents "might seem incredible, if not preposterous, to most people," but the Court cannot be responsible for "finding their truth or falsity" without questioning the beliefs of every other religious sect. As Cuomo states it, the definition of religion—and thus the grounds for any public consensus about the role of religion—must be expanded beyond traditional, organized religions to include all belief systems, including those such as secular humanism that reject religious and moral precepts in favor of ethical relativism. As such, for the sake of individual autonomy, government must be wholly secular and neutral not just between religious sects but also toward religion generally.

Another line of interpretation seems to be represented by Mark Souder. Although the American Founders separated church and state, the "so-called wall-of-separation argument" expounded by the modern Supreme Court has gone too far in forcing the removal of religion from the public square, leaving a secular state to replace the church as the primary moral agent of society. But in this case it is the solution, not the problem, that is unclear. There is no "common denominator" between reason and revelation, forcing religious liberty to rely on one or the other for its justification and defense. Indeed, Souder writes, "The notion of a natural law common to all religions is in fact a worldview and a moral view that is different from a Christian worldview and moral view." This argument seems to reject the rational or natural rights grounding of religious liberty in favor of a sectarian view of politics. Or at least a politics seen through an exclusively sectarian lens.

Neither of these interpretations, in my opinion, fully grasps the Founders' understanding of religious liberty. Taking a broader view of their intentions tells a different story and suggests a different policy for today's politics.

Far from turning to the rights argument in order to remove religion from public life, the Founders saw religion as a necessary and vital element of their experiment in republican government. They sought the official separation of church and state in order to establish civil and religious liberty, but they never intended—indeed, roundly rejected the idea of—separating religion and politics. There would be no formal established or state-sponsored national church (though the federal government would not do away with state establishments), and church doctrine would not determine the laws (or laws determine church doctrine), but they favored government encouragement and support of religion in public laws, official speeches and ceremonies, on public property and in public buildings, and even in public schools.

Despite their strong nonsectarianism, the American Founders did not believe for a moment—concerned as they were about the moral character of citizens—that government should be neutral toward religion generally. "And can the liberties of a nation be thought secure when we have removed their only firm basis, a conviction in the minds of the people that these liberties are a gift of God?" Thomas Jefferson asks in his *Notes on the State of Virginia*.[2]

Indeed, the separation of church and state allows and encourages (just as true religious freedom depends upon) a certain mixing of religion and politics on the level of political action. As when the day after it approved the Bill of Rights Congress calls upon the president to "recommend to the people of the United States a day of public thanksgiving and prayer, to be observed by acknowledging, with grateful hearts, the many signal favors of Almighty God." (President Washington responds by noting that "it is the duty of all nations to acknowledge the providence of Almighty God, to obey his will, to be grateful for his benefits, and humbly implore his protection and favor.")[3]

Even after the "republican revolution" of 1800, Thomas Jefferson praises America's "benign religion, professed, indeed, and practiced in various forms, yet all of them inculcating honesty, truth, temperance, gratitude, and the love of man; acknowledging and adoring an overruling Providence, which by all its dispensations proves that it delights in the happiness of man here and his greater happiness hereafter."[4] President Jefferson (whose famous "wall of separation" letter was written to explain his refusal to proclaim days of prayer and thanksgiving) regularly attended church services held in the House of Representatives and allowed executive branch buildings to be used for the same purpose. Jefferson, for one, seemed to think there was nothing wrong with the federal government supporting religion in a nondiscriminatory and noncoercive way.

The reason the Founders supported the blending of religion and politics is the following syllogism: Morality is necessary for republican government; religion is necessary for morality; therefore religion is necessary for republican government. "Of all the dispositions and habits which lead to political prosperity," Washington writes in his Farewell Address, "religion and morality are indispensable supports. In vain would that man claim the tribute of Patriotism who should labor to subvert these great Pillars of human happiness—these firmest props of the duties of Men and citizens."[5]

Think about those two sentences. Religion and morality are the props of duty, the indispensable supports of the dispositions and habits that lead to political prosperity and the great pillars of human happiness. They aid good government by teaching men their moral obligations and creating the conditions for decent politics. And while there might be particular cases in which morality does not depend on religion, Washington argues, this is not the case for the morality of the nation: "And let us with caution indulge the supposition, that morality can be maintained without religion."

In the end, while it is often thought that the separation of church and state marks the divorce of religion and politics in America, and that they must be discussed as if they are radically separate spheres, the Founders' conception of religious liberty is almost exactly the opposite. It actually requires the moralization of politics, which includes—and requires—the expansion and endorsement of religion's influence in our politics. It also means allowing, within the context of religious liberty, for legitimate moral decisions by duly constituted political majorities.

At the same time, religious liberty does depend on principles, standards, and morals common to all religions. By acknowledging the realm where reason and faith agree and can cooperate about morality and politics, religious liberty unites civic morality and the moral teachings of religion, thereby establishing common standards of morality required in republican government to guide private and public life. By recognizing the need for morality, and the prominent role that religion plays in nurturing morality, the Founders invite churches to cooperate at the political level in sustaining the moral consensus underlying their theological differences. It is by separating sectarian conflict from the political process and then strengthening this moral consensus that religious liberty makes self-government possible.

The stability of the volatile combination of politics and religion depends on there being more areas of agreement than disagreements, to say the least. Individuals can worship freely according to the dictates of their consciences, but there is a common understanding of morality underlying their religious differences. America does not depend on a shared theology, but it does depend on a shared morality. The First Inaugural of the first president— written with the assistance of James Madison—says that "there exists in the economy and course of nature, an indissoluble union between virtue and happiness" and that no nation can prosper that "disregards the external rules of order and right, which Heaven itself has ordained."[6] Jefferson puts it more succinctly: The people, who are the source of all lawful authority, "are inherently independent of all but the moral law."[7]

What the separation of church and state does, then, is free religion—in the form of morality and the moral teachings of religion—to exercise an unprecedented influence over private and public opinion by shaping mores, cultivating virtues, and in general providing an independent source of moral reasoning and authority. Even though religion "never intervenes directly in the government of American society," as Tocqueville observes, it directs the mores and is "the first of their political institutions."[8] The result is that in America, throughout its history, religion has flourished—and so has liberty.

Today it is increasingly evident that there is a close connection between America's deepest social ills—divorce and fatherlessness, illegitimacy and abortion, drugs and suicide—and the weakening of religious participation and the abandonment of traditional moral norms taught by religion. Rebuilding a postwelfare state society demands the return of religion and faith-based institutions to their central role in our nation's civic and public life. But we must abandon the interpretation, maintained by the Supreme Court, that religion is in conflict with freedom and that any "endorsement" of religion creates an unconstitutional religious establishment—thus preventing government from advancing or endorsing religion generally. At the same time we must not look to sectarian politics as the way to restore and strengthen our religious heritage. A better course is to return to the more reasonable, historically accurate, and faith-friendly view of religious liberty that upholds religion and morality as indispensable supports of good habits, the firmest props of the duties of citizens, and the great pillars of human happiness.

Notes

1. "Letter to the Hebrew Congregation in Newport, R.I., August 1790," in *George Washington: Writings* (New York: Library of America, 1997), pp. 766–67.

2. "Notes on the State of Virginia, Query XVIII," in *Thomas Jefferson: Writings* (New York: Library of America, 1984), p. 289.

3. "Thanksgiving Proclamation, October 3, 1789," in *Washington: A Collection* (Indianapolis: Liberty Classics, 1988), p. 534.

4. "Inaugural Address, March 4, 1801," in *Thomas Jefferson: Writings*, p. 494.

5. "Farewell Address, September 19, 1796," in *George Washington: Writings*, p. 791.

6. "Inaugural Address, April 30, 1789," in *George Washington: Writings*, p. 733.

7. "Letter to Judge Spencer Roane, September 6, 1819," in *Thomas Jefferson: Writings*, p. 1426.

8. Alexis de Tocqueville, vol. 1, pt. 2, of *Democracy in America*, ed. J. P. Mayer (Harper Perennial, 1988), p. 292.

THOUGHTS ON RELIGION
AND POLITICS

JEFFREY STOUT

All citizens should feel free to express the ideas that lead them to their political conclusions. The right to do so is protected by the First Amendment's ideal of free speech. When those ideas are religious in content, the First Amendment's provision for the free exercise of religion also kicks in. Many citizens are religiously committed to expressing their religious views in public and to pressing for policies that are consistent with those views. When such citizens speak freely, they are also exercising their religious freedom. The Bill of Rights protects them twice over.

It is imprudent, as well as against the spirit of the First Amendment, to tell such people to shut up or to demand that they filter out the religious content of their thinking before they address the public. As Mark Souder makes clear, religious people are going to rely on religious premises when reasoning about political questions regardless of what the secularists say.

For most religious people, integrity requires that they refuse to "separate their lives into a private sphere and a public sphere." The "wall of separation" between church and state does not run through the heart of believers. So unless these people stop being religious, as seems unlikely, the pundits and philosophers who want political deliberation to be conducted in a completely secularized way are fighting a losing battle. But if that is true, and a large segment of the citizenry is in fact relying on religious premises when making political decisions, it behooves all of us to know what those premises are. Premises left unexpressed are often premises left unchallenged.

Among the great achievements of American history is the abolition of slavery. How did it come about? Not by argument cast in a thoroughly secularized vocabulary. The abolitionists had to persuade American Christians that biblically grounded defenses of slavery were not compelling, despite Saint Paul's advice that slaves should obey their masters and the notion that God had punished blacks as descendants of Ham. The abolitionists did not say to their opponents, Keep your religious views to yourselves. They said, Speak your minds, so that we can test the soundness of your argument and its coherence with the rest of what you have said and done. And then they talked about the exodus from Egyptian slavery and the rights that every child of God has.

A debate is now raging over the issue of same-sex coupling. Like the debate over slavery, it is full of fear, hatred, and paranoid fantasy. It is too early to know how it will turn out, but there is no way to avoid having it. If you look at the debate closely, you will see that it is not a dispute between Christians and non-Christians. Much of the debate is among Christians who are perfectly orthodox in their conception of God and revelation. Some of the same biblical passages that mattered greatly in the debate over slavery, such as Galatians 3:28, are receiving extensive attention again.

These examples should teach us something about how real political discussions work in a religiously diverse democratic republic. Each of us is free to say why we accept the political conclusions we do. We can filter out the religious content of our reasoning or not, as we wish. But when we have expressed an argument, we should expect our interlocutors to pick it apart and to test its fit with other arguments we have made and other proposals we have favored. We do not just express our own views; we criticize one another's views. Sometimes minds change in the process, and we reach a consensus. Sometimes the discussion grinds to a halt, the votes are counted, and we go home determined to press our case a bit differently the next time. Even when consensus is out of reach for the time being, however, we can show each other respect as the particular people we are by hearing each other out and grappling with the arguments that have actually been made.

A free-wheeling exchange of views in the public square can be a dangerous thing. The debate over slavery led to civil war. The debates over same-sex coupling and abortion have inspired some to speak of cultural warfare. Whenever a political proposal appears to threaten an entire way of life to which some people are deeply committed, passions will inevitably flare. At these moments, much depends on the determination of citizens to speak the truth as they see it, to address each other with civility and respect, to avoid manipulation and demagoguery, and to interpret each other's actions and words charitably. Political leaders in particular are obliged to exemplify the virtues of democratic citizenship when they decide what to say and how to say it. Mario Cuomo and Mark Souder have behaved better than many, but the overall record of our political leaders since the mid-1990s has been grim indeed. The House of Representatives, in particular, has become a den of discursive iniquity.

The next generation of aspiring leaders will have to decide whether they want to exploit the culture wars for political advantage or rise above them in a way that helps the people see what they have in common. Research shows that the citizenry is not nearly as divided along cultural lines as many politicians and opinion makers would have us believe. Ideologues on the Right and the Left are dragging the people toward a dualistic struggle that need not and should not take place.

Immediately after September 11 citizens spontaneously identified with one another and expressed their love for the civic nation as a whole; for a time our ethnic, religious, and political differences mattered less than knowing that we share a democratic heritage. But our leaders missed the opportunity to transcend the logic of blue states and red states; they failed to articulate a vision of our common fate or demand sacrifices on an equal basis at the very moment when the people were most prepared to respond favorably to high statesmanship. One party exploited our fear of terrorism to justify a war that had little to do with terrorism, while the other party held its moistened finger in the wind. Meanwhile, the rich have received tax cuts so massive that government's ability to help the old and the poor is jeopardized for the foreseeable future.

Mario Cuomo's appeal to natural law promises to lift us above the disputes among particular religious perspectives by focusing on what everybody knows, whatever their upbringing and subsequent experiences might be. But he makes the task of reaching consensus seem easier than it is. Natural law is just one tradition among others. Even within this tradition, one finds a wide spectrum of views concerning what the content of the natural law is—as the differences between Cuomo and the bishops who used to reprimand him make clear. Mark Souder is right to resist the idea that the principles of individuality and community are the ethical core of all great religious traditions. Individuality, in particular, has long been a sticking point in dialogue across cultural boundaries. Muslim traditionalists, among many others, often deny its legitimacy as a value. Pretending otherwise is wishful thinking.

Still, most Americans, including most Muslim Americans, do see value in both individuality and community. Unless overwhelmed by fear of terrorism, they would resist any redefinition of political community that failed to show respect for individual rights. And they recognize that their welfare as individuals depends on the security, prosperity, and justice of the local, state, and national communities in which they live and work. September 11 could have been an occasion to fortify these commitments and rethink what it means for a democratic people to honor them. But the opportunity is being squandered.

Contemporary conservatism claims to honor both commitments. It does so by combining libertarian hatred of interference with traditionalist longing for community. William F. Buckley Jr. concocted the unstable mixture half a century ago, and Presidents Ronald Reagan and George W. Bush sold it successfully to the electorate as an elixir for everything that ails us. But what do libertarians and traditionalists have in common besides their suspicion of government? Only by repeatedly stigmatizing government— thus undermining the legitimacy of the institutions they wish to administer—can conservatives hold the coalition together. That is why they propose deregulation and tax cuts as solutions to all economic problems, for these are the only measures on which they can agree. But such measures can be pressed only so far without bringing democratic government down and leaving ordinary people defenseless against unconstrained economic power.

The heirs of Barry Goldwater make strange bedfellows with today's religious Right. The incoherence of today's conservatism renders the movement vulnerable to attack. Libertarians and traditionalists are natural enemies. No coherent movement could have both Ayn Rand and Edmund Burke as patron saints. Libertarianism first thrived among those who moved to America or to the western frontier to escape religiously uniform communities. Its motto, directed simultaneously against governments, churches, and communities, was Don't Tread on Me!

To enlist the religious Right, the conservatives have adopted policies that restrict civil liberties while liberating from political oversight giant corporations and the elites responsible for running them. A strange new doctrine of freedom it is that so easily loses sight of individuals in any capacity but that of consumer, manager, or stockholder. We now have government by the corporations and for the corporations but hardly any government of the corporations. The corporations, no less than government agencies, are large-scale bureaucracies wielding massive power. It makes no sense to denounce big government while leaving ourselves unprotected against big business. The collapse of Soviet communism and the failures of state socialism have made us forget about the need for a balance of power between citizens and large corporations outside the sphere of government.

Few people ask what role the increasingly unchecked corporations have played in destroying the communities whose values conservatism lauds. It

197

is easy to see what kind of nostalgia such conservatism expresses, but nobody can say what it succeeds in conserving. It is not the social safety net for the poor and the elderly. It is not the environment. Neither is it the culture of small towns, tightly knit neighborhoods, and family farms.

"Compassionate" conservatism professes love of such things. The adjective seemed necessary only when citizens began to notice the harsh consequences of the programs being enacted. They want reassurance that those proposing the programs are not themselves unfeeling and find such reassurance in the professedly Christian motivations of men like Souder. But the motives of conservative leaders seem increasingly beside the point. The real question is whether conservative policies—by bankrupting government at the local, state, and national levels—are likely to destroy much of what the people wish to conserve and defend.

Why have the opponents of conservatism done so little to exploit the inconsistency and blindness at the heart of the coalition now in power? Is it a lack of political imagination, a lack of courage, a lack of eloquence? All of these factors contribute to the explanation. You will have trouble displacing an incoherent vision without a more attractive one to offer, and this is something that liberals have failed to provide. Cuomo's address to the Democratic National Convention in 1984 lifted many hearts for a moment, but it has not issued in a vision capable of restoring coherence and conviction to progressive political struggle. The liberal coalition was already falling apart, in no small part because it had come to be viewed as the carrier of a secularist ideology rooted in New York and California—an impression mitigated only when apparently sincere children of the Bible Belt like Presidents Jimmy Carter and Bill Clinton served as its standard-bearer.

The truth of the matter is that neither conservatism nor liberalism in their current forms can avoid running negative campaigns. Neither appears to possess a positive vision that is sufficiently coherent and attractive to withstand explicit statement and examination.

Time will tell whether new leaders will arise who can revive the ideal of democracy in the wake of September 11. In the meantime, it will not help for our judges to display the Ten Commandments in our courthouses or for our representatives to stand on the steps of the Capitol and sing "God Bless America." The kings and queens of ages past made a mockery of religion by presuming to be its caretakers; what most of them really wanted was a kind of religion that would justify their rule while pacifying the populace. Our elected representatives are prone to the same temptations and are no more likely to resist them.

The religion that politicians practice in public blurs the line between piety and nationalism; it smells of self-idolatry. Its symbolic gestures make for bad religion and bad politics. Claiming to speak for the people as a whole on religious topics, the politicians imply that citizens who refuse to be spoken for in this way are less than full-fledged members of the people. When dissenters object, they are demonized as secularists. Symbolic sacrifice of the secularist scapegoat is itself a ritual essential to the public religion that some politicians would have the nation adopt. Here too the spirit of the First Amendment is as important to keep in mind as the letter. Even when such rites do not add up to the literal establishment of a religion, they rend the body politic at the very moment that they purport to be binding it together symbolically.

A country that has preachers, prophets, poets, houses of worship, and open air does not need politicians expressing its piety in public places. Individual citizens can be trusted to find appropriate ways to express their own religious convictions and train the young in virtue. What the people need from political leaders are the virtues of truthfulness, justice, practical wisdom, courage, vision, and a kind of compassion whose effects can actually be discerned in the lives of the poor and the elderly. Politics is the art of tending to the arrangements we make for ourselves. In our constitutional democracy, it is the art of taking collective responsibility for those arrangements in light of a tradition in which reasons have long been exchanged.

Today, that means at least three things. First, it means holding accountable any political leader who deceives the people and the Congress about the reasons for going to war. Second, it means finding a way to make government just powerful enough to hold corporations and their leaders responsible for their conduct. And third, it means refusing to permit either governmental or corporate power to deprive individuals of the liberties essential to maintaining a democratic culture. Among those liberties are the freedoms protected by the First Amendment. If we wish to conserve something of our heritage, let us start there.

BELIEF AND POWER

ROBERTO SURO

In his initial discourse Mario Cuomo invokes Abraham Lincoln on behalf of what he terms "the simplest and most useful instruction" for resolving religion's place in public life, and that is the interplay of "individuality and community." Indeed this is an oft-cited distinction perhaps because it is so labile it can be put to many purposes. Cuomo uses the device to reduce all of Judaism and then all of religion to two words. Adopting that standard for what is acceptably facile, I would argue that the essential juxtaposition between Cuomo and Mark Souder in the inspirational text for this volume is between a highly individualistic, solitary view of the role of religion in public life and one that emphasizes communal action.

Cuomo, in his best Hamlet-on-the-Hudson mode, focuses on the personal dilemmas he has faced reconciling his individual beliefs and the demands of public life. Souder speaks of communal political action on behalf of a religious agenda. Cuomo fades and shrinks his beliefs in a quest for a lowest common denominator—some natural law—that will erase any differences between his faith and the faiths of all other human beings. Souder boldly proclaims his Anabaptist creed yet states his goal of creating a community of like-minded voters large enough to win elections and enact laws. "When should I argue to make my religious value your morality, my rule of conduct your limitation?" says Cuomo, summarizing his dilemma as a Roman Catholic holding public office. Cuomo resolves that problem by subsuming his individual beliefs in a search for universal truths. "Religious values will not be accepted as part of the public morality unless they are shared by the community at large," he says. "The plausibility of achieving that consensus is a relevant consideration in deciding whether or not to make the effort to impose those values officially."

For Cuomo the role of the political leader is to articulate a consensus view of moral and religious positions. This revelation helps explain why Cuomo gave up the effort of trying to win elective office. In a society as pluralistic and as sharply divided on religious and moral issues as the United States, Cuomo is proposing an impossible project, in my view. It has two inescapable results: The individual leader must dilute his or her beliefs, as Cuomo does in his search for natural law, to the point of disappearance. And even in the hands of an individual as rhetorically gifted as Cuomo, the consensus view is so vague and so compromised that it fails to serve as a rallying point for political action.

Souder departs from cold political practicality: "In a republic, disagreements are decided in the public arena." Listing a variety of issues from abortion to marijuana use that provoke starkly different moral and religious judgments among Americans, Souder says that they will be decided by "the worldview of legislators, of the president, and of the courts." While Cuomo seeks the mantle of the prophet who speaks for "the community at large," Souder states flatly, "I do not believe there is a common denominator that is workable in the American political system."

Instead of taking his individual beliefs as the starting point, Souder is focused on the need to assemble that political community of 50-percent-plus-one that governs and that in governing decides moral disputes for everyone. Viewed philosophically it might seem ironic that the leader who starts by weighing his individual views against those of the polity ends up diluting those views, while the leader bent on assembling a community for governance paints his beliefs in loud colors. But this discussion is ultimately about politics and religion, not philosophy. The stump always values clarity and sharply drawn beliefs, and so does the pulpit. Moral compromises, as intellectually appealing as they may be, rarely inspire. Souder touts his political success, saying, "I have a far more diverse base than establishment liberals or Democrats do." To explain it, he says, "I have strong views, and so I respect the strong views of others, and people sense that."

Souder understands the difference between tolerance and acceptance. The right to express minority views must be respected, but in the realpolitik of the republic, that does not mean that those views have to be taken into account by the governing majority. This modus operandi is hardly unique to today's conservative Christians; it has been practiced by many faiths in many circumstances. The one regulator is the need to avoid alienating enough voters to tip an election. And indeed, beyond the happy world of our Republic, the more common model is one of repressing the minority views before they are stated. The history of religion in public life, if written honestly, centers on the process through which competing belief systems have assembled and exercised power over each other. That is religion as a basis for communal action. The individuals who posit universal truths are few and far between, and the credos of the most successful of them have all been used as instruments of power, eventually.

DIGNITY IN WORK
AS AN ARTICLE OF FAITH

JOHN SWEENEY

Few of us have the opportunities to act on our faith and to honor God in the prominent ways that elected officials do. Of course, neither do we carry the burden of publicly trying to balance faith values and the obligations of democratically chosen representatives.

But even if we all do not share the faith opportunities and burdens of a Mario Cuomo or a Mark Souder we nonetheless have the occasion as well as the challenge to live out our faith values in daily life. I have been blessed with a life's work on behalf of working families struggling to improve their lot and advance the possibilities for their children. My work provides occasions every day to speak and act on such social justice workplace issues as living wages, health benefits, nondiscrimination, and the rights of immigrant workers. And I have also had my values challenged in the course of my work.

My own thinking about the intersection of religion and politics runs closer to the views of Mario Cuomo than those of Mark Souder, although I find much to appreciate in Souder's remarks. Maybe it is the New Yorker in me, or my Irish ancestry, but I have always been more comfortable with Cuomo's distinction between religious life and life "in the public square" than Souder seems to be. Which is not to say I believe in a great degree of separation between the two. But I also think that our Founding Fathers had it pretty much right when they kept a respectful distance in this regard.

In fact, I want to suggest in this short essay that we would all benefit if both religious denominations and our political structures recognized and encouraged a *greater* connection of faith and everyday life—especially work life—however an individual may choose to make that connection. In today's parlance, I guess I want to argue for more and better "space" for the connection, however individuals may define it. I believe that what we do at our jobs and in our community life is every bit as much a part of our faith expression as what we do in more formal religious activities, such as worship services and prayer. And living our faith is a key dimension of our secular lives, indeed often a driving force. We need the guidance and support of our religious and political leaders to help us make everyday life a spiritual path and to bring our values into the public square. Speaking and preaching to the spiritual dimensions of work and daily life are key to enabling us to honor God in our daily activities and fully participating in the nation's political life.

Honoring work and respecting the people who do the work is the responsibility of political and religious leaders alike. Doing so not only recognizes the dignity of each person but also honors God by helping to advance the kingdom of God on earth. Unfortunately, both religious and political institutions generally do a poor job of this. With the exception of those congregations that champion the struggles of their members for social and economic justice, the nearest thing most churches offer is the occasional sermon on charitable work or respect-for-life issues. And for all the debates over social policy within the political structures, those structures are way, way more responsive to moneyed special interests than to average working families. Similarly (some individual elected officials notwithstanding), political debates, at least at the federal level, sadly lack acknowledgement of or attention to the justice gospel.

Mario Cuomo's and Mark Souder's presentations provide useful and illuminating examples of different approaches that elected officials with deep religious conviction take in balancing faith and public duties in secular institutions. How striking the difference between a leading product of U.S. Catholic assimilation and a prominent representative of conservative Evangelical Christians! What a rich diversity indeed exists among people of faith, even people who identify themselves as Christians, as Mark Souder points out. We all would benefit from more such exchanges.

The Cuomo-Souder dialogue contains hints about participation of voters of faith but nothing much in depth. Without taking anything away from their excellent exchange, I note that their remarks largely reflect today's media focus on Left versus Right and on the conservative views and criticisms that dominate politics, at least in Washington. I suspect that the most useful contribution I can make to this exchange lies in reflections about the relationship between religious values and political participation among working families—the people I am honored to represent as president of the AFL-CIO.

My own faith journey began in baptism, was made official through confirmation, and is rooted week in and week out in the Eucharist. I have been blessed with rich opportunities for participation in both the sacramental and the public life of the church. Throughout all the years my faith has sustained me—although not without question and at times not without doubt—as a constant sign of the forgiveness and the love of God and as a redemptive force. Faith is (as my bishop, Cardinal Theodore McCarrick, constantly reminds us) the key to it all.

I have received a great gift from God, in being able to pursue a life dedicated to justice. I get daily nourishment from my encounters with working women and men as I travel the country. Time spent with immigrant workers in Chicago, Los Angeles, or New York, a few hours with workers hurt by repetitive stress injuries but fighting to protect their co-workers, or a session with former Enron employees who want to warn others about blind faith in their company stock, restores the energy I can lose from repeated encounters with partisans in Washington, where the influence of money and the dominance of special interests cast a pall on our nation's capital as a place of the people's business.

My growing up in the Bronx as a child of working-class immigrants from County Leitrim, Ireland, was an early version of this experience. James, my father, was a bus driver who was active in the Transport Workers Union. Agnes, my mother, was a domestic worker in the employ of a well-to-do Fifth Avenue household. In my upbringing, the family was the source of unfailing love and support, the union the source of a living wage and inspiring social justice work, and the church the path to redemption. Almost as regular as attending Mass with my parents was the experience of going to union meetings and walking picket lines with my father. The Transport Workers Union was then headed by the legendary Mike Quill. One of my father's pet phrases was, "Thank God for Mike," when the latest union contract meant more food for the family, an extra day's vacation on the beaches of New York, or more time with us because the workweek shrank from forty-eight to forty hours (after a tough strike).

As a young officer of the janitors' union in New York City, I led the organizing and contract bargaining for service workers at the World Trade Center. How often have the cold days of December 1976, when workers picketed in stiff winter winds, come back to me as I visited that site after September 11, when 633 members of New York union families lost their lives. Those workers, and the many more who were left without jobs, were contemporaries of those earlier workers—and of my family and my neighbors, immigrants to the New World in search of a better way of life for them and for the generations to follow. For us, faith was the rock, and belief in the ultimate triumph of God's reign the beacon, in a harsh and often troubling world.

For us, participation in the life of the church was anchored in the Eucharist and other sacraments but also extended into the more social dimensions of church life, such as the parish community and the mission of the church in the wider world. Most prominent within this participation is work life. Work takes up a large amount of our waking hours and accounts for a significant portion of our social interactions—indeed, the overwhelming part for many Americans. Given the steady rise in two- and three-wage-earner families, total work time dwarfs other categories of activity in many families. In its spiritual and ethical dimensions, work offers a rich path of participation in the kingdom of God outside the church proper.

Whatever else our jobs may be, work provides the opportunity for spiritual participation in God's ongoing act of creation. Through our own creativity, ingenuity, diligence, commitment to service, solidarity with co-workers, and stewardship of resources we are given the chance to emulate God's love for us all, thereby honoring him as we fulfill the mission of the church in the world. Do we, as "church," represent Christ in the world of work? This is the mission question we face in our daily work lives.

Participation at work takes many forms. First, work itself is a form of participation in the life of Christ, since all creative effort stems from and reflects God's love. Second, the manner in which work is done—how skillfully, diligently, honestly, effectively, responsibly—reflects ethical values. Third, the social dimensions of work—service to family and community, faithfulness to the work enterprise, collegiality and solidarity with co-workers of all stripes—mark degrees of participation in the mission of the church in the world.

The social dimensions involve both rights and responsibilities. Workers are entitled to participate fully in the decisions that affect their work lives and their work organizations. They have a concomitant responsibility to participate fully and to do so with deep respect for the rights of co-workers to also participate and with the need for effective work organization (like division of labor and decisionmaking among co-workers), whether we are peers, supervisors, or subordinates. In practical terms, workers' primary responsibility is to provide quality products and services to the public they serve—the customers, in today's parlance. A closely allied responsibility is captured in the old phrase, a fair day's work for a fair day's pay. That is, an equitable relationship with the owner of the enterprise in which they work. All workers have a stewardship responsibility for the time, material, equipment, and reputation of the enterprise as well as an obligation to work cooperatively with superiors.

Owners need to live up to their end of the bargain and provide fair pay and benefits, consistent with industry and area standards, and a healthful and discrimination-free workplace. They also have a responsibility, to the extent possible, to encourage the human development of their work force through skill development. Last, they have the responsibility to provide avenues of participation for workers and to respect their freedom to choose their own voice at work without interference.

While genuine participation can exist in various types of workplace—under different management styles and work cultures—the traditional form of participation is worker self-organization through unions. While workplaces do not need unions to have fair policies, nondiscriminatory practices, and decent wages and benefits, unionization is the most common—and I would argue by far the most effective—path to worker rights there is in capitalist societies.

There are many practical reasons for workers to turn to unions. The most common is a perceived lack of respect and fairness. Another is that the scope of the business enterprise may require collective action across many workplaces. But even in individual workplaces and in relatively respectful work relationships workers may choose a union to help them establish a voice at work independent from management, with access to skills in collective action and resources to support their interests.

Today, unionization efforts among American workers range across industries and skill levels, from airline pilots and aerospace engineers to nurses, hotel staff, poultry-processing workers, janitors, and home health aides. The common denominator among these groups is that belief in collective action (solidarity) overcomes both the deep individualism of American culture and the common fear of reprisal for doing so. In one sense, union organization brings a worker culture and participation to enterprises that are often strongly hierarchical, with little accountability to the bulk of the people who produce the goods and the wealth. What workers realize from unions in a material sense is well documented: additional dollars per hour, largely employer-paid family health benefits, traditional pension plans with guaranteed benefits, safer workplaces, and additional opportunities for skill development. These kinds of gain take time and hard work in bargaining contracts that give a greater share of the economic benefits to workers. But what workers gain more immediately is a sense of self-respect that comes from acts of solidarity and empowerment.

Traditionally, most religious denominations have supported labor unions based on their adherence to the principle of solidarity. This remains true today, although some conservatives oppose unions because we give greater support to Democrats than to Republicans and they incorrectly link this to support for abortion. (For the record, the AFL-CIO and individual unions commonly endorse Republicans who support working-family issues, and the AFL-CIO has rejected taking a position on the abortion question despite repeated requests by prochoice union members.)

Union members select the candidates they support the same way non-union Americans do: through personal judgment based on how candidates present themselves and by evaluating candidates' positions against their own values. The age of continuous communication has made it harder, not easier, for all Americans to make these judgments because of the sophisticated manipulation of the public by spinmeisters, constant misrepresentation by many candidates, and the universal practice of negative campaigning. The AFL-CIO is proud of our record of communicating with members on a factual basis about the positions of candidates on issues of importance to working families. We have helped union members to assess the candidates' strengths and weaknesses and to judge their relative merits based on members' own values and beliefs. Faith values are central to those decisions—values related to individual morality, social issues, and justice issues. Our responsibility is to provide members with information on the issues directly related to the reasons that workers join unions: wages, worker protections, health care coverage, pensions, Social Security, and so forth.

Unions are a mediating force and, in that respect, share some characteristics with both religious denominations and political structures. Recognition of and respect for the dignity of work and the contribution of workers is a responsibility we all share.

Our faith communities and our political structures would both be enriched by more explicit and concrete support for the dignity of work and the contributions of workers.

IT'S THE CONTENT THAT COUNTS

W. DOUGLAS TANNER JR.

Polls indicate that American voters increasingly want their president to be a person of faith. Religious mooring among public officials appears to have become more valuable in the public mind as a source of confidence amid our current anxieties and uncertainties. Even before September 11, 2001, though, religion had come on stage as a supporting actor in the 2000 presidential election. In 2004 it may vie for more prominent casting. The enduring questions in any election year have to do with the content of its role.

I spend most of my time and energy trying to help members of Congress and others related to Capitol Hill seriously consider the connections between faith and politics. The task is neither simple nor easy. Discerning the proper place of religious faith in electoral politics and public policy is complex and challenging, as is living authentically and effectively in the political arena as a person of mature faith. The complexity and challenge surrounding such work underscores its significance. Mario Cuomo and Mark Souder recognize the nature of the task and meet its challenge with clarity and courage. Their differing conclusions demonstrate the impact of different religious perspectives on politics and policy.

The vision, the values, and the spirit of public officials have a major bearing on the quality of life in our nation. Sometimes they are creative and constructive; sometimes they are damaging and destructive. Vision, values, and spirit tend to be reflections of faith. Those of us who encourage the active engagement of religious faith in the political arena of a constitutional democracy, I believe, are under an obligation to pay close attention to the qualities such engagement brings into the arena, to support it when it serves the goals of human dignity and human community, and to question it when it does disservice to either.

We Americans usually have been more comfortable with the appearance of a certain measure of personal piety among our politicians than with the idea of their faith being the source of their policy decisions. Among a substantial segment of the electorate that clearly has changed: Particular policy positions are treated as litmus tests for candidates seeking support from particular parts of the religious community. I suspect, though, that a great number of those who now want a visibly religious president are more drawn to the image of someone who will turn to a higher source of wisdom and guidance in time of crisis than to direct connections between the president's faith and his or her platform.

My hope and prayer is that the increased attention to the role of faith and religion in electoral politics may lead to a deeper understanding of both its value and its threat. If that happens, I believe it will be at least as much through the accurate telling of real human stories as through theoretical analysis: stories of political leaders whose faith has given them remarkable strength, courage, and largeness of spirit in profoundly difficult times— leaders who help to heal the wounds of divided societies even as they address injustices that must be confronted and challenged; stories as well of leaders whose interpretation of their faith has led to a narrowness of spirit, who divide the body politic, reinforce injustices, and increase alienation.

Lincoln surely is representative of the first category, though he was hardly recognized as such by most Americans during most of his lifetime. He presided over a terribly traumatic period with grace, wisdom, and wit even as he endured extreme periods of sadness and depression. The depth of Lincoln's religious faith and its power as a healing force are evidenced vividly in his Second Inaugural Address.

Hitler is an extreme twentieth-century example of the second. Knowing well the importance of religion in Germany's public life, his Nazi Party went to incredible lengths to shape a purportedly Christian theology supportive of their policies. It denied Jesus was Jewish and argued that he was Aryan, thereby enabling storm troopers to consider themselves both Nazi and Christian.

Some leaders undergo experiences that transform their understandings and enlarge their spirits. Such journeys merit celebration; their stories particularly can offer hope for constructive political engagement that is informed and shaped by religious faith.

I recently traveled with a congressional delegation to South Africa to study that nation's experience in the transition from apartheid to a nonracial democracy honoring human rights, promoting sustainable economic development, and supporting effective solutions to long-standing conflicts. Former President F. W. de Klerk spoke to us about the connections between faith and politics in South Africa's history. He described the Afrikaner worldview that had prevailed until the late 1980s and how it began to change:

We [Afrikaners] clung to the concept of being free as a nation with our own culture, with our own language, in our land . . . but we failed to bring justice. And we had to take a hard look at ourselves. . . . [Our] religion at certain times justified apartheid. And the three main Afrikaner churches, with great effectiveness, read the Bible to justify the concept of separateness. . . . Politics and faith should go hand in hand. But at all times we should be critical, because in faith and in religion you can go the wrong way and in politics you can become obsessed with the wrong ideas and the wrong principles. . . . Fundamental principles—justice, integrity, love, forgiveness— should be the guiding light if you talk about reconciliation.

Respect for those fundamental principles brought the Nobel Peace Prize jointly to de Klerk and Nelson Mandela. Mandela probably has embodied them more dramatically and thoroughly than any other living statesman. He is a deeply spiritual man who brought his faith to his politics in ways that have become transparent and that have served both his former adversaries and his continual allies extraordinarily well. But throughout his presidency, Mandela was reticent about speaking of the connection between his religion and his politics because he was acutely, painfully aware of the way in which the wedding of religion and politics could serve evil ends.

Perhaps there is a significant measure of privacy to be reserved for one's religious faith if it is to have its optimal value in public life. Its authenticity can thereby be shielded from the polluting, diluting effect of its use as a campaign theme. But this appears to be a season in which the American public will not trust a candidate perceived as too private about his or her religion. Our task, again, is to discern both the authenticity and the content of the religious allegiance claimed by politicians. If it is not authentic, it may not matter beyond the consequences of any other dishonesty along the campaign trail. On the other hand, if I judge a candidate to be truly religious, questions of content become important to me. What vision originates from this person's religious perspective? What values accompany it? Perhaps most important of all, what spirit flows from it?

Reinhold Niebuhr's contribution to mature consideration of issues at the nexus of faith and politics remains unsurpassed. Niebuhr was intensely aware of the deleterious role hubris plays in both our personal and our public lives. Nowhere can hubris find more running room than it does in politics, and nowhere can it be more destructive. It is a spirit that should evoke wariness at all times—but more than ever during dangerous times.

Niebuhr's wisdom is contained in numerous volumes of his writing, one brief excerpt of which I deem an especially valuable guide for those who labor in the political vineyard: "Nothing worth doing can be achieved in a lifetime; therefore we must be saved by hope. Nothing that is true or beautiful or good makes complete sense in any immediate context of history; therefore we must be saved by faith. Nothing that we do, however virtuous, can be accomplished alone; therefore we must be saved by love."[1]

May we choose political leaders who will live with such awareness—and who will use their positions to call it forth among those of us who have chosen them.

Note

1. Reinhold Niebuhr, quoted in Elizabeth Sifton, *The Serenity Prayer: Faith and Politics in Times of Peace and War* (Norton, 2003), p. 349.

FAITH AND THE PUBLIC SQUARE

JIM TOWEY

When President George W. Bush promotes his faith-based initiative by extolling the power of faith to change lives, or makes mention of God in his public remarks, most Americans are comfortable with this policy of treating faith-based institutions fairly and with expressions of personal faith. However, well-publicized critics take issue with the president and protest that he is tearing down the wall that separates church and state—that he is injecting religion into public affairs.

It helps to place the issue in historical perspective. Start with the oft-cited "wall" between church and state. The wall of separation can sometimes be a useful metaphor, but it does not capture our government's long and respected tradition of accommodating the religious beliefs and activities of its citizens and of cooperating with religious groups in the provision of social services. For decades, federal dollars have reached religiously affiliated organizations through Medicare, Medicaid, Pell grants, the GI bill, and a host of other programs. Indeed, if you go back to the earliest days of America, you would see the federal government giving money to faith-based groups to provide services to those in need. So the idea that faith-based organizations can deliver social services without violating the U.S. Constitution is neither new, nor is it some sneak assault on church-state separation.

A cursory look at the statements of earlier presidents would debunk the myth that President Bush has gone overboard with his frequent references to God. Thomas Jefferson referred to liberties as a "gift of God." George Washington spoke of religion and morality as "indispensable supports" of political prosperity. James Madison said that before a man could be "a member of Civil Society, he must be considered as a subject of the Governor of the Universe." And Abraham Lincoln's references to God are too numerous to cite.

Often it seems that criticisms of politicians who make public professions of religious belief divide along partisan lines. Republicans typically get accused of talking too much about God, while Democrats have a reputation for silence on matters of faith. It is worth mentioning here that there were many twentieth-century Democrats (besides Jimmy Carter) who spoke easily of Almighty God. Here is an excerpt from the 1942 State of the Union address of Franklin Roosevelt. In speaking of Nazi Germany, he said, "They know that victory for us means victory for religion. And they could not tolerate that. The world is too small to provide adequate living room for both Hitler and God. In proof of that, the Nazis have now announced their plan for enforcing their new German, pagan religion all over the world—a plan by which the Holy Bible and the Cross of Mercy would be displaced by Mein Kampf and the swastika of the naked sword."

Robert Kennedy, too, did not separate his belief in God from his politics. In his "Day of Affirmation" address, he said, "At the heart of . . . Western freedom and democracy is the belief that the individual man, the child of God, is the touchstone of value, and all society, groups, the state, exist for his benefit."

Yet when President Bush says things like "the liberty we prize is not America's gift to the world, it is God's gift to humanity," some single him out and accuse him of pandering to the religious vote. President Clinton signed into law protections for religious groups to receive tax dollars and still be able to hire according to their religious beliefs, but when President Bush proposed the same thing, he was accused of supporting so-called federally funded discrimination. Why the double standard?

I think that the church-state pendulum had swung markedly to the Left by the end of the twentieth century, and the religious voice or influence had all but vanished from the public square. By contrast, this makes President Bush's sensible move toward the middle—where government would not favor faith but would not oppose it either—seem controversial.

My predecessor, John DiIulio, outlined in detail in the August 2001 White House report he prepared, "Unlevel Playing Field," how faith-based groups have been systematically discriminated against in the federal grant-making process. Among the numerous examples in recent years is that of the Old North Church in Boston, where Paul Revere was signaled from the steeple, "One if by land, two if by sea," at the dawn of the American Revolution. This church building, a popular tourist site, applied for a grant from the Save America's Treasures program to restore its windows. It was turned down. Other historic landmarks—hospitals, museums, train stations, and so forth—had received these grants, but the existing policy said, "Not Old North Church. Not any active church or synagogue." What you had was a federal policy that said secular places were worth preserving but not sacred places. President Bush decided that such a policy was unfair, and he changed it. Now, not only Old North Church but also Tuoro Synagogue in Newport, Rhode Island (the oldest synagogue in America) have been deemed American treasures and worthy of preservation for future generations. More should follow, and will, thanks to President Bush's intervention.

Another example could be found in the Department of Housing and Urban Development (HUD) regulations that were on the books when President Bush took office. These regulations barred "religious influences" of any kind in certain HUD-funded programs. I worked for twelve years with Mother Teresa of Calcutta. When I read that regulation for the first time, I wondered: If she had operated a homeless shelter funded by HUD under those rules, would her smile have been deemed an impermissible "religious influence"?

This purposefully vague regulatory language had the effect of chasing away some of the most qualified and effective providers of housing services. Others were forced to form secular nonprofits (for example, Saint John's shelter became John's shelter) if they wanted HUD funding. But the reality was that many groups were not willing to dramatically alter their identities in order to provide a public service.

The sad consequence of such an imbalanced approach to the First Amendment was that America's social service network was ruthlessly secularized—a person could be written up for a violation of regulations if they had so much as a scriptural quotation taped to a computer screen. I heard just such a story from a woman working in a YWCA shelter for victims of domestic violence in South Bend, Indiana.

Because faith-based organizations were driven away from the federal table, the poor were denied access to some of the most effective drug treatment, prisoner reentry, and job training programs in America. President Bush launched his faith-based and community initiative to bring fairness and accountability to the provision of taxpayer-funded social services. He made clear in his regulatory reforms that there could be no proselytizing with tax dollars, that you could not discriminate against beneficiaries on the basis of religion or a refusal to worship, and that faith-based groups that received public money had to account for it, just like any other grantee. Fundamental to the president's approach was this tenet: One could honor the dictates of the First Amendment without treating faith-based groups unfairly.

There is more to President Bush's faith-based and community initiative than the goal of leveling the playing field. It is also about results. The president has said repeatedly that government cannot love, and that is why he sees great promise in the ability of faith-based organizations and other community groups to touch the lives of people in lasting ways. That is not injecting God into government, nor is it politicizing religion. It is recognizing that public dollars are often spent in vain if the spiritual dimension of life is ignored. The fundamental question is not whether social service organizations believe in God or not but whether their programs work. Are addicts recovering? Are the homeless finding places to live? And are they rediscovering their great human dignity and connecting with the lives of others in positive, life-giving ways?

A Dartmouth Medical School study shows that there is a biological basis for religious cravings and the need to find moral meaning in life. The report looked at the basic structure of the brain and determined that humans are born to find meaning through attachment to others. George Will, in reporting on the study, concludes that "the Bush administration's belief in the wisdom of delivering social services through faith-based institutions is not just a matter of faith."[1]

I am no scientist, but I have to say that the study's findings confirm my own experiences in working with the poor for nearly twenty years: Human beings *are* hardwired to connect. In the fall of 1986 Mother Teresa asked me to work in her Washington home for people with AIDS, and I was in the first group of volunteers when we took in Andy and Cliff, two wonderful but terribly broken men. I learned a lot from them and the lovely souls who followed in their footsteps to the Gift of Peace home, particularly during 1990 when I was a full-time volunteer there. Many of the residents had been drug addicts, some had lived like animals on the street, and they all had AIDS. But their greatest pain was that they felt unloved, unwanted, and rejected. If we did not get to know them—that is, connect with them—and discover why they had put needles in their arms or sold their bodies in the first place, all of our social service efforts on their behalf were doomed to be of little or no benefit.

President Bush's willingness to speak of God, as his predecessors have, and to welcome faith into the social service delivery system, as our country's Founders envisioned, is driven by a heartfelt desire to bring balance to matters of faith in the public square and hope to the lives of individuals seeking to connect with others—and in the process reclaim their lives. He knows the power of America's "armies of compassion" and believes that our country is stronger and better because of their efforts.

Note

1. George Will, "Hardwired to Connect," *Washington Post,* September 21, 2003, p. B7.

FAITH COMMUNITIES
AND AMERICAN DEMOCRACY

MARK R. WARREN

Below the firing line in the debate about religion and American politics, a quiet movement is building. In this movement, faith communities engage in day-to-day struggles to improve the quality of life for children and families. The issues are not hot-button moral controversies. Instead, they concern affordable housing, better schools, safe neighborhoods, and economic opportunities for low-income workers. The action is not focused on the election of candidates to represent people. Rather, it is directed toward the active engagement of the people themselves in the art of political action. Its significance, I believe, lies in its long-range potential to revitalize the foundation of American democracy, to build an organized constituency to place the social and economic needs of poor and working Americans at the top of the nation's agenda.

Perhaps *movement* is the wrong term, since these efforts are mainly local and sometimes link to each other only at state or regional levels. But they are powerful at the local level—and are spreading across the country. A survey conducted in 1999 shows that faith-based organizing is now a truly national phenomenon, with a broad reach into American congregations.[1] According to the survey, more than 130 local faith-based community organizations operate in thirty-three states across all regions of the country and claim more than 4,000 institutions as members. About 3,500 of those institutions are religious congregations, which means that more than 1 percent of all American congregations are involved in a faith-based organizing group. The field may reach as many as three million people through these congregations.

The Industrial Areas Foundation (IAF), founded by Saul Alinsky, pioneered the development of this kind of faith-based organizing, especially through its work in Texas. Ernesto Cortes Jr., along with faith leaders in his native San Antonio and the IAF's national director Ed Chambers, reworked Saul Alinsky's community organizing tradition to create what I term a *theology of organizing*.[2] With this faith-based strategy, Cortes built Communities Organized for Public Service (COPS) in San Antonio into the nation's most powerful community-based organization. Rooted in Hispanic Catholic parishes, COPS addresses a wide range of issues of concern to its low-income Mexican American constituents, including affordable housing, job training, school reform, after-school programs, neighborhood safety, public health, and citizenship. Although COPS does not endorse candidates, it registers voters, holds "accountability nights" with candidates, and publicizes their stances on issues of concern to its constituents. Since its inception in 1974, COPS has garnered more than a billion dollars in public and private resources. Hundreds of lay leaders work on its campaigns; and 3,000 participants attend its annual conventions.

From San Antonio, the IAF spread across Texas and into other parts of the Southwest with its nonpartisan, faith-based strategy.[3] The network now includes organizations in more than twenty localities and operates as a statewide political force in Texas. In 1999 the IAF celebrated twenty-five years of organizing in Texas and the Southwest; 6,000 clergy and lay leaders, not professional political activists, filled the San Antonio municipal auditorium. They outlined a "human development" platform, which includes issues like those addressed by COPS.

What does all this have to do with religion? The anniversary celebration closed with the following remarks. A white Catholic priest, Richard Beck, asked, "What will fuel our efforts for the next twenty-five years? The same thing that has fueled the last twenty-five: faith in God and faithfulness to God's demand for justice. . . . We cannot stand by and watch our cities and our children crumble." Terry White, a black minister, added, "As we leave this place may the power of God's Holy Spirit be the fire that burns within us and fuels us in our efforts to do God's justice." Finally, the interfaith group on stage asked all delegates to hold hands. Drawing upon a Jewish tradition, the delegates declared, "We stand together as citizens. We work within our communities. Our feet may be tired, but our souls are rested. Our faith will give us strength to mend our world. *Tikkun olam.* Let us mend our world. *Tikkun olam. Tikkun olam!*"

As this vignette suggests, faith is central to this political phenomenon; and it is so both for institutional and for theological reasons. Faith institutions continue to anchor community life, playing the largest single role of any set of American institutions in structuring charitable donations, volunteering, civic engagement, and community action. And churches are certainly our most egalitarian form of group participation, with low-income people and people of color well represented in the pews.[4] If we want to find a place from which to engage Americans broadly, religious congregations represent an unparalleled resource.

Moreover, faith traditions call their believers to act for the broader community and for social justice. The extent to which any particular faith community decides to answer that call, and how it decides to define its community, varies a great deal of course. Nevertheless, for many the call is profound and provides a powerful motivation for action. In the face of the relentless promotion of consumerism and individualism in American life, faith traditions offer coherent frameworks for community. Certainly the participants in the Texas IAF whom I interviewed draw deeply from their faith commitments when explaining their motivations for action.

Internally, faith communities involved in this form of political organizing interrogate their religious traditions for inspiration and to anchor their community-building agenda. In the public sphere, however, they are careful to argue their proposals on more interest-based criteria. In fact the IAF and other organizing networks are famous for training their participants to examine the self-interest of all stakeholders and opponents in their campaigns. Realism is prized, as groups search for winnable goals that will make significant improvements in the lives of their constituents. In this way, organizing fuses faith-based values, material interests, and the common good. In other words, IAF organizations argue for affordable housing because low-income families need it, because it is the right thing to do, and because it is necessary to the health and viability of a diverse society. Building affordable housing is good public policy.

Although much of the public debate about religion and politics focuses on the divisiveness it can cause, this is only one side of the story. In faith-based organizing, communities of different faiths, social classes, and racial backgrounds have found a way to work together. In many of the local organizations of the Texas IAF, Hispanic Catholics and black Protestants from low-income communities regularly work together with more affluent white congregants from the suburbs around an agreed-upon agenda. Racial and religious differences are not necessarily buried here; rather, people are encouraged to learn from other traditions and experiences as part of the search for a solid consensus on shared concerns.

From the national standpoint, the field of faith-based organizing is remarkably diverse racially and religiously.[5] The field combines three large sectors of the American people: black Protestants, Hispanic Catholics, and white mainline Protestants. Other racial or religious groupings participate although to a much lesser extent; and there is a small but significant presence of Jewish and other non-Christian faiths. One of the field's challenges will be to see if faith-based organizing can really encompass the full range of American religious and community experience. At the same time, the phenomenon remains one of our most significant, almost unique, venues for multiracial cooperation and political action.

Faith-based organizing in 2004 remains intensely focused locally and rather disengaged from the national election scene. This is not all bad. American politics has become so focused at the top that little attention is ever devoted to building at the bottom. Yet poor and working Americans will seldom jump straight from local activity to political action in Washington. If we want to build an infrastructure for American democracy, we have to start locally and build seriously there for the long term. Of course local work alone is not sufficient, but we are now paying the costs of ignoring the local for so long.

The 2004 election will not likely concentrate on lack of affordable housing or the continued stagnation of wages for the working poor. But if faith communities continue to organize an infrastructure for democratic politics and find a way to cohere at the national level, our next national election could develop quite differently. The faith-based movement may be our best hope to put the social and economic needs of poor and working families and their communities into the center of our nation's political agenda.

Notes

1. See Mark R. Warren and Richard L. Wood, *Faith-Based Community Organizing: The State of the Field* (Jericho, N.Y.: Interfaith Funders, 2001).

2. For a treatment of the historical development of the theology of organizing and an analysis of the contemporary work of the Texas IAF, see Mark R. Warren, *Dry Bones Rattling: Community Building to Revitalize American Democracy* (Princeton University Press, 2001). For other accounts of the Texas IAF, see Mary Beth Rogers, *Cold Anger: A Story of Faith and Power Politics* (University of North Texas Press, 1990); Paul Osterman, *Gathering Power: The Future of Progressive Politics in America* (Boston: Beacon Press, 2002); and Dennis Shirley, *Community Organizing for Urban School Reform* (University of Texas Press, 1997).

3. Although I use the term *faith-based organizing,* the IAF prefers *broad-based organizing,* in part because the network wants to make clear it is not a religious group pursuing an agenda derived directly from scripture. Moreover, the IAF seeks

to incorporate into its local organizations a wider range of institutions beyond faith congregations—for example, schools and unions.

4. For some evidence, see Sidney Verba, Kay Lehman Schlozman, and Henry E. Brady, *Voice and Equality: Civic Voluntarism in American Politics* (Harvard University Press, 1995).

5. See Warren and Wood, *Faith-Based Community Organizing,* for the details.

FAITH, FREEDOM, AND TOLERATION

ALAN WOLFE

Once upon a time—that is to say, in the 1950s—religion in American public life was widely accepted and appreciated, even if religions in American public life frequently raised concern and controversy. It was the most liberal justice ever to serve on the Supreme Court, William O. Douglas, who said, in *Zorach* v. *Clausen* (1952), that "we are a religious people whose institutions presuppose a Supreme Being." Perhaps craftily, Douglas never indicated precisely who that Supreme Being was. In so doing, he expressed the widespread consensus of his time. In private, Christians may have prayed to a Christian God and Jews to a Jewish one. But in public they were careful to avoid identifying the God of some as the God of all. Thus it is that when we added those famous words to the Pledge of Allegiance in 1954, we proclaimed ourselves one nation "under God," not "under Christ." In Dwight D. Eisenhower's America, it was important that you believe in something, whatever that something happened to be.

But this is George W. Bush's America. And in this era of heightened religiosity, it seems that we fooled ourselves in thinking that we could get by with this distinction between religion and religions. Although religion in general may be fine for public occasions, the devout believe in religion in particular. And of all America's religions, Evangelicals have taken the lead in mentioning, unapologetically and without circumlocution, the divinity who, in their views, saves souls. An appropriate example has been offered by Mark Souder in his remarks in this volume. His is not the "God talk" of the wishy-washy set. "To ask me to check my Christian beliefs at the public door is to ask me to expel the Holy Spirit from my life when I serve as a congressman, and that I will not do," is how he put it. "Either I am a Christian or I am not. Either I reflect His glory or I do not." These are the words of a man deeply devoted to his religion. And they are also words that would likely offend someone devoted to another religion—or to no religion at all.

Because they speak about God in ways different from mainline Protestants, Catholics, and Jews, Evangelicals raise anew questions about the proper relationship between religion and politics. Should we praise Souder for bringing his faith so resolutely to the public square? Or should we worry that his specifically Christian language will be found offensive by others? I believe that the answer to that question depends on how religion is practiced in everyday life.

Souder tells us he was raised in a fundamentalist church. Were he to practice his faith in line with his fundamentalist upbringing, his overt religiosity would indeed be worrisome to those who did not share his specific faith convictions. Fundamentalists in the period between the 1920s and the 1970s rejected modernity—that is what made them fundamentalist—and, with it, the idea of respect for all faiths. After all, if you have the truth, and fundamentalists were persuaded that they did, and if only one truth can be true at any one time, then your obligation as a believer is to do whatever is in your power to help others see their truth, not to sit and "dialogue" with them about whose truth is really true.

Some conservative Christians continue to speak like fundamentalists of old; Jerry Vines, Franklin Graham, Jerry Falwell, and Pat Robertson made comments in the wake of September 11 indicating in one way or another that Islam was a false religion. The first thing to be noted about Mark Souder's comments is that, unlike those of the faithful four, they were made by a congressman. When fundamentalists turned their back on modernity, they withdrew from public life, perhaps stung by the defeat of their one-time hero William Jennings Bryan in the 1925 Scopes trial. Having cut themselves off from the world, they were free to develop their own institutions: schools and colleges teaching biblical literalism, parachurch revivalist movements, Christian summer camps, gospel radio and television. Because these organizations were self-enclosed, they were also intolerant. Fundamentalists could believe that the Catholic Church embodied the Antichrist because they met so few Catholics. They could likewise be persuaded of Zionist influence because their paths never crossed with those of Jews.

But Catholics and Jews, needless to say, exist aplenty in Congress and also in any other institution, public or private, that has made its peace with modernity, which means that by the very nature of his job Souder will find himself in a position quite unlike the ones in which previous generations of fundamentalists found themselves. If we believe in exposing people to a wide variety of others with different points of view, it is far better to have conservative Christians in Congress than having them out.

Souder himself illustrates how public service complicates fundamentalist certainties. When casting his vote on the impeachment of Bill Clinton, he found a higher source of authority than the Bible; his vote was guided by the Constitution. Nor would his votes involving war and peace be determined by the pacifist principles central to the Anabaptist faith in which he was raised; if a war were just, he would support it even if doing so "will never, ever, be easy for me because of my fundamental beliefs." And he reaches out to the non-Christians in his distinct manner, including a substantial number of subcontinent Indians and a small group of Iraqis. As a Christian, Mark Souder asks himself what he, as a humble sinner, should do. As a congressman, he decides what he should do by turning not only to his God but to many other sources and texts as well.

The important question is whether the majority of America's Evangelicals continue to live in self-selected worlds composed almost entirely of people like themselves or whether, like Mark Souder, they have entered into the mainstream of American institutional life. Fortunately there now exists a significant body of empirical sociological work devoted to this question, and the answer it provides is unambiguous: Evangelicals are now part of the American mainstream: upwardly mobile, career oriented, suburban dwelling, and college attending. Along with their changing demography has come a new political sensibility. While strongly committed to their faith, Evangelicals accept the separation of church and state and share the culture of toleration of the rest of their society.

In my book *The Transformation of American Religion* I examine some of the implications of the ways in which Evangelicals have made their peace with American culture. Contrary to the fears of many liberals and secularists, Evangelicals these days practice their religion in ways that people of all faiths share. Their forms of worship, because they emphasize an up-front-and-personal relationship with Jesus, owe much to the individualistic character of American society. They resist strong identification with congregations and denominations because, like Americans in other areas of life, they tend to be distrustful of institutions. Although conservative in their theology and to a lesser but significant degree in their politics, they value authenticity of faith over tradition and in that sense do not serve as a force of resistance against the innovative character of American life. They insist on the importance of strong moral dispositions and watchfulness against sin, but they are also part of a society that wants to emphasize the positive and uplifting over the negative and depressing. And perhaps most important of all, although they are under an obligation to witness their faith, the form their proselytizing takes is reluctant to be offensive and intrusive.

The fact that Evangelicals are now part of the American mainstream does not mean that all issues regarding religion and politics can now be settled in favor of religion. When, to take one prominent example, a judge constructs a 5,000-pound monument of the Ten Commandments and puts it in a courtroom, his in-your-face assertions of his religious convictions clearly violate the rights of others and should not be permitted. But when politicians bring their religious convictions to bear on whether they favor limiting research into stem cells or support public assistance to faith-based charities, we ought to respect them for elevating the seriousness of our public conversation even if we disagree with the positions they take.

Americans believe in God and they believe in freedom. They take religion seriously, but unlike many other societies in history that have also given a prominent place to God, they do not enshrine any one religion as the official religion of their society. They also take freedom seriously, but unlike many other countries in the world that also do, they have not used their freedom to create a society in which faith plays no especially visible role. It is never easy to balance faith and freedom, which is one reason that our courts and legislatures revisit these issues so often. Finding the right balance between them may not therefore involve discovering some constitutional secret or passing a piece of extraordinary legislation. That balance can only come if believers and nonbelievers act out of toleration for each other. Some on both sides of the divide never will, but the great majority find ways to live together. And as long as they do, we need fear neither the triumph of secular humanism nor the establishment of a theocracy.

CONTRIBUTORS

JOANNA ADAMS is senior minister of the Trinity Presbyterian Church in Atlanta, Georgia. She has served as a preacher for the General Assembly of the Presbyterian Church USA, the *Protestant Hour,* and the Chautauqua Institution. She previously served as a trustee of Columbia Theological Seminary and as a board member of the Presbyterian Investment and Loan Program.

AZIZAH Y. AL-HIBRI is a professor at the T. C. Williams School of Law at the University of Richmond. She is founder and executive director of KARAMAH: Muslim Women Lawyers for Human Rights. She serves on the editorial boards of the *Journal of Law and Religion,* the *American Journal of Islamic Social Sciences,* and *Studies in Contemporary Islam.*

DOUG BANDOW is a senior fellow at the Cato Institute in Washington. He worked in the Reagan administration as a special assistant to the president. He has contributed to several publications, including the *Washington Post,* the *Washington Times,* the *Los Angeles Times,* and the *Christian Science Monitor.*

MICHAEL BARONE is a senior writer for the *U.S. News & World Report* and principal coauthor of *The Almanac of American Politics,* published every two years by the *National Journal.* He has written for many publications, including the *New York Times,* the *Weekly Standard,* the *New Republic,* the *Economist,* and the *National Review.*

GARY L. BAUER is president of American Values as well as a founder and chairman of the Campaign for Working Families. He has served as president of the Family Research Council and as a domestic policy adviser and undersecretary of education under President Reagan. He is the author or coauthor of several publications, including: *Our Journey Home, Our Hopes, Our Dreams,* and *Children at Risk.*

PAUL E. BEGALA is cohost of two political shows on television, CNN's *Crossfire* and MSNBC's *Equal Time.* He is also a professor of government at Georgetown University. He served as adviser to President Clinton during the 1992 election campaign. His recent publications include *Is Our Children Learning? The Case against George W. Bush* and *Buck Up, Suck Up . . . and Come Back When You Foul Up.*

ROBERT BELLAH is an emeritus professor of sociology at the University of California, Berkeley. He was awarded the National Humanities Medal by President Clinton in 2000. He is author of numerous articles, including "Civil Religion in America" and "Religious Evolution" and is author or coeditor of several books, including *Habits of the Heart, Beyond Belief, The Broken Covenant,* and *The Good Society.*

DAVID BROOKS is a columnist for the *New York Times.* He is a senior editor at the *Weekly Standard,* a contributing editor to *Newsweek,* and a correspondent for *Atlantic Monthly.* He has contributed to the *New Yorker, Forbes,* the *Washington Post, Commentary,* and the *Public Interest.* He is author or editor of several publications, including *Bobos in Paradise* and *Backward and Upward.*

HARVEY COX is a professor at Harvard Divinity School. An American Baptist minister, he previously held positions at several universities, including Temple University, Oberlin College, and the University of Michigan. A columnist for beliefnet.com, he is author of *The Secular City, Common Prayers,* and *The Reshaping of Religion in the Twenty-First Century.*

MICHAEL CROMARTIE is vice president of the Ethics and Public Policy Center in Washington, where he directs two of its programs: Evangelicals in Public Life and Religion and the Media. He is an adjunct professor at the Reformed Theological Seminary and an advisory editor for *Christianity Today.* His publications include *A Public Faith, A Preserving Grace,* and *Caesar's Coin Revisited.*

MARIO CUOMO was elected New York State's fifty-second governor in 1982 and won reelection in both 1986 and 1990. He has served as a cochairman and board member of the Partnership for a Drug-Free America. He is author of several publications, including *Why Lincoln Matters Today More than Ever, Reason to Believe,* and *More than Words.*

JOHN J. DIIULIO JR. is a professor of politics, religion, and civil society and professor of political science at the University of Pennsylvania as well as a nonresident senior fellow at the Brookings Institution. He served as first director of the White House Office of Faith-Based and Community Initiatives. He is coeditor of *What's God Got to Do with the American Experiment?*

E.J. DIONNE JR. is a senior fellow at the Brookings Institution and a professor at Georgetown University. He is a syndicated columnist with the *Washington Post* and cochair, with Jean Bethke Elshtain, of the Pew Forum on Religion and Public Life. He is editor or coeditor of several Brookings volumes, including *Lifting up the Poor, United We Serve,* and *Sacred Places, Civic Purposes,* and author of *Why Americans Hate Politics* and *Stand up, Fight Back.*

KAYLA M. DROGOSZ is a senior research analyst for the Religion and Civil Society Project at the Brookings Institution. She is also coeditor of *United We Serve: National Service and the Future of Citizenship* and the *Pew Forum Dialogues on Religion and Public Life* and has served with the policy offices of United Jewish Communities and in the U.S. mission to the United Nations.

TERRY EASTLAND is publisher of the *Weekly Standard.* Previously he was a senior fellow at the Ethics and Public Policy Center, director of public affairs at the Department of Justice, and a special assistant to the attorney general. His is author of several books, including *Ending Affirmative Action* and *Ethics, Politics, and the Independent Counsel.*

ROBERT EDGAR is general secretary of the National Council of Churches USA in the United States. An ordained elder in the United Methodist Church, he served six terms in the United States House of Representatives for Pennsylvania's Seventh District. He has also served as president of Claremont School of Theology.

JEAN BETHKE ELSHTAIN is a professor of social and political ethics at the University of Chicago. She is a member of the National Commission for Civic Renewal and currently serves as chair of both the Council on Families in America and the Council on Civil Society and cochair, with E. J. Dionne, of the Pew Forum on Religion and Public Life.

RICHARD WIGHTMAN FOX is a professor of history at the University of Southern California. He has also held positions at Boston University, Reed College, and Yale University. He is author of numerous publications, including *Reinhold Niebuhr: A Biography,* and is coeditor of *In the Face of Facts: Moral Inquiry in American Scholarship.*

WILLIAM GALSTON is a professor of civic engagement and director of the Institute for Philosophy and Public Policy at the University of Maryland. He serves as director of the Center for Information and Research on Civic Learning and Engagement (CIRCLE) and is a founding member of the board of the National Campaign to Prevent Teen Pregnancy. Previously he served as executive director of the National Commission on Civic Renewal.

ROBERT P. GEORGE is a professor of jurisprudence and director of the James Madison Program in American Ideals and Institutions at Princeton University. He has served as a presidential appointee to the United States Commission on Civil Rights and as a judicial fellow at the Supreme Court of the United States. He currently serves on the President's Council on Bioethics.

ANDREW GREELEY is a professor of social sciences at the University of Chicago and the University of Arizona as well as a research associate at the National Opinion Research Center at the University of Chicago. He is author of numerous publications, including *The Catholic Revolution, Confessions of a Parish Priest, Furthermore,* and *Bishop Goes to the University.*

JOHN C. GREEN is a professor of political science and director of the Ray C. Bliss Institute of Applied Politics at the University of Akron. He is editor of *Vox Pop,* the newsletter of the Political Organizations and Parties section of the American Political Science Association. He is coauthor of several volumes, including *The Bully Pulpit,* and coeditor of *The State of the Parties.*

ANNA GREENBERG is vice president of Greenberg Quinlan Rosner Research. Formerly an assistant professor of public policy at Harvard University, she has also worked on a special project at the National Opinion Research Center and on campaigns for Senators Christopher Dodd and Joseph Lieberman and Representative Rosa DeLauro. She will teach in the School of Public Affairs at American University in the fall of 2004.

SUSANNAH HESCHEL is chair of Jewish studies and serves as an associate professor in the Department of Religion at Dartmouth College. Previously she held positions at Southern Methodist University, Case Western Reserve University, and the University of Frankfurt. She is author and coeditor of several books, including *Abraham Geiger and the Jewish Jesus.*

AMORY HOUGHTON JR. is a United States congressional representative, serving New York's Twenty-Ninth District. The fifth-ranking Republican on the House Ways and Means Committee, he chairs its Oversight Subcommittee and serves on the Subcommittee on Trade. He also is a member of the International Relations Committee and serves as cochair of the board of the Faith and Politics Institute.

MICHAEL KAZIN is a professor of history at Georgetown University and a member of the editorial board of *Dissent*. He has held positions at numerous universities, including American University and Stanford University. He is series coeditor of *Politics and Culture in Modern America* and coauthor of *America Divided: The Civil War of the 1960s*.

M. A. MUQTEDAR KHAN is a visiting fellow at the Brookings Institution as well as an assistant professor of political science and director of International Studies at Adrian College in Michigan. He serves on the board of the Center for the Study of Islam and Democracy and is vice president of the Association of Muslim Social Scientists. He is author of *American Muslims: Bridging Faith and Freedom*.

GLENN C. LOURY is a professor of economics and founding director of the Institute on Race and Social Division at Boston University. He previously held positions at Northwestern University, the University of Michigan, and Harvard University. He is author of *The Anatomy of Racial Inequality* and *One by One from the Inside Out*.

MARTHA MINOW is a professor at Harvard Law School. She previously served as acting director of Harvard University's Program on Ethics and the Professions, where she also was a visiting professor. She is author or coeditor of several books, including *Between Vengeance and Forgiveness, Not Only for Myself, Making All the Difference,* and *Law Stories*.

STEPHEN V. MONSMA is a professor of political science and holds the chair in social science at Pepperdine University. He is also a nonresident fellow at the Center for Public Justice and at the Center for Research on Religion and Urban Civil Society at the University of Pennsylvania. Previously he served in both the Michigan House of Representatives and the Michigan Senate.

MARK A. NOLL is a professor of Christian thought at Wheaton College and cofounder and director of the school's Institute for the Study of American Evangelicals. In recent years he has been a visiting professor at Harvard Divinity School, the University of Chicago Divinity School, Westminster Theological Seminary, and Regent College of Vancouver.

DAVID NOVAK holds the chair of Jewish studies at the University of Toronto. He also serves as secretary-treasurer of the Institute on Religion and Public Life and is on the editorial board of its monthly journal, *First Things*. He is a founder of the Union for Traditional Judaism and a former pulpit rabbi. He is author of several publications, including *Covenantal Rights* and *Natural Law in Judaism.*

RAMESH PONNURU is a senior editor for the *National Review,* where he covers national politics. Previously a fellow at the Institute of Economic Affairs in London, he is author of the monograph *The Mystery of Japanese Growth.* He has also written for numerous publications, including the *Wall Street Journal,* the *New York Times,* the *Financial Times,* and *Newsday.*

DAVID E. PRICE is a Democratic member of the United States House of Representatives, serving North Carolina's Fourth District. He holds a bachelor of divinity degree and a Ph.D. in political science from Yale University. Before his election to Congress in 1986, he was a professor of political science and public policy at Duke University.

JEFFREY ROSEN is an associate professor at the George Washington University Law School. Legal affairs editor of the *New Republic* since 1992, he has also contributed to the *New York Times Magazine* and the *New Yorker.* He is author of *The Unwanted Gaze: The Destruction of Privacy in America* and frequently appears on National Public Radio.

CHERYL J. SANDERS is a professor of ethics at Howard University School of Divinity and serves as senior pastor at the Third Street Church of God in Washington. She is author of several books, including *Ministry at the Margins, Youth and the Poor, Saints in Exile, Living the Intersection, Empowerment and Ethics for a Liberated People,* and *Slavery and Conversion.*

JULIE A. SEGAL is president of Civic Action Strategies and specializes in mobilizing citizens to participate in the political process. She previously served as legislative counsel of Americans United for Separation of Church and State. She is a frequent spokesperson and writer on First Amendment law and policy.

RON SIDER is a professor of theology and culture at Eastern Baptist Seminary and president and founder of Evangelicals for Social Action. He is a founding board member of the National Religious Partnership for the Environment and author of several publications, including *Rich Christians in the Age of Hunger* and *Cup of Water, Bread of Life.*

JAMES W. SKILLEN is president of the Center for Public Justice. Previously he served as the organization's executive director. He also is a trustee for Bread for the World, Institute for Prison Ministries, and Free the Children Trust. He is an editorial consultant for *Regeneration Quarterly, Third Way,* and *Philosophia Reformata.*

MARK SOUDER is a United States congressional representative serving Indiana's Third District. He is chairman of the Government Reform Subcommittee on Criminal Justice, Drug Policy, and Human Resources. He has also served on the Committee on Resources as well as the Select Committee on Homeland Security.

MATTHEW SPALDING is director of the B. Kenneth Center for American Studies at the Heritage Foundation. He is also a visiting assistant professor of government at Claremont McKenna College and a fellow at the Claremont Institute. He has contributed, authored, or edited several publications on the subject of government reform and civil society, including the *National Review,* the *Washington Times,* and *A Sacred Union of Citizens.*

MARGARET O'BRIEN STEINFELS is editor of *Commonweal.* She has written for several publications, including the *New York Times,* the *Los Angeles Times,* and the *New Republic.* She has served on the boards of Georgetown University and the Catholic Press Association. She currently serves on the advisory committee to the Catholic Common Ground Initiative.

JEFFREY STOUT is a professor of religion and acting chair of the Department of Religion at Princeton University. He also serves on the editorial board and the board of trustees' Finance Committee of the Princeton University Press. He is a contributing editor to the *Journal of Religious Ethics* and is author of *Ethics after Babel.*

ROBERTO SURO is director of the Pew Hispanic Center, a Washington-based think tank. Previously he served as a foreign correspondent with the *Washington Post, Time Magazine,* and the *New York Times.* His publications include *Strangers among Us: Latino Lives in a Changing America, Watching America's Door,* and *Remembering the American Dream.*

JOHN SWEENEY is president of the AFL-CIO, a position he has held since 1995. He has served as a vice president of the organization as well as president of the Service Employees International Union, one of the largest organizations within the AFL-CIO. He is author of *America Needs a Raise: Fighting for Economic Security and Social Justice.*

W. DOUGLAS TANNER JR. is president and cofounder of the Faith and Politics Institute in Washington. A United Methodist minister, he has served as a campus chaplain and a parish minister and has additional experience as a congressional campaign manager, a congressional aide, and a Senate campaign consultant.

JIM TOWEY is director of the White House Office of Faith-Based and Community Initiatives. An attorney, he previously served as legal counsel to Mother Teresa of Calcutta and established Aging with Dignity. He led Florida's health and social services agency and served in the cabinet of Governor Lawton Chiles.

J. BRENT WALKER is executive director of the Washington-based Baptist Joint Committee on Public Affairs, where he previously served as the committee's general counsel. An ordained minister, adjunct professor at Georgetown University Law Center, and attorney, Walker is a frequent commentator on church-state issues in the national media.

MARK R. WARREN is associate professor at Harvard's Graduate School of Education. Previously he was professor of sociology at Fordham University. He is a fellow at the W. E. B. DuBois Institute for African American Research at Harvard and has published several books, including *Dry Bones Rattling* and *Faith-Based Community Organizing*.

ALAN WOLFE is a professor of political science and director of the Boisi Center for Religion and American Public Life at Boston College. He served as an adviser to President Clinton and twice has conducted U.S. State Department programs that bring Muslim scholars to the United States to learn about separation of church and state.

INDEX